Praise for *America's Contin...*   *le East*

"I prefer a friend who tells me the ugly truth to a friend who tells me beautiful lies. Chas Freeman belongs to the first category. Without sentiments and with a clear analytical mind, he shows us how it happened and why. Perhaps he can help to save us from ourselves."

—URI AVNERY
Veteran Israeli peace activist; former member of the Knesset

"With unsparing wit and relentlessly clear-eyed analysis, Chas Freeman once more demonstrates why he is America's best-informed and most incisive critic of U.S. foreign policy in the Middle East. You could read the editorial pages of the *New York Times* and *Washington Post* for ten years, and you won't find the wisdom contained in this very short but exceedingly shrewd book."

—ANDREW BACEVICH
Author of *America's War for the Greater Middle East: A Military History*

"Chas Freeman's latest volume offers a characteristically sharp and unapologetic critique of America's role in the Middle East. For those who care deeply about this increasingly complicated region, whatever their perspectives, these thoughtful essays will challenge, provoke and illuminate."

—AMB. WILLIAM J. BURNS
President, Carnegie Endowment for International Peace;
former U.S. deputy secretary of state

"With laser-sharp clarity and shrewd analysis, Amb. Chas Freeman offers a frank, no-holds-barred assessment of recent U.S. policy and involvement in the Middle East. Thoughtful and compelling, Freeman dissects virtually every aspect of the complicated American engagement in the region. This seminal work by one of our most insightful diplomats provides a vivid portrayal of events and lucid explanations of cause and effect. A 'must read' for anyone with a desire to understand Middle East policy, this book offers a comprehensive and peerless appreciation of what has transpired and straightforward prescriptions for the way ahead."

—WILLIAM FALLON
Admiral, U.S. Navy (Retired); Former commander, U.S. CENTCOM;
Senior fellow, Center for Naval Analyses

"This is a trenchantly stated, carefully...well-worded series of analyses and assessments, mainly of U.S. policy over the last half decade, presented in a collection of important speeches by one of America's diplomatic stars, focused on the Middle East, but with important insights into China and its relations to the region. Freeman is tough on all comers in the region—not just the United States, but also on Israel, Iran, the Gulf states, and others. At rock bottom, this is a key exposition of major errors and foibles of policy and execution along with critical ideas for the major course corrections that should be pursued to get us out of the deep holes Freeman shows clearly we and others have dug for ourselves."

—THOMAS R. PICKERING
Former U.S. under secretary of state; former U.S. ambassador
to Jordan, Israel, Russia, India and the United Nations

"Ambassador Freeman knows first hand what he writes about. This is an important book for us all. Better, he brings to a depth of knowledge that adds up to wisdom."

—WILLIAM R. POLK
Former president of the Adlai Stevenson Institute of International Affairs

"Chas Freeman's new book, *America's Continuing Misadventures in the Middle East*, should be required reading for all presidential candidates. A veteran diplomat who served as U.S. ambassador to Saudi Arabia during the 1991 Gulf War, Freeman's verdict on U.S. foreign policy is harsh and largely justified. With bipartisan scorn, he faults Bill Clinton's 'dual containment' of Iran and Iraq in the 1990s, George Bush's disastrous invasion of Iraq in 2003, and both parties' enablement of Israeli settlement expansion and repression of Palestinians. In this compendium of speeches delivered from 2010–15, Freeman occasionally fails to foresee fast-moving developments, such as Egypt's U-turn to authoritarian rule. But his prescription for U.S. policy is on the mark...."

—BARBARA SLAVIN
Acting director of the Future of Iran Initiative, the Atlantic Council

"In *America's Continuing Misadventures in the Middle East*, Amb. Chas Freeman brings his unparalleled experience, vast erudition, and enormous intelligence to bear on the sorry tale of U.S. Middle East policy. This clear-eyed collection of essays and speeches explains why the United States has repeatedly failed to achieve its main goals in this vital region, usually at considerable human, economic, and political cost. Readers will enjoy Freeman's elegant and often witty prose, but not the parade of illusions and follies that he recounts. If you want to know why the United States has erred in the past and how it might do better in the future, read this book."

—**STEPHEN WALT**
Robert and Renee Belfer Professor of International Affairs,
Harvard University

AMERICA'S CONTINUING MISADVENTURES IN THE MIDDLE EAST

CHAS W. FREEMAN, JR.

Just World Books
Charlottesville, Virginia

Just World Books
Timely Books for Changing Times

Just World Books is an imprint of Just World Publishing, LLC.

Cover design by CStudio Design.
Typesetting by Diana Ghazzawi for Just World Publishing, LLC.

Publisher's Cataloging in Publication
(Provided by Quality Books, Inc.)

Freeman, Charles W., author.
    America's continuing misadventures in the Middle East
/ by Chas W. Freeman, Jr. -- Second edition.
    pages cm
    Includes bibliographical references.
    LCCN 2015953817
    ISBN 9781682570050 (paperback)
    ISBN 9781682570043 (hardcover)
    ISBN 9781935982951 (ePub)
    ISBN 9781935982975 (PDF)
    ISBN 9781935982968 (Mobi)

    1. Middle East--Foreign relations--United States.
2. Middle East--Foreign relations--1979- 3. United States
--Foreign relations--Middle East. 4. United States--
Foreign relations--1989- 5. National security--Middle
East. I. Title.

DS63.2.U5F733 2016   327.56073
                QBI15-600235

Contents

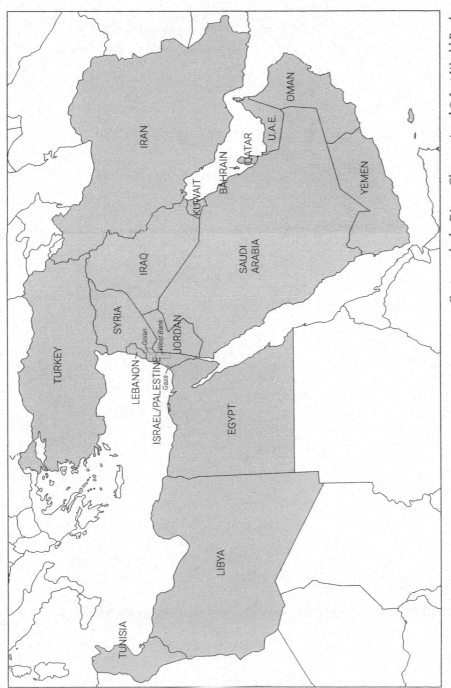

9

Introduction

Lessons from America's Continuing Misadventures in the Middle East

Twenty-six years ago, when the elder President Bush asked me to be his ambassador to Saudi Arabia, he assured me that "nothing much ever happens in Arabia." That had been the case for quite a while. Now no one would refer to any part of the Middle East—not even the Arabian Peninsula—as a zone of tranquility. It was a different world back then.

Mistakes made in Washington had a great deal to do with why and how that relative stability disappeared.

In 1993, the United States unilaterally replaced reliance on the balance between Iraq and Iran with so-called "dual containment" of both directly by the U.S. armed forces. This created an unprecedented requirement for a large, long-term U.S. military presence in the Gulf. That, in turn, stimulated the birth of anti-American terrorism with a global reach. One result: 9/11.

From 2003 to date, Americans have racked up $6 trillion in outlays and unfunded liabilities for two wars, which we have lost. That $6 trillion—much of it yet to be borrowed—might otherwise have been invested in America's human and physical infrastructure. We live amidst the falling educational standards, collapsing bridges, man-eating potholes, transportation gridlock, and declining international competitiveness that are the consequences of our not spending that money here.

After September 11, 2001, in America's zeal to track down and kill our enemies and terrorize their supporters, we embraced practices like kidnapping, torture, and political assassination. By doing so, we voluntarily surrendered the moral high ground the United States had long occupied in world affairs and forfeited our credentials as exemplars and advocates of human rights.

In 2003, the United States decapitated and destabilized Iraq, erasing the inhibitions to sectarian strife there and in Syria. This fostered anarchy and religious extremist movements that have brought untold suffering to millions, driving them to seek refuge first in neighboring countries, then beyond.

Since 2001, Washington has quixotically attempted to exclude both militant Islam and the Pashtun plurality from a significant role in governing Afghanistan, while making it safe for homegrown "narcocrats." Afghanistan is now a political debacle, a human-rights disaster, a terrorist training camp, or a drug bust waiting to happen.

For almost five decades, the United States aided and abetted a fraudulent "peace process" and the institutionalization of intolerable injustice for the Arabs of the Holy Land. This has enabled Israel to keep expanding but eroded the Jewish state's democracy, alienated the majority of the world's Jews from it, delegitimized it in the eyes of the international community, and placed its long-term survival in doubt.

In 2011, Americans mistook mob rule in the streets of the Middle East for democracy and turned our back on leaders we had previously supported. This cost us our reputation as a reliable ally and helped install incompetent government in Egypt, state collapse and anarchy in Libya, and civil war in Yemen.

For most of the past twenty years, Washington has demanded that Iran end its nuclear program but declined to speak with it. By the time American diplomats finally did sit down with the Iranians, their program had expanded and advanced. Despite some rollback, we ended up accepting Iranian nuclear capabilities much beyond what they had earlier offered.

Over the course of this decade, instead of a strategy to combat Islamist violence, the Obama administration has executed a campaign plan involving the promiscuous use of drone warfare. This has multiplied America's enemies and spread terrorism to ever more parts of West Asia and North Africa. One result: the so-called "Islamic State"—Da'esh—now has more foreign recruits than it can induct or train.

Since 2011, Americans have put neither our military power nor our money where our mouths were in Syria. The continued mass death and dislocation there is in part a result of a uniquely American combination of policy overreach, operational hesitancy, and ideologically palsied diplomacy. The strife we helped kindle in Syria (and Iraq) continues to have unforeseen knock-on effects, like the incubation of Da'esh, the destabilization of the European Union by overwhelming refugee flows, and the reappearance of Russian power in the Middle East.

By now, the consequences of multiple U.S. missteps are obvious to all but the most determined American partisans of diplomacy-free foreign policy. Our many bruising encounters with the inconvenient realities of the Middle East should have taught us a lot about how to conduct—or not conduct—diplomacy and war, as well as the limitations of purely military solutions to political problems. But, for the most part, American politicians and pundits have been more comfortable reaffirming ideological preconceptions and tendentious partisan narratives than facing up to what the policies and actions they have advocated actually produce and why. Our continuing misadventures in the Middle East and much of the turmoil there are consequences of this evasion of any "after-action review" process. The misadventures began with our affirmation of the United Nations Charter and international law. They continue amidst our studied disregard of both.

It has been a quarter-century since Saddam Hussein decided to celebrate the end of the Cold War and his assault on Iran by invading, looting, and annexing Kuwait. Iraq's brazen aggression unified the United Nations behind Western and Muslim coalitions that came to Kuwait's rescue. The rescue took place in the name of defending the sovereignty and independence of the weak and their immunity from bullying or invasion by the strong. That's what the UN Charter was meant to guarantee.

Since then, almost no one in American public office has referred to either the charter or international law. When President Obama did so in the UN General Assembly at the end of September, there was stunned silence in the hall as other countries' leaders marveled at his chutzpah. He was, after all, extolling principles Americans once upheld but now refuse to apply ourselves. The president's castigation of other great powers for their deviations from the charter and international law simply reminded many present of the U.S. actions in Bosnia, Kosovo, Iraq, Libya, and Syria, which have marked the relapse to a state of international disorder in which the strong do what they will and the weak suffer what they must. That was, of course, precisely the post–Cold War norm that the war to liberate Kuwait was meant to preclude.

What might we learn from our continuing misadventures in the Middle East?

One key conclusion is that, just as diplomacy without military backing is hamstrung, military power, however great, has limited utility unless it is informed and accompanied by diplomacy. We have shown that force can remove regimes. We have seen that it cannot replace them or the political structures it destroys. Our armed forces can shock, awe, and vanquish their foes on the battlefield, but we have learned the hard way in Afghanistan and Iraq that wars do not end until the defeated accept defeat and stand down their resistance.

Translating military outcomes into lasting adjustments in the behavior of those we have defeated is the job of diplomats, not warriors. For the most part, we have not called on our diplomats to do that job. Judging by the plague of incompetent campaign gerbils and carpetbaggers we appointed to manage Iraq and Afghanistan after we occupied them, our government lacks the diplomatic professionalism, expertise, and skills—as well as the politico-military backing and resources—needed to craft peace. We have no war termination strategies and no one who would know how to implement them if we did, so our wars never end.

We have also come to understand that threats to attack projects like Iran's nuclear program are more likely to stiffen the backs of those we are trying to intimidate than to bring them to their knees. Threats offend the pride of their targets even as they menace their security. As the German proverb cautions: "The best enemies are those that make threats." Warning that you plan to attack an adversary stimulates military countermeasures and efforts at deterrence on its part. It also promotes hatred and bravado, not thoughts of surrender. If you are serious about attacking a foreign adversary, better get on with it!

We have learned, however, from studying our options vis-à-vis Iran, that bombing can destroy program infrastructure, but probably not all of it. Assassination can murder key project personnel, but most likely not all of them. Cyberattacks can cripple software and even destroy some equipment, but invite retaliation in kind. None of these aggressive measures can erase a society's scientific, technological, engineering, and mathematical skills. The competencies that created complex programs remain available to reconstitute them.

Short of occupation and pacification, the only way to eliminate or at least mitigate latent menaces like that of the Iranian nuclear program is through the negotiation of a binding framework of undertakings to constrain them, subject to impartial verification. That is what we have finally worked out with Iran. In negotiations, though, the perfect is often the enemy of the good and ripe moments soon rot away. In 2005, Iran offered a deal. We rejected it, refused to talk to Iran directly, and doubled down on sanctions. Ten years later, we settled for much less than what was originally offered. It's important to know when time is on your side and when it isn't—and it's important to understand what sanctions can do and what they can't.

A century ago, Woodrow Wilson declared that "a nation that is boycotted is a nation that is in sight of surrender. Apply this economic, peaceful, silent, deadly remedy and there will be no need for force."[1] We've spent a hundred years testing this alluring theory. It's now clear that, when he articulated it, Wilson was out to lunch.

If sanctions are not linked to a diplomatic process aimed at dispute resolution, they entrench differences rather than bridge them. Our recent experience with Iran bears this out. So, by the way, do the results of sanctions against Mao's China, Kim Il-sung's north Korea, Castro's Cuba, and Putin's Russia. Sanctions make some people poor and others rich, but on their own they neither bring about regime change nor break the will of foreign nationalists.

Dean Acheson was right when he said that "to determine the pattern of rulership in another country requires conquering it.... The idea of using commercial restrictions as a substitute for war in getting control over somebody else's country is a persistent and mischievous superstition in the conduct of foreign affairs."[2]

Sanctions quite predictably did not suffice to bring about Saddam's withdrawal from Kuwait. Air and ground attacks were needed to achieve that. Nor could sanctions topple the regimes in Iraq and Libya. For that, the direct use of force was required. Syria has since underscored the reality that sanctions also come up short even when buttressed by covert action to foment and intensify rebellion. Despite tough sanctions, ostracism, and multiple foreign-supported insurgencies, President Bashar al-Assad is still the head of what passes for a national government in his country.

The case of Iran further buttresses Acheson's point. Thirty years of escalating sanctions on Iran did nothing but reinforce its obduracy. Only after the reopening of direct diplomatic dialogue finally enabled hard bargaining were we able to trade sanctions relief for restrictions on the

1. Quoted in Saul K. Padover, *Wilson's Ideals* (New York: American Council on Public Affairs, 1942), 108.
2. Quoted in Chas W. Freeman, Jr., *The Diplomat's Dictionary, 2nd ed.* (Washington, D.C.: United States Institute of Peace Press, 2009), 340.

Iranian nuclear program. Ironically, it turns out, the only utility of sanctions in terms of changing behavior lies in their agreed *removal*. Imposing them doesn't accomplish much and may even be counterproductive. Yet, as a political cheap shot, sanctions, combined with diatribe and ostracism, remain the preferred response of the United States to foreign defiance.

That's because, as someone wise in the ways of Washington once pointed out, "sanctions always succeed in their principal objective, which is to make those who impose them feel good."[3] But gratifying as it may be to politicians trying to show how tough they are, the pain inflicted by sanctions is meaningless unless it leads to agreement by their target country to change its policies and practices. Agreed change can only be achieved through trade-offs. And these need to be arranged in negotiations focused on a "yes-able" proposition. Sanctions relief can be a useful part of the bargaining process, but sanctions that are imposed to give the appearance of changing behavior without bargaining with those on whom they are imposed are diplomatic and military cowardice tarted up as moral outrage.

Which brings me to our recent experiences with the deployment and use of the U.S. military in the Middle East. These ought to have taught us a lot about strategy and the conduct of war as well as what is required to translate the results of war into a better peace. They have certainly demonstrated beyond a reasonable doubt that strategic incoherence invites punishment by the uncontrolled course of events.

A strategy is a plan for actions that can achieve a desired objective with the minimum investment of effort, resources, and time. The objective must be clear and attainable. The operational concept must be realistic and reasonably simple. To promote efficiency, it should draw on the synergies of all relevant elements of national and international power—political, economic, informational, and military. For a strategy to succeed, the tactics by which it is implemented must be both feasible and flexible. The strategy must weigh the interests and changing perceptions of affected parties and consider how best to accommodate, counter, or correct these.

Since we became a world power seventy years ago, the United States has sought to sustain stability in the Persian Gulf. A related objective has been to preclude monopoly control of the region's energy resources by a hostile power. We accomplished these tasks successfully for decades—without stationing significant forces in the region—by ensuring that Iraq and Iran balanced each other, by arming the countries of the Gulf Cooperation Council (GCC) to buttress that balance, and by showing that

---

3. Quoted in ibid., 204.

if our friends in the GCC were threatened, we could arrive in time and with sufficient firepower to defend them. Our strategy protected the Arab societies of the Gulf at minimal cost, with a minimal U.S. troop presence and minimal social or religious friction.

The Gulf War (1990–91) validated this strategy. The United States led forces that joined with a Saudi-led coalition to liberate Kuwait and chastise Iraq. Together, Western and Islamic coalition air forces and armies reduced the military power of Iraq to levels that enabled it once again to balance Iran without threatening its other neighbors.

But in 1993, the Clinton administration abruptly abandoned the effort to use Iraq to balance Iran. With no prior consultation with the U.S. military or our security partners in the Gulf, the White House suddenly proclaimed a policy of "dual containment," under which the United States undertook unilaterally to balance both Baghdad and Tehran simultaneously. This made sense in terms of protecting Israel from either Iraq or Iran, but not otherwise. It deprived the Gulf Arabs of a role in determining a low-cost national security strategy for their region and required the creation of a long-term American military presence in the Gulf. The irritations that presence entailed gave birth to al-Qaeda and led to 9/11. The subsequent U.S. invasion and destruction of Iraq's power and independence from Iran ensured that there was no way to sustain a stable balance of power in the Gulf that did not require the continuation of a huge, expensive, and locally burdensome American military presence there. So there we are, and there we will remain.

No one openly questions this situation, but no one is comfortable with it—and with good reason. It presupposes a degree of congruity in U.S. and Arab views that no longer exists. It is politically awkward for all concerned. Notwithstanding the Obama administration's considerable efforts to allay Gulf Arabs' concerns, they suspect that the logic of events in the region could yet drive America toward rapprochement with Iran and strategic cooperation with it against Sunni Islamism.

In assessing American reliability, our partners in the Gulf cannot forget what happened to Hosni Mubarak. Not surprisingly, they want to reduce their dependence on America for protection as much as they can. This is leading to a lot of arms purchases and outreach by Saudi Arabia and other GCC members to countries like China, India, and Russia. It has also stimulated assertively independent foreign policies on their part.

But the GCC countries' capacity for self-reliance is limited. No matter how heavily they arm themselves, they cannot match either the population or the potential for subversive trouble-making that their Iranian adversary and its fellow travelers possess. Sadly, for the GCC, there is no great power other than the United States with power-projection capabilities and an inclination to protect the Gulf Arab states from external challenges. There is no escape from their reliance on America.

Meanwhile, however, the apparent contradictions between U.S. interests and policies and those of our GCC partners are widening. The United States now asserts objectives in the region that do not coincide with those of most GCC members. These include support of the Shiite-dominated Iraqi government against its Sunni opposition and assigning priority in Syria to the defeat of Da'esh over the ouster of President Assad. U.S. support for the Kurds disturbs our Arab friends as well as our ally Turkey. America supports the GCC's military operations in Yemen less out of conviction than out of a perceived need to sustain solidarity with Saudi Arabia.

The United States and Gulf Arab governments have in effect agreed to disagree about the sources of instability in Bahrain and Egypt and how to cure them. Where a common ideology of anticommunism once united us or caused us to downplay our disagreements, passionate differences between Americans and Arabs over Salafism, Zionism, feminism, religious tolerance, sexual mores, and democratic versus autocratic systems of governance now openly divide us. Neither side harbors the sympathy and affection for the other that it once did. The ultimate sources of mutual discomfort are the strategic conundrums of what to do about Syria and how to deal with Iran.

Wishful thinking about the region's strategic geometry and determination to exclude powerful governments and leaders from participation in its politics have failed to curb endless warfare, mass flight, and extremist ideologies. Diplomatic processes that leave out those who must agree to an altered status quo or acquiesce in it for it to last are exercises in public relations flimflam, not serious attempts at problem solving. No party with proven strength on the ground, however odious, can be ignored. All parties, including what's left of the Syrian government led by President Assad, must sign on to a solution for it to take hold. As long as one or more of the external and internal parties in Syria is willing to fight to the last Syrian to get its way, the anarchy will continue. So will the refugee flows. Assad will remain in power in part of the country; Da'esh and its like will flourish in the rest. This situation is and should be acceptable to no one.

It is almost certainly too late to put the Syrian Humpty Dumpty together again. The same is likely true of Iraq (as well as Libya). The future political geography of the Fertile Crescent now looks to be a mosaic of religiously and ethnically purified principalities, statelets, and thugdoms. If this is indeed what comes to pass in the region, Iran, Israel, Turkey, and great powers outside the area will be able to divide and rule it. Conceivably, Da'esh could forge a viable Levantine "Sunnistan" that balances both Iran and Israel, but that is hard to imagine and would be unacceptable to all but the most religiously constipated Muslims. Even less plausibly, portions of Iraq and Syria could come together in some sort of federal structure that can play a regional balancing role.

With Turkey sidelined, Russia allied with the Assad government, and no potential Arab partner to help balance Iran, the GCC states have been driven to harmonize some of their Iran policies clandestinely with Israel. However, Israel's treatment of its captive Arab population and neighbors makes it morally and politically anathema to other actors in the region. Its use of negotiations to deceive its negotiating partners and others interested in brokering peace for it with the Palestinians and other Arabs has gained it a worldwide reputation for diplomatic chicanery it will not soon live down. As long as it continues to oppress its captive Arab population, Israel will disqualify itself as any country's public partner in strategy and diplomacy in the Middle East.

Meanwhile, in Iraq and Syria, the attempt to use air power to stop Da'esh and to train a ground force to oppose it, without fixing the broken political environment in which extremism flourishes, has failed. This should not be a surprise. Analogous Israeli campaigns against Hamas and Hezbollah had earlier failed. The Saudi-led GCC campaign in Yemen is unlikely to prove the exception to the rule that you can't accomplish objectives you can't define. Nor can you overthrow or install a regime from the air, even when you totally dominate the airspace. The Iran nuclear deal shows that diplomacy can solve problems that bombing cannot. Political problems, including those with a religious dimension, require political solutions—and political solutions depend on political strategies that inform sound policies.

There is no such strategy or agreed-upon policy for dealing with Iran now that its nuclear program has been constrained and sanctions will be lifted. The United States seems to have no clear idea of what it now wants from Iran. The GCC would like Iran isolated and contained, as it was before the United States helped install a pro-Iranian government in Baghdad and connived with Israel to propel Hezbollah to the commanding heights of Lebanese politics. But there is no GCC strategy with any prospect of achieving this result. Wars of religion, not strategy, are shaping the future of the Middle East.

As refugees overwhelm Europe and Da'esh continues to hold its own against the forces arrayed against it, the world is moving toward the conclusion that any outcome in Syria—any outcome at all that can stop the carnage—is better than its continuation. The ongoing disintegration of the Fertile Crescent empowers Iran; drives Iran, Iraq, Russia, and Syria together; weakens the strategic position of the GCC; vexes Turkey; and leaves the United States stuck in the Gulf. The region seems headed, after still more tragedy and bloodshed, toward an unwelcome inevitability— the eventual acknowledgment of Iran's hegemony in Iraq and Syria and political influence in Bahrain, Gaza, Lebanon, and Yemen. That is not where Americans and our Gulf Arab friends imagined we would end up twenty-five years after liberating Kuwait from Iraqi aggression, but it is where protracted strategic incoherence has brought us. We can no longer avoid considering whether an opening to Iran is not the key to peace and stability in the Middle East.

Whatever our answer to that question, the seventy-year-old partnership between Americans and Gulf Arabs has never faced bigger challenges. We will not surmount these challenges if we do not learn from our mistakes and work together to cope with the unpalatable realities they have created. Doing so will require intensified dialogue between us, imagination, and openness to novel strategic partnerships and alignments. There are new realities in the Middle East. It does no good to deny or rail against them. We must now adjust to them and strive to turn them to our advantage.

—Chas W. Freeman
September 2015

1

The Role of the
Israel-Palestine Conflict

To be disillusioned, one must first have illusions. Few things have been as disillusioning to partisans of the consolidation of a secure homeland for Jews in the Middle East (the most important objective of U.S. diplomacy in the region for decades) as the evolution of Israeli policies and practices over the past quarter-century.

This period began with an internationally sponsored conference in Madrid from October 30 to November 1, 1991. The Madrid Conference brought Israel, its Arab neighbors, and the Palestine Liberation Organization together for the first time in an effort to achieve regional acceptance for the Jewish state. This led by circuitous means to the signing in Washington (on September 13, 1993) of the Oslo accords, which envisaged Palestinian elections to establish self-government, Israeli withdrawal from Palestinian lands, and a process of self-determination that would culminate within five years in the establishment of a Palestinian state alongside Israel.

This era may be said to have definitively ended on October 26, 2015, when Israeli prime minister Binyamin Netanyahu told the Knesset that, while he rejected the idea of a binational state, Israeli Jews "need to control all of the territory [of historic Palestine] for the foreseeable future." Mr. Netanyahu showed that he understood that this would preclude a secure peace for Israel with Palestinians, other Arabs, and the world's Muslims when he added, "I'm asked if we will forever live by the sword—yes."

The essays that follow reveal my own gradual and grudging realization that I had been wrong in my presumption that Israel desired peace and reconciliation with those its Western-backed establishment and military consolidation in the Middle East had injured or offended. As events unfolded, it became increasingly hard to deny that the absence of peace was explained not by the unwillingness of the victims of Israeli colonialism to compromise, but by Israel's own view that it had no need to make concessions as long as it had the backing of the United States.

With great reluctance, I came to see that, given U.S. enablement, Israel has never been prepared to risk peace with those it displaced from their homes in Palestine. When faced with a choice between territorial expansion and advances toward reconciliation with Arabs, Israel always chooses land over peace. The now-defunct American-sponsored "peace process"—on which the United States staked its reputation in the Middle East and elsewhere, and which I labored to support—has been revealed to all as part of an elaborate diplomatic deception, intended to provide political cover for Israel's continued territorial expansion at Palestinian expense.

To be clear, this hypocrisy matters to me as a patriotic American less because of its injustice to the Palestinians than because of its political and military consequences for Israel and the United States. Israel can enjoy neither domestic tranquility nor security from non-hostile neighbors and the world's Muslims if it continues to deal with its captive Arab population through the culling of their leaders by targeted assassination, the tyranny of occupation, and the persecution of checkpoints and separation walls, punctuated by sniper attacks and occasional bombing campaigns against defenseless Palestinian civilians. Such an approach guarantees violent resistance by Palestinians and hostility by those who identify with them.

Equally, or perhaps more importantly, it represents a secession by Israel from both Western civilization and the humane values of the Judeo-Christian moral tradition. As such, it delegitimizes Israel internationally and alienates it from Jews in other countries. This is a prescription for escalating regional enmity and declining support for Israel in Europe and America. It is a suicidal strategy for Zionism. Given American solidarity with Israel, it foretells rising politico-military costs for the United States from anti-American terrorism by estranged Muslims, accompanied by division between the United States and major European allies. It is in the interest of the United States that citizens raise their voices to head off this scenario. That is what I have tried to do.

Is Israel a Strategic Asset or Liability for the United States?
July 20, 2010[1]

I s Israel a strategic asset or liability for the United States?

In my view, there are many reasons for Americans to wish the Jewish state well. Under current circumstances, strategic advantage for the United States is not one of them. If we were to reverse the question, however, and to ask whether the United States is a strategic asset or liability for Israel, there would be no doubt about the answer.

American taxpayers fund between 20 and 25 percent of Israel's defense budget (depending on how you calculate it). Twenty-six percent of the $3 billion in military aid we grant to the Jewish state each year is spent in Israel on Israeli defense products. Uniquely, Israeli companies are treated like American companies for purposes of U.S. defense procurement. Thanks to congressional earmarks, we also often pay half the costs of special Israeli research and development projects, even when—as in the case of defense against very short-range unguided missiles—the technology being developed is essentially irrelevant to our own military requirements. In short, in many ways, American taxpayers fund jobs in Israel's military industries that could have gone to our own workers and companies. Meanwhile, Israel gets pretty much whatever it wants in terms of our top-of-the-line weapons systems, and we pick up the tab.

Identifiable U.S. government subsidies to Israel total over $140 billion since 1949. This makes Israel by far the largest recipient of American giveaways since World War II. The total would be much higher if aid to Egypt, Jordan, Lebanon, and support for Palestinians in refugee camps and the occupied territories were included. These programs have complex purposes but are justified in large measure in terms of their contribution to the security of the Jewish state.

Per capita income in Israel is now about $37,000—on a par with the UK. Israel is nonetheless the largest recipient of U.S. foreign assistance, accounting for well over a fifth of it. Annual U.S. government transfers run at well over $500 per Israeli, not counting the costs of tax breaks for private donations and loans that aren't available to any other foreign country.

These military and economic benefits are not the end of the story. The American government also works hard to shield Israel from the international political and legal consequences of its policies and actions

---

1. Remarks at the Nixon Center, Washington, D.C.

in the occupied territories, against its neighbors, or—most recently— on the high seas. The nearly forty vetoes the United States has cast to protect Israel in the UN Security Council are the tip of the iceberg. We have blocked a vastly larger number of potentially damaging reactions to Israeli behavior by the international community. The political costs to the United States internationally of having to spend our political capital in this way are huge.

Where Israel has no diplomatic relations, U.S. diplomats routinely make its case for it. As I know from personal experience (having been thanked by the then-government of Israel for my successful efforts on Israel's behalf in Africa), the U.S. government has been a consistent promoter and often the funder of various forms of Israeli programs of cooperation with other countries. It matters also that America—along with a very few other countries—has remained morally committed to the Jewish experiment with a state in the Middle East. Many more Jews live in America than in Israel. Resolute American support should be an important offset to the disquiet about current trends that has led more than 20 percent of Israelis to emigrate, many of them to the United States, where Jews enjoy unprecedented security and prosperity.

Clearly, Israel gets a great deal from us. Yet it's pretty much taboo in the United States to ask what's in it for Americans. I can't imagine why. Still, the question I've been asked to address today is just that: What's in it—and not in it—for us to do all these things for Israel?

We need to begin by recognizing that our relationship with Israel has never been driven by strategic reasoning. It began with President Truman overruling his strategic and military advisers in deference to personal sentiment and political expediency. We had an arms embargo on Israel until Lyndon Johnson dropped it in 1964 in explicit return for Jewish financial support for his campaign against Barry Goldwater. In 1973, for reasons peculiar to the Cold War, we had to come to the rescue of Israel as it battled Egypt. The resulting Arab oil embargo cost us dearly. And then there's all the time we've put into the perpetually ineffectual and now long defunct "peace process."

Still, the U.S.–Israel relationship has had strategic consequences. There is no reason to doubt the consistent testimony of the architects of major acts of anti-American terrorism about what motivates them to attack us. In the words of Khalid Sheikh Mohammed, who is credited with masterminding the 9/11 attacks, their purpose was to focus "the American people...on the atrocities that America is committing by supporting Israel against the Palestinian people." As Osama bin Laden, purporting to speak for the world's Muslims, has said again and again: "The cause of our dis-agreement with you is your support to your Israeli allies who occupy our land of Palestine." Some substantial portion of the many lives and the tril-lions of dollars we have so far expended in our escalating conflict with the Islamic world must be apportioned to the costs of our relationship with Israel.

It's useful to recall what we generally expect allies and strategic part-ners to do for us. In Europe, Asia, and elsewhere in the Middle East, they provide bases and support the projection of American power beyond their borders. They join us on the battlefield in places like Kuwait and Afghanistan or underwrite the costs of our military operations. They help recruit others to our coalitions. They coordinate their foreign aid with ours. Many defray the costs of our use of their facilities with "host na-tion support" that reduces the costs of our military operations from and through their territory. They store weapons for our troops' use. They pay cash for the weapons we transfer to them.

Israel does none of these things and shows no interest in doing them. Perhaps it can't. It is so estranged from everyone else in the Middle East that no neighboring country will accept flight plans that originate in or transit it. Israel is therefore useless in terms of support for American power projection. It has no allies other than us. It has developed no friends. Israeli participation in our military operations would preclude the cooperation of many others. Meanwhile, Israel has become accustomed to living on the American military dole. The notion that Israeli taxpayers might help defray the expense of U.S. military or foreign assistance operations, even those undertaken at Israel's behest, would be greeted with astonishment in Israel and incredulity on Capitol Hill.

Military aid to Israel is sometimes justified by the notion of Israel as a test bed for new weapons systems and operational concepts. But no one can identify a program of military R&D in Israel that was initially pro-posed by our men and women in uniform. All originated with Israel or members of Congress acting on its behalf. Moreover, what Israel makes it sells not just to the United States but to China, India, and other major arms markets. It feels no obligation to take U.S. interests into account when it transfers weapons and technology to third countries and does so only under duress.

Meanwhile, it's been decades since Israel's air force faced another in the air. It has come to specialize in bombing civilian infrastructure and militias with no air defenses. There is not much for the U.S. Air Force to learn from that. Similarly, the Israeli navy confronts no real naval threat.

Its experience in interdicting infiltrators, fishermen, and humanitarian aid flotillas is not a model for the U.S. Navy to study. Israel's army, however, has had lessons to impart. Now in its fifth decade of occupation duty, it has developed techniques of pacification, interrogation, assassination, and drone attack that inspired U.S. operations in Fallujah, Abu Ghraib, Somalia, Yemen, and Waziristan. Recently, Israel has begun to deploy various forms of remote-controlled robotic guns. These enable operatives at faraway video screens summarily to execute anyone they view as suspicious. Such risk-free means of culling hostile populations could conceivably come in handy in some future American military operation, but I hope not. I have a lot of trouble squaring the philosophy they embody with the values Americans have traditionally aspired to exemplify.

It is sometimes said that, to its credit, Israel does not ask the United States to fight its battles for it; it just wants the money and weapons to fight them on its own. Leave aside the question of whether Israel's battles are, or should be, America's. It is no longer true that Israel does not ask us to fight for it. The fact that prominent American apologists for Israel were the most energetic promoters of the U.S. invasion of Iraq does not, of course, prove that Israel was the instigator of that grievous misadventure, but the very same people are now urging an American military assault on Iran explicitly to protect Israel and to preserve its nuclear monopoly in the Middle East. Their advocacy is fully coordinated with the government of Israel. No one in the region wants a nuclear-armed Iran, but Israel is the only country pressing Americans to go to war over this.

Finally, the need to protect Israel from mounting international indignation about its behavior continues to do grave damage to our global and regional standing. It has severely impaired our ties with the world's 1.6 billion Muslims. These costs to our international influence, credibility, and leadership are, I think, far more serious than the economic and other burdens of the relationship.

Against this background, it's remarkable that something as fatuous as the notion of Israel as a strategic asset could have become the unchallengeable conventional wisdom in the United States. Perhaps it's just that as Hitler once said, "People...will more easily fall victim to a big lie than a small one." Be that as it may, the United States and Israel have a lot invested in our relationship. Basing our cooperation on a thesis and narratives that will not withstand scrutiny is dangerous. It is especially risky in the context of current fiscal pressures in the United States. These seem certain soon to force major revisions of both current levels of American defense spending and global strategy, in the Middle East as well as elsewhere. They also place federally funded programs in Israel in direct competition with similar programs here at home. To flourish over the long term, Israel's relations with the United States need to be grounded in reality, not myth, and in peace, not war.

America's Faltering Search for Peace in the Middle East: Openings for Others?

September 1, 2010[2]

The declaration of principles worked out in Oslo seventeen years ago was the last direct negotiation between Israelis and Palestinian Arabs to reach consequential, positive results. The Oslo accords were a real step toward peace, not another deceptive pseudo-event in an endlessly unproductive, so-called "peace process." If that one step forward in Oslo in 1993 was followed by several steps backward, there is a great deal to be learned from how and why that happened.

There can be no doubt about the importance of today's topic. The ongoing conflict in the Holy Land increasingly disturbs the world's conscience as well as its tranquility. The Israel-Palestine issue began as a struggle in the context of European colonialism. In the postcolonial era, tension between Israelis and the Palestinians they dispossessed became, by degrees, the principal source of radicalization and instability in the Arab East and then the Arab world as a whole. It stimulated escalating terrorism against Israelis at home and their allies abroad. Since the end of the Cold War, the interaction between Israel and its captive Palestinian population has emerged as the fountainhead of global strife. It is increasingly difficult to distinguish this strife from a war of religions or a conflict of civilizations.

For better or ill, the United States has played and continues to play the key international part in this contest. American policies, more than those of any other external actor, have the capacity to stoke or stifle the hatreds in the Middle East and to spread or reverse their infection of the wider world. American policies and actions in the Middle East thus affect much more than that region.

Yet, as I will argue, the United States has been obsessed with *process* rather than substance. It has failed to involve parties who are essential to peace. It has acted on Israel's behalf to preempt rather than enlist international and regional support for peace. It has defined the issues in ways that preclude rather than promote progress. Its concept of a "peace process" has therefore become the handmaiden of Israeli expansionism rather than a driver for peace. There are alternatives to tomorrow's diplomatic peace

---

2. Remarks to staff of the Royal Norwegian Ministry of Foreign Affairs and, separately, to members of the Norwegian Institute of International Affairs, Oslo

pageant on the Potomac.[3] As Norway has shown, there is a role for powers other than America in crafting peace in the Holy Land.

Over thirty years ago, at Camp David, Jimmy Carter pushed Israel through the door to peace that Egypt's Anwar Sadat had opened. Twenty years ago, the first Bush administration pressed Israel to the negotiating table with Palestinian leaders, setting the stage for their clandestine meetings in Oslo. The capacity of the United States to rally other governments behind a cause that it espouses may have atrophied, but American power remains far greater than that of any other nation. Nowhere is this more evident than in the Middle East.

For more than four decades, Israel has been able to rely on aid from the United States to dominate its region militarily and to sustain its economic prosperity. It has counted on its leverage in American politics to block the application of international law and to protect itself from the political repercussions of its policies and actions. Unquestioning American support has enabled Israel to put the seizure of ever more land ahead of the achievement of a *modus vivendi* with the Palestinians or other Arabs. Neither violent resistance from the dispossessed nor objections from abroad have brought successive Israeli governments to question, let alone alter the priority they assign to land over peace.

Ironically, Palestinians too have developed a dependency relationship with America. This has locked them into a political framework over which Israel exercises decisive influence. They have been powerless to end occupation, pogroms, ethnic cleansing, and other humiliations by Jewish soldiers and settlers. Nor have they been able to prevent their progressive confinement in checkpoint-encircled ghettos on the West Bank and in the great open air prison of Gaza.

Despite this appalling record of failure, the American monopoly on the management of the search for peace in Palestine remains unchallenged. Since the end of the Cold War, Russia—once a contender for countervailing influence in the region—has lapsed into impotence. The former colonial powers of the European Union, having earlier laid the basis for conflict in the region, have largely sat on their hands while ringing them, content to let America take the lead. China, India, and other Asian powers have prudently kept their political and military distance. In the region itself, Iran has postured and exploited the Palestinian cause without doing anything to advance it. Until recently, Turkey remained aloof.

---

3. President Obama began talks on September 1, 2010, with Mahmoud Abbas, Binyamin Netanyahu, King Abdullah II, and Hosni Mubarak.

On rare occasions, as in the case of the 1973 Arab oil embargo, the Arabs have backed their verbal opposition to Israel with action. Egypt and Jordan have settled into an unpopular coexistence with Israel that is now sustained only by U.S. subventions. Saudi Arabia has twice taken the initiative to offer Israel diplomatic concessions if it were to conclude arrangements for peaceful coexistence with the Palestinians. Overall, though, Arab governments have earned the contempt of the Palestinians and their own people for their lack of serious engagement. For the most part, Arab leaders have timorously demanded that America solve the Israel-Palestine problem for them, while obsequiously courting American protection against Israel, each other, Iran, and—in some cases—their own increasingly frustrated and angry subjects and citizens.

Islam charges rulers with the duty to defend the faithful and to uphold justice. It demands that they embody righteousness. The resentment of mostly Muslim Arabs at their governing elites' failure to meet these standards generates sympathy for terrorism directed not just at Israel but at both the United States and Arab governments associated with it.

The perpetrators of the September 11, 2001, terrorist attack on the United States saw it in part as reprisal for American complicity in Israeli cruelties to Palestinians and other Arabs. They justified it as a strike against Washington's protection of Arab governments willing to overlook American contributions to Muslim suffering. Washington's response to the attack included suspending its efforts to make peace in the Holy Land as well as invading and occupying Afghanistan and Iraq. All three actions inadvertently strengthened the terrorist case for further attacks on America and its allies. The armed struggle between Americans and Muslim radicals has already spilled over to Pakistan, Yemen, Somalia, and other countries. Authoritative voices in Israel now call for adding Iran to the list of countries at war with America. They are echoed by Zionist and neoconservative voices in the United States.

The widening involvement of Americans in combat in Muslim lands has inflamed anti-American passions and catalyzed a metastasis of terrorism. It has caused a growing majority of the world's 1.6 billion Muslims to see the United States as a menace to their faith, their way of life, their homelands, and their personal security. American populists and European xenophobes have meanwhile undercut liberal and centrist Muslim arguments against the intolerance that empowers terrorism by equating terrorism and its extremist advocates with Islam and its followers. The current outburst of bigoted demagoguery over the construction of an Islamic cultural center and mosque in New York is merely the most recent illustration of this.[4] It suggests that the blatant racism and Islamophobia of contemporary Israeli politics is contagious. It rules out the global alliances against religious extremists that are essential to encompass their political defeat.

President Obama's inability to break this pattern must be an enormous personal disappointment to him. He came into office committed to crafting a new relationship with the Arab and Muslim worlds. His first interview with the international media was with Arab satellite television. He reached out publicly and privately to Iran. He addressed the Turkish parliament with persuasive empathy. He traveled to a great center of Islamic learning in Cairo to deliver a remarkably eloquent message of conciliation to Muslims everywhere. He made it clear that he understood the centrality of injustices in the Holy Land to Muslim estrangement from the West. He promised a responsible withdrawal from Iraq and a judicious recrafting of strategy in Afghanistan. Few doubt Mr. Obama's sincerity. Yet none of his initiatives has led to policy change anyone can detect, let alone believe in.

It is not for me to analyze or explain the wide gaps between rhetoric and achievement in the Obama administration's stewardship of so many aspects of my country's affairs. American voters will render their first formal verdict on this two months from tomorrow, on the second of November. The situation in the Holy Land, Iraq, Afghanistan, and adjacent areas is only part of what they will consider as they do so, but I do think it worthwhile briefly to examine some of the changes in the situation that ensure that many policies that once helped us to get by in the Middle East no longer do this.

Let me begin with the "peace process," a hardy perennial of America's diplomatic repertoire that the Obama administration will put back on public display tomorrow. During the Cold War, the appearance of an earnest and "even-handed" American search for peace in the Holy Land was the price of U.S. access and influence in the Middle East. It provided political cover for conservative Arab governments to set aside their anger at American backing of Israel so as to stand with America and the Western bloc against Soviet Communism. It kept American relations with Israel and the Arabs from becoming a zero-sum game. It mobilized domestic Jewish support for incumbent presidents. Of course, there hasn't been an American-led "peace process" in the Middle East for at least a decade. Still,

4. In 2010, a Muslim community center and prayer space was proposed to be built on Park Place in lower Manhattan. An Islamophobic controversy erupted, with right-wing media referring to the complex (originally named Cordoba House in honor of that Spanish city's history of tolerance, then called Park51) as the "Ground Zero Mosque" and portraying it as an insult to the victims of the 9/11 attacks.

the conceit of a "peace process" became an essential political convenience for all concerned. No one could bear to admit that the "peace process" had expired. It therefore lived on in phantom form.

Even when there was no "peace process," the possibility of resurrecting one provided hope to the gullible, cover to the guileful, beguilement for the press, an excuse for doing nothing to those gaining from the status quo, and—last but far from least—lifetime employment for career "peace processors." The perpetual processing of peace without the requirement to produce it has been especially appreciated by Israeli leaders. It has enabled them to behave like magicians, riveting foreign attention on meaningless distractions as they systematically remove Palestinians from their homes, settle half a million or more Jews in newly vacated areas of the occupied territories, and annex a widening swath of land to a Jerusalem they insist belongs only to Israel.

Palestinian leaders with legitimacy problems have also had reason to collaborate in the search for a "peace process." It's not just that there has been no obviously better way to end their people's suffering. Playing "peace process" charades justifies the international patronage and Israeli backing these leaders need to retain their status in the occupied territories. It ensures that they have media access and high-level visiting rights in Washington. Meanwhile, for American leaders, engagement in some sort of Middle East "peace process" has been essential to credibility in the Arab and Islamic worlds, as well as with the ever-generous American Jewish community. Polls show that most American Jews are impatient for peace. Despite all the evidence to the contrary, they are eager to believe in the willingness of the government of Israel's to trade land for it.

Previous "peace processes" have exploited all these impulses. In practice, however, these diplomatic distractions have served to obscure Israeli actions and evasions that are more often prejudicial to peace than helpful in achieving it. Behind all the blather, the rumble of bulldozers has never stopped. Given this history, it has taken a year and a half of relentless effort by U.S. special envoy George Mitchell to persuade the parties even to meet directly to *talk about talks* as they first did here in Oslo, seventeen years ago. When the curtain goes up on the diplomatic show in Washington tomorrow, will the players put on a different skit? There are many reasons to doubt that they will.

One is that the Obama administration has engaged the same aging impresarios who staged all the previously failed "peace processes" to produce and direct this one, with no agreed script. The last time these guys staged such an ill-prepared meeting, at Camp David in 2000, it cost both

delegation heads, Ehud Barak and Yasser Arafat, their political authority. It led not to peace but to escalating violence. The parties are showing up this time to minimize President Obama's political embarrassment
in advance of midterm elections in the United States, not to address his
agenda—and still less to address each other's agendas. These are indeed
difficulties. But the problems with this latest—and possibly final—iteration of the perpetually ineffectual "peace process" are more fundamental.

The Likud Party charter flatly rejects the establishment of a Palestinian
Arab state west of the Jordan River and stipulates that "the Palestinians
can run their lives freely in the framework of self-rule, but not as an independent and sovereign state." This Israeli government is committed to
that charter as well as to the Jewish holy war for land in Palestine. It has no
interest in trading land it covets for a peace that might thwart further territorial expansion. It considers itself unbound by the applicable UN resolutions, agreements from past peace talks, the "Road Map," or the premise
of the "two-state solution."

The Palestinians are desperate for the dignity and security that
only the end of the Israeli occupation can provide, but the authority of
Palestinian negotiators to negotiate rests on their recognition by Israel and
the United States, not on their standing in the occupied territories, Gaza,
or the Palestinian diaspora. Fatah is the ruling faction in part of Palestine.
Its authority to govern was repudiated by voters in the last Palestinian
elections. Mahmoud Abbas's administration retains power by grace of the
Israeli occupation authorities and the United States, which prefer it to the
government empowered by the Palestinian people at the polls. Mr. Abbas's
constitutional term of office has long since expired. He presides over a parliament whose most influential members are locked up in Israeli jails. It is
not clear for whom he, his faction, or his administration can now speak.

So the talks that begin tomorrow promise to be a case of the disinter-
ested going through the motions of negotiating with the mandateless. The
parties to these talks seek to mollify an America that has severely lessened international credibility. The United States government had to borrow the modest reputations for objectivity of others—the EU, Russia, and
the UN—to be able to convene this discussion. It will be held under the
auspices of an American president who was publicly humiliated by Israel's
prime minister on the issue that is at the center of the Israel-Palestine dispute: Israel's continuing seizure and colonization of Arab land.

Vague promises of a Palestinian state within a year now waft through
the air. But the "peace process" has always sneered at deadlines, even much,
much firmer ones. A more definitive promise of an independent Palestine

within a year was made at Annapolis three years ago. Analogous promises of Palestinian self-determination have preceded or resulted from previous meetings over the decades, beginning with the Camp David accords of 1979. Many in this audience will recall the five-year deadline fixed at Oslo. The talks about talks that begin tomorrow can yield concrete results only if the international community is prepared this time to insist on the one-year deadline put forward for recognizing a Palestinian state. Even then, there will be no peace unless long-neglected issues are addressed.

Peace is a pattern of stability acceptable to those with the capacity to disturb it by violence. It is almost impossible to impose. It cannot become a reality, still less be sustained, if those who must accept it are excluded from it. This reality directs our attention to who is *not* at this gathering in Washington and what must be done to remedy the problems these absences create.

Obviously, the party that won the democratically expressed mandate of the Palestinian people to represent them—Hamas—is not there. Yet there can be no peace without its buy-in. Egypt and Jordan have been invited as observers. Yet they have nothing to add to the separate peace agreements each long ago made with Israel. (Both these agreements were explicitly premised on grudging Israeli undertakings to accept Palestinian self-determination. The Jewish state quickly finessed both.) Activists from the Jewish diaspora disproportionately staff the American delegation. A failure to reconcile either American Jews or the Palestine diaspora to peace would doom any accord. But the Palestinian diaspora will be represented in Washington only in tenuous theory, not in fact.

Other Arabs, including the Arab League and the author of its peace initiative, Saudi Arabia, will not be at the talks tomorrow. The reasons for this are both simple and complex. At one level they reflect a conviction that this latest installment of the "peace process" is just another in a long series of public entertainments for the American electorate, as well as a lack of confidence in the authenticity of the Palestinian delegation. At another level, they result from the way the United States has defined the problems to be solved and the indifference to Arab interests and views this definition evidences. Then, too, they reflect disconnects in political culture and negotiating style between Israelis, Arabs, and Americans.

To begin with, neither Israel nor the conveners of this proposed new "peace process" have officially acknowledged or responded to the Arab peace initiative of 2002. This offered normalization of relations with the Jewish state, should Israel make peace with the Palestinians. Instead, the United States and the Quartet have seemed to pocket the Arab offer, ignored its precondition that Israelis come to terms with Palestinians, and gone on to levy new demands.

In this connection, making Arab recognition of Israel's "right to exist" the central purpose of the "peace process" offends Arabs on many levels. In framing the issue this way, Israel and the United States appear to be asking for something well beyond pragmatic accommodation of the reality of a Jewish state in the Middle East. To the Arabs, Americans now seem to be insisting on Arab endorsement of the idea of the state of Israel, the means by which that state was established, and the manner in which it has comported itself. Must Arabs really embrace Zionism before Israel can cease expansion and accept peace?

Arabs and Muslims familiar with European history can accept that European anti-Semitism justified the establishment of a homeland for traumatized European Jews. But asking them, even implicitly, to agree that the forcible eviction of Palestinian Arabs was a morally appropriate means to this end is both a nonstarter and seriously off-putting. So is asking them to affirm that resistance to such displacement was and is sinful. Similarly, the Arabs see the demand that they recognize a Jewish state with no fixed borders as a clever attempt to extract their endorsement of Israel's unilateral expansion at Palestinian expense.

The lack of appeal in this approach has been compounded by a longstanding American habit of treating Arab concerns about Israel as a form of anti-Semitism and tuning them out. Instead of hearing out and addressing Arab views, U.S. peace processors have repeatedly focused on soliciting Arab acts of kindness toward Israel. They argue that gestures of acceptance can help Israelis overcome their Holocaust-inspired political neuroses and take risks for peace.

Each time this notion of Arab diplomacy as psychotherapy for Israelis has been trotted out, it has been met with incredulity. To most in the region, it encapsulates the contrast between Washington's sympathy and solicitude for Israelis and its condescendingly exploitative view of Arabs. Some see it as a barely disguised appeal for a policy of appeasement of Israel. Still others suspect an attempt to construct a "peace process" in which Arabs begin to supply Israel with gifts of carrots so that Americans can continue to avoid applying sticks to it.

The effort to encourage Arab generosity as an offset to American political pusillanimity vis-à-vis Israel is ludicrously unpersuasive. It has failed so many times that it should be obvious that it will not work. Yet it was a central element of George Mitchell's mandate for "peace process" diplomacy. And it appears to have resurfaced as part of the proposed follow-up to tomorrow's meeting between the parties in Washington. It should be no puzzle why the Saudis and other Arabs could not be persuaded to join this gathering.

Arabic has two quite different words that are both translated as "negotiation," making a distinction that doesn't exist in either English or Hebrew. One word, *musaawama,* refers to the no-holds-barred bargaining process that takes place in bazaars between strangers who may never see each other again and who therefore feel no obligation not to scam each other. Another, *mufaawadhat,* describes the dignified formal discussions about matters of honor and high principle that take place on a basis of mutual respect and equality between statesmen who seek a continuing relationship.

Egyptian president Anwar Sadat's travel to Jerusalem was a grand act of statesmanship to initiate a process of *mufaawadhat*—relationship-building between leaders and their polities. So was the Arab peace initiative of 2002. It called for a response in kind. The West muttered approvingly but did not act. After a while, Israel responded with intermittent, somewhat oblique suggestions of willingness to haggle over terms—but an offer to bicker over the terms on which a grand gesture has been granted is, not surprisingly, seen as insultingly unresponsive.

I cite this not to suggest that non-Arabs should adopt Arabic canons of thought, but to make a point about diplomatic effectiveness. To move a negotiating partner in a desired direction, one must understand how that partner understands things and help him to see a way forward that will bring him to an end he has been persuaded to want. One of the reasons we can't seem to move things as we desire in the Middle East is that we don't make much effort to understand how others reason and how they rank their interests. In the case of the Israel-Palestine conundrum, we Americans are long on empathy and expertise about Israel—and very, very short on these for the various Arab parties. The essential militarism of U.S. policies in the Middle East adds to our difficulties. We have become skilled at killing Arabs. We have forgotten how to listen to them or persuade them.

I am not myself an "Arabist," but I am old enough to remember when there were more than a few such people in the American diplomatic service. These were officers who had devoted themselves to the cultivation of understanding and empathy with Arab leaders so as to be able to convince these leaders that it was in their own interest to do things we saw as in our interest. If we still have such people, we are hiding them well; we are certainly not applying their skills in our Middle East diplomacy.

This brings me to a few thoughts about the Western and Arab interests at stake in the Holy Land and their implications for what must be done.

In foreign affairs, interests are the measure of all things. My assumption is that Americans and Norwegians, indeed Europeans in general, share common interests that require peace in the Holy Land. To my mind, these interests include—but are, of course, not limited to—gaining security and acceptance for a democratic state of Israel; eliminating the gross injustices and daily humiliations that foster Arab terrorism against Israel and its foreign allies and supporters, as well as friendly Arab regimes; and reversing the global spread of religious strife and prejudice, including, very likely, a revival of anti-Semitism in the West if current trends are not arrested. None of these aspirations can be fulfilled without an end to the Israeli occupation and freedom for Palestinians.

Arab states, like Saudi Arabia, also have compelling reasons to want relief from occupation as well as self-determination for Palestinians. They may not be concerned to preserve Israel's democracy, as we are, but they share an urgent interest in ending the radicalization of their own populations, curbing the spread of Islamist terrorism, and eliminating the tensions with the West that the conflict in the Holy Land fuels. These are the concerns that have driven them to propose peace, as they very clearly did eight years ago. For related reasons, Saudi Arabia's King Abdullah has made interfaith dialogue and the promotion of religious tolerance a main focus of his domestic and international policy.

As the custodian of two of Islam's three sacred places of pilgrimage, Mecca and Medina, Saudi Arabia has long transcended its own notorious religious narrow-mindedness to hold the holy places in its charge open to Muslims of all sects and persuasions. This experience, joined with Islamic piety, reinforces a Saudi insistence on the exemption of religious pilgrimage to Jerusalem from political interference or manipulation. The Ottoman Turks were careful to ensure freedom of access for worship to adherents of the three Abrahamic faiths when they administered the city. It is an interest that Jews, Christians, and Muslims share.

There is, in short, far greater congruity between Western and Arab interests affecting the Israel-Palestine dispute than is generally recognized. This can be the basis for creative diplomacy. The fact that this has not occurred reflects pathologies of political life in the United States that paralyze the American diplomatic imagination. Tomorrow's meeting may well demonstrate that, the election of Barack Obama notwithstanding, the United States is still unfit to manage the achievement of peace between Israel and the Arabs. If so, it is in the American interest as well as everyone else's that others become the pathbreakers, enlisting the United States as best they can in support of what they achieve, but not expecting America to overcome its incapacity to lead.

Here, I think, there is a lesson to be drawn from the Norwegian experience in the 1990s. The Clinton administration was happy to organize the public relations for the Oslo accords but did not take ownership of them. It did little to protect them from subversion and overthrow, and nothing to insist on their implementation. Only a peace process that is protected from Israel's ability to manipulate American politics can succeed.

This brings me to how Europeans and Arabs might work together to realize the objectives both share with most Americans: establishing internationally recognized borders for Israel, securing freedom for the Palestinians, and ending the stimulus to terrorism in the region and beyond it that strife in the Holy Land entails. I have only four suggestions to present today. I expect that more ideas will emerge from the discussion period. A serious effort to cooperate with the Arabs of the sort that Norway is uniquely capable of contriving could lead to the development of still more options for joint or parallel action on behalf of peace.

Now to my suggestions, presented in ascending order of difficulty, from the least to the most controversial.

First, *get behind the Arab peace initiative*. Saudi Arab culture frowns on self-promotion, and the Kingdom is less gifted than most at public diplomacy. Political factors inhibit official Arab access to the Israeli press. The Israeli media have published some (mostly dismissive) commentary on the Arab peace initiative but have left most Israelis ignorant of its contents and unfamiliar with its text. Why not buy space in the Israeli media to give Israelis a chance to read the Arab League declaration and consider the opportunities it presents? I suspect the Saudis, as well as other members of the Arab League, would consider it constructive for an outside party to do this. It might facilitate other sorts of cooperation with them in which European capabilities can also compensate for Arab reticence. The Turks and other non-Arab Muslims should be brought in as full participants in any such efforts. This wouldn't be bad for Europe's relations with both. By the way, given the U.S. media's notorious one-sidedness and American ignorance about the Arab peace plan, a well-targeted advertising campaign in the United States might not be a bad idea either.

Second, *help create a Palestinian partner for peace*. There can be no peace with Israel unless there are officials who are empowered by the Palestinian people to negotiate and ratify it. Israel has worked hard to divide the Palestinians so as to consolidate its conquest of their homeland.

Saudi Arabia has several times sought to create a Palestinian peace partner for Israel by bringing Fatah, Hamas, and other factions together. On
each occasion, Israel, with U.S. support, has acted to preclude this. Active
organization of non-American Western support for diplomacy aimed at
restoring a unity government to the Palestinian Authority could make a
big difference. The Obama administration would be under strong domestic political pressure to join Israel in blocking a joint European-Arab effort
to accomplish this. Under some circumstances, however, it might welcome
being put to this test.

Third, *reaffirm and enforce international law.* The UN Security
Council is charged with enforcing the rule of law internationally. In the
case of the Middle East, however, the Council's position at the apex of
the international system has served to erode and subvert the ideal of a
rule-bound international order. Almost forty American vetoes have prevented the application to the Israeli occupying authorities of the Geneva
Conventions, the Nuremberg precedents, human rights conventions, and
relevant Security Council directives. American diplomacy on behalf of the
Jewish state has silenced the collective voice of the international community as Israel has illegally colonized and annexed broad swaths of occupied
territory, administered collective punishment to a captive people, assassi-
nated their political leaders, massacred civilians, barred UN investigators,
defied mandatory Security Council resolutions, and otherwise engaged
in scofflaw behavior, usually with only the flimsiest of legally irrelevant
excuses.

If ethnic cleansing, settlement activity, and the like are not just "un-
helpful" but illegal, the international community should find a way to say
so, even if the UN Security Council cannot. Otherwise, the most valuable legacy of Atlantic civilization—its vision of the rule of law—will be
lost. When one side to a dispute is routinely exempted from principles, all
exempt themselves, and the law of the jungle prevails. The international
community needs collectively to affirm that Israel, both as occupier and as
regional military hegemon, is legally accountable internationally for its actions. If the UN General Assembly cannot "unite for peace" to do what an
incapacitated Security Council cannot, member states should not shrink
from working in conference outside the UN framework. All sides in the
murder and mayhem in the Holy Land and beyond need to understand
that they are not above the law. If this message is firmly delivered and enforced, there will be a better chance for peace.

Fourth, *set a deadline linked to an ultimatum*. Accept that the United States will frustrate any attempt by the UN Security Council to address the continuing impasse between Israel and the Palestinians. Organize a global conference outside the UN system to coordinate a decision to inform the parties to the dispute that if they cannot reach agreement in a year, one of two solutions will be imposed. Schedule a follow-up conference for a year later. The second conference would consider whether to recommend universal recognition of a Palestinian state in the area beyond Israel's 1967 borders or recognition of Israel's achievement of de jure as well as de facto sovereignty throughout Palestine (requiring Israel to grant all governed by it citizenship and equal rights at pain of international sanctions, boycott, and disinvestment). Either formula would force the parties to make a serious effort to strike a deal or to face the consequences of their recalcitrance. Either formula could be implemented directly by the states as members of the international community. Admittedly, any serious deadline would provoke a political crisis in Israel and lead to diplomatic confrontation with the United States as well as Israel, despite the Obama administration itself having proclaimed a one-year deadline in order to entice the Palestinians to tomorrow's talks. Yet both Israel and the United States would benefit immensely from peace with the Palestinians.

Time is running out. The two-state solution may already have been overtaken by Israeli land grabs and settlement activity. Another cycle of violence is likely in the offing. If so, it will not be local or regional, but global in its reach. Israel's actions are delegitimizing and isolating it even as they multiply the numbers of those in the region and beyond who are determined to destroy it. Palestinian suffering is a reproach to all humanity that posturing alone cannot begin to alleviate. It has become a cancer on the Islamic body politic. It is infecting every extremity of the globe with the rage against injustice that incites terrorism.

It is time to try new approaches. That is why the question of whether there is a basis for expanded diplomatic cooperation between Europeans and Arabs is such a timely one.

Failed Interventions and What They Teach
October 21, 2010[5]

I feel honored to have been asked to open this conference on U.S.-Arab relations and America's ties with the broader Middle East. But I confess that, as an American, the results of U.S. policies in the Middle East remind me of a T-shirt someone once gave me that said, "Sinatra is dead. Elvis is dead. And me, I don't feel so good."

The Middle East is a constant reminder that a clear conscience is usually a sign of either a faulty memory or a severe case of arrogant amorality. It is not a badge of innocence. These days, we meticulously tally our own battlefield dead; we do not count the numbers of foreigners who perish at our hands or those of our allies. Yet each death is a tragedy that extinguishes one soul, wounds others, and diminishes the world. If we do not grieve for those we slay, we may justly be charged with inhumanity. If we cannot understand the consequences for ourselves of the manner in which they died, we are surely guilty of strategic ineptitude.

All that is required to be hated is to do something hateful. Apparent indifference to the pain and humiliation one has inflicted further outrages its victims, their families, and their friends. As the Golden Rule, which is common—in one phrasing or another—to all religions, implicitly warns, moral blindness is contagious. That is why warring parties engaged in tit-for-tat come in time to resemble each other rather than to sharpen their differences.

I want to speak to you today about three things. First, why militarized U.S. policies and the actions we are taking pursuant to them in the broader Middle East risk provoking terrorist retaliation against the United States and its citizens. Second, why our military and quasi-diplomatic interventions in the region have failed or are failing. And, third, how our current policy course is changing us for the worse without changing the Arab and Islamic worlds for the better. I will end with a thought or two on the prospects for changed policies that could produce better results.

War is not the spectator sport that the fans who watch it here on television imagine. Nor is it the "cakewalk" that its armchair advocates like to suggest it could be. War is traumatic for all its participants. Recent experience suggests that 30 percent of troops develop serious mental health problems that dog them after they leave the battlefield. But what of the

---

5. Remarks to the National Council of U.S.-Arab Relations, Washington, D.C.

peoples soldiers seek to punish or pacify? To understand the hatreds war unleashes and its lasting psychological and political consequences, one has only to translate foreign casualty figures into terms we Americans can relate to. You can do this by imagining that the same percentages of Americans might die or suffer injury as foreigners have. Then think about the impact that level of physical and moral insult would have on us.

Consider, for example, the two sides of the Israel-Palestine struggle. So far in this century—since September 29, 2000, when Ariel Sharon marched into al-Aqsa and ignited the Intifada of that name—about 850 Israeli Jews have died at the hands of Palestinians, 125 or so of them children. In proportion to population, that's equivalent to 45,000 dead Americans, including about 6,800 children. It's a level of mayhem we Americans cannot begin to understand. But, over the same period, Israeli soldiers and settlers have killed 6,600 or so Palestinians, at least 1,315 of whom were children. In American terms, that's equivalent to 460,000 U.S. dead, including 95,000 children. Meanwhile, the American equivalent of almost 500,000 Israelis and 2.9 million Palestinians have been injured. To put it mildly, the human experiences these figures enumerate are not conducive to peace or goodwill among men and women in the Holy Land or anywhere with emotional ties to them.

We all know that events in the Holy Land have an impact far beyond it. American sympathy for Israel and kinship with Jewish settlers assure that Jewish deaths there arouse anti-Arab and anti-Muslim passions here, even as the toll on Palestinians is seldom, if ever, mentioned. Among the world's 340 million Arabs and 1.6 billion Muslims, however, all eyes are on the resistance of Palestinians to continuing ethnic cleansing and the American subsidies and political support for Israel that facilitate their suffering. The chief planner of 9/11, Khalid Sheikh Mohammed, testified under oath that a primary purpose of that criminal assault on the United States was to focus "the American people...on the atrocities that America is committing by supporting Israel against the Palestinian people." The occupation and attempted pacification of other Muslim lands like Iraq and Afghanistan as well as the shocking hate speech about Islam that now pervades American politics lend credence to deepening Muslim perception of an escalating U.S. crusade against Islam and its believers.

No one knows how many Iraqis have died as a direct or indirect result of the U.S. invasion and the anarchy that followed it. Estimates range between a low of something over 100,000 to a high of well over 1 million. Translated to American proportions, that equates to somewhere between 1 and 13 million dead Americans. More than 2.25 million Iraqis fled to neighboring countries to escape this bloodbath. Only 5 percent have returned. An equal number sought temporary refuge inside Iraq. Most of them also remain displaced. In our terms, this equals a flight to Canada and Mexico of 24 million Americans, with another 24 million still here but homeless. I think you will agree that, had this kind of thing happened to Americans, religious scruples would not deter many of us from seeking revenge and engaging in reprisal against whoever had done it to us.

The numbers in Afghanistan aren't quite as frightful but they make the same point. We're accumulating a critical mass of enemies with personal as well as religious and nationalistic reasons to seek retribution against us. As our violence against foreign civilians has escalated, our enemies have multiplied. The logic of this progression is best understood anecdotally.

I am grateful to Bruce Fein (a noted constitutional scholar here in Washington) for calling attention to the colloquy of convicted Times Square car bomber Faisal Shahzad with U.S. District Judge Miriam Cedarbaum. She challenged Shahzad's self-description as a "Muslim soldier" because his contemplated violence targeted civilians,

"Did you look around to see who they were?"

"Well, the people select the government," Shahzad retorted. "We consider them all the same. The drones, when they hit...."

Judge Cedarbaum interrupted, "Including the children?"

Shahzad countered, "Well, the drone hits in Afghanistan and Iraq, they don't see children, they don't see anybody. They kill women, children, they kill everybody. It's a war, and in war, they kill people. They're killing all Muslims."

Later, he added, "I am part of the answer to the U.S. terrorizing the Muslim nations and the Muslim people. And, on behalf of that, I'm avenging the attack. Living in the United States, Americans only care about their own people, but they don't care about the people elsewhere in the world when they die."

No amount of public diplomacy, no matter how cleverly conducted, can prevail over the bitterness of personal and collective experience. The only way to reverse trends supporting anti-American violence by the aggrieved is to reverse the policies that feed it.

We are now a nation with unmatched military capabilities. Perhaps that is why we are the only country in the world to have proclaimed that our conflict with terrorists is a "war" or to have dismissed civilian victims of our violence as "collateral damage." Few allies joined us in Iraq. Those that joined us in Afghanistan did so to demonstrate their solidarity with us, not because they see the piecemeal pacification of the Muslim world as the answer to the extremist nonstate actors in its midst. They know, even if we do not, that terrorism is a tactic, not a cause against which one can wage war. Weapons are tools with which to change men's minds, but the inappropriate use of them can entrench animosity and justify reprisal against the citizens of the nations that wield them. No other people has so powerful a military establishment that it could even begin to persuade itself, as many Americans have, that guns can cure grudges or missiles erase militancy.

If you view the world through a bomb sight, everything looks like a target. Yet the lesson of 9/11 is that if you drop bombs on enough people—even peoples with no air force—the most offended among them will do their best to bomb you back. Thus our destabilization of places remote from our shores has already blown back to challenge our own domestic tranquility. There is no reason to doubt that it could do so again. Then, too, one of the main lessons of Iraq and Afghanistan is that there are some problems for which invasion and occupation are inappropriate and ineffective responses. Far from demonstrating the irresistible might of the United States, as their neoconservative champions intended, these wars have revealed the considerable limits of American power.

As a case in point, the use of force in Iraq has neither shaped that country to our will nor vindicated our values. We have so far given 4,500 American lives, suffered the maiming of 32,000 American bodies, disordered many tens of thousands of young American minds, and spent at least $900 billion in Iraq. Our one clear achievement—the removal from power of Saddam Hussein—culminated in a tragicomic trial and execution that mocked rather than celebrated the rule of law. We will leave behind a traumatized society, brutalized by anarchy, sectarian violence, and terrorism spawned by resentment of foreign occupation. Iraq's constitutional order, prospects for domestic tranquility, relations with its neighbors, and international orientation all remain in doubt.

The Iranian-influenced, Shiite Arab–dominated regime we brought to power in Baghdad is—for now, at least—at peace with Iraq's Kurds. But this regime has not shown that it can coexist peacefully with the country's Sunni Arab minority. More than half a year after national elections, no new government has been formed. Many in the region suspect that the army we Americans are training and equipping may in time emerge, like its predecessors, as the principal institution of government in Iraq as well as the violent enforcer of its national unity under Shiite Arab majority rule. Will Iraq once again balance Iran or will it collude with it? We do not know.

What does seem clear is that neither the Iraqi nor the American people will remember Iraq's close encounter with the United States proudly or fondly. The years to come are more likely to produce intermittent reminders of Iraq's agonies and America's witlessness as this century began than to furnish reasons for nostalgia about shared experience. Nor is the U.S. experience with war in Iraq of much value to the formulation of campaign plans for pacifying other countries.

The "surge" of more troops into Iraq is now presented by some as a model for plucking impasse from the maw of military disgrace in Afghanistan too. But that "success," such as it was, cannot be translated to Afghanistan. The concentration of U.S. forces in Baghdad froze the pattern of sectarian urban enclaves that had emerged from four years of savage confessional cleansing. It allowed warring Iraqi religious groups to barricade the Baghdad neighborhoods into which they had retreated. This both reduced the level of mayhem and fixed sectarian divisions in place. But Afghanistan cannot be stabilized by such religious apartheid. Its divisions have always been primarily ethnic, rural, and regional rather than confessional.

In parts of Iraq, a surge of U.S. cash helped Iraq's conservative Sunni tribesmen to recognize the U.S. Marines as allies against the murderous, foreign jihadis in their midst. Tribes and localities in Afghanistan are also fond of cash, but the context is very different. The foreign jihadis who were in Afghanistan have withdrawn to neighboring Pakistan, and no one wants or expects them to return. The Taliban are Afghan traditionalists, not foreign radicals.

Afghanistan has always defined itself as a confederation of tribes and localities that cooperate for limited purposes while resisting central or foreign control. The only alien presence in Afghanistan at present is U.S. and NATO forces and associated aid agencies and NGOs. But they are there to impose allegiance to Kabul and to challenge tribal customs, not to make common cause with the tribal and local authorities on these matters. Many at the local level see their presence as a nuisance that attracts unwanted attention from homegrown, not foreign, guerrillas—and one that disturbs, not preserves, the peace.

Counterinsurgency doctrine is an implausible answer to the situation in Afghanistan. It was developed to defend postcolonial governments in newly independent states modeled on those of their erstwhile colonial masters. It was never intended to replicate colonialism by building such states in traditional societies that lack and don't much want them. It presumes that foreign forces are assisting a national government to defeat rebels attempting to overthrow it or secede from it. In Afghanistan, the national government is a barely established creature of foreign intervention that is attempting to extend central authority in unprecedented ways. The Hamid Karzai regime has been happy to leave the task of imposing its rule on the country at large to Americans and other foreigners, while profiting as best it can from our efforts. By all accounts, it hasn't done at all badly at such profiteering.

Afghanistan is one of the poorest countries on earth. Its nearly 30 million people have a GDP of about $10 billion. Over the past nine years, we have put $350 billion into making war there and spent another $54 billion on developing the place. Not surprisingly, some Afghans, including not a few in positions of authority, have seen no reason to restrain their enthusiasm about the opportunities for rake-offs that this level of spending sustains.

Nine years after it began, the U.S. intervention in Afghanistan has strayed far from its original objectives of suppressing al-Qaeda and punishing the Taliban to deter them from ever again accommodating anti-American "terrorists with global reach." Our war now seems to be mostly about suppressing reactionary Islam and securing some measure of deference for feminist values. In practice, our primary enemy is no longer al-Qaeda but the Taliban and other Islamists—in both Afghanistan and adjacent areas of Pakistan. Pakistan remains very wary of longstanding Indian ties to the Northern Alliance from which the current Kabul regime emerged. For Islamabad, the war in Afghanistan has come to be as much about forestalling Indian encirclement and destabilization of its strategic rear as it is about appeasing the United States, controlling Pashtun and Baluchi nationalism, and preventing destabilization by Islamic militants. To Pakistanis, we seem to be part of these problems, not part of their solutions.

Meanwhile, the growing U.S. focus on combating Muslim extremism, broadly defined, is drawing our covert warriors and armed forces into military operations in an ever-lengthening list of countries. The American *dar al-harb* (realm of war) has already grown beyond Afghanistan, Iraq, south Lebanon, and Palestine to embrace Pakistan, Somalia, and Yemen. Nowhere in the domain of Islam are we succeeding in dividing or reducing our enemies, still less diminishing the threat they represent to us and our homeland.

As if this were not enough, the very same people who "neo-conned" us into war with Iraq seven years ago are working hard to get the United States into yet another war—this one with Iran. Their reasoning mixes bluff with blackmail. They insist that the United States must risk regional catastrophe by launching its own war with Iran, because Israel will otherwise drag us into an even more catastrophic one. For their part, Israel's military planners are quite rationally concerned about the loss of their nuclear monopoly and the limits this would place on their freedom of action against Arab neighbors like Lebanon and Syria, but they know there is nothing much they can do to prevent this. Military frustration plus popular hysteria about Iran in Israel produces repeated threats by Israeli politicians to bomb Iran. Their supporters here faithfully echo these threats. This, of course, increases Iran's perceived need to develop a nuclear deterrent to such attack. And so it goes.

Ironically, the primary strategic effect of the policies these neoconservative warmongers advocated in the past was to eliminate Iran's enemies in Afghanistan and Iraq, while greatly enhancing Iranian influence in Iraq, Lebanon, and Palestine and cementing Iran's alliance with Syria. As a result, while the United States remains focused on Iran's nuclear program, it is becoming apparent to countries in the region that Iranian cooperation or acquiescence is essential to address a lengthening list of problems of concern to them. These include issues relating to Iraq, Lebanon, and Syria as well as Palestine.

The self-defeating actions and statements of both sides over the course of the thirty-year impasse in Iranian-American relations prove many basic rules of diplomacy. Unilateral suspensions of international law and comity (whether through hostage-taking or demands that rights conferred by the Nuclear Non-Proliferation Treaty regime be set aside) are quite naturally resented as inherently illegitimate by the affected side. Neither humiliation nor invective will induce reflection; both inspire brooding about how to show unyielding determination, indirectly hurt the other side, or retaliate directly against it. Sanctions that are not in support of a negotiating process constitute mindless pressure rather than leverage and invite defiance rather than compromise. Offers of talks premised on the need to check the diplomatic box before proceeding to coercive measures understandably meet with rebuff. (As a case in point: why should Iran cooperate in legitimizing the use of force against it on the spurious grounds that measures short of war have been exhausted?) And so forth. I'm tempted to go on, but this is not the occasion for a lecture on strategic self-frustration through diplomatic mismaneuver.

In sum, our military interventions in the greater Middle East have been both unproductive and counterproductive. And we have hardly tried diplomacy. That is no less true in the context of the Israel-Palestine conflict than with other issues. The political pantomime on the Potomac known as the "peace process" bears the same relationship to diplomacy that Bernie Madoff's operations did to wealth management. The hopes invested in the transaction alter neither its hollowness nor its cynical insincerity. It seems to serve the interests of its participants but does not lead to anything real—just more of the same. For Israel, the so-called "peace process" provides cover for more land grabs. For the Palestinian Authority, it earns international aid to make up for the lack of legitimacy at home. For the United States, it gives the illusion of activism on behalf of peace while avoiding the politically costly decisions necessary actually to produce it.

Israel has yet to attempt an answer to the question Prime Minister David Ben-Gurion asked Nahum Goldmann in 1956:

> Why should the Arabs make peace? If I were an Arab leader I would never make terms with Israel. That is natural: we have taken their country. Sure, God promised it to us, but what does that matter to them? Our God is not theirs. We come from Israel, it's true, but two thousand years ago, and what is that to them? There has been anti-Semitism, the Nazis, Hitler, Auschwitz, but was that their fault? They only see one thing: we have come here and stolen their country. Why should they accept that?[6]

We have no answer to that question either—but we need one. If no peaceful path to justice and dignity is available to Palestinians, they will see no reason not to return to violence. There is a mounting danger that many elsewhere will support them as they do so.

Americans seem to sense the growing risk of violent blowback from the Arab world and the broader Middle East. What else can explain our willingness to surrender the very values that have defined us as a society and that we claim to be defending? Our violent interaction with the Arab and Muslim worlds is clearly changing us much more than it is changing Arabs and Muslims. Our obsession with homeland security is corroding our values at home while increasing enmity and disregard for us abroad. If this makes us safer in the short term, it makes us both less free and less safe in the long term. It is also a prescription for diminished international prestige and support amid continuing worsening of our country's relations with Arabs and Muslims. It neither preserves our liberties nor advances our security.

---

6. Quoted in Nahum Goldmann, *The Jewish Paradox* (New York: Grosset & Dunlap, 1978).

The founding fathers knew that acceptance of a measure of risk is the prerequisite for freedom. The checks and balances of the American constitution were instituted to prevent attempts by our government to make us less free in order to make us safer. Yet, not quite 210 years after we enacted them, we Americans are setting aside the protections of individual rights enshrined in the Bill of Rights. In our pursuit of a zero-risk security environment, we are slowly but steadily substituting the elements of a garrison state for constitutionally ordained freedoms. Increasingly, we seek to achieve national security by impairing the security of individual Americans. Our citizens and foreign residents may take comfort from being told that foreign terrorists are under American military pressure, but they can no longer feel secure from arbitrary and capricious actions by government agencies and officials in their homeland.

Let me be specific. The Fourth Amendment's ban on searches and seizures of persons, houses, papers, and effects without probable cause has been vitiated by universal electronic eavesdropping, warrantless seizure of paper and electronic records at the border, and intrusive inspection of anything and everything in the possession of passengers using public transportation.

The Eighth Amendment's ban on "cruel and unusual punishments" has yielded to the expediencies of torture and the officially contrived disappearances of "extraordinary rendition."

The Fifth Amendment's protections against deprivation "of life, liberty, or property, without due process of law" have not prevented the suspension of habeas corpus or executive branch assertions of a right to detain American citizens as well as foreigners indefinitely without charge or trial.

The Sixth Amendment's guarantee of the right of anyone accused of a crime to be informed of the charges and confronted with the witnesses against him has given way to trials based on "secret evidence" and sequestered witnesses.

The president now claims the right to act as judge, jury, and executioner of anyone abroad, including Americans, whom he thinks may be aiding or abetting individuals or organizations our political process has listed as "terrorists."

Meanwhile, talk itself is being criminalized. Advocacy of causes also espoused by so-called "terrorists" risks prosecution for conspiracy to abet terrorism. Lawyers who defend people charged with connections to allegedly terrorist movements can themselves be charged with aiding terrorism. As any American Muslim can attest, the neutrality of the government with respect to religion is everywhere under attack. Whatever happened to the First Amendment's guarantees of freedom of speech and religious belief or the Sixth Amendment's right to be represented by a lawyer when detained or on trial?

These are the domestic effects of an approach to international affairs that is fundamentally at odds with the philosophy on which American foreign policy was long based. Our original idea was that we could best secure our own sovereignty and freedom by respecting the sovereignty and diverse ways of life of other nations. This view was best stated by John Quincy Adams, who said with pride in his speech to the U.S. House of Representatives of July 4, 1821:

> America...has abstained from interference in the concerns of others, [even] when the conflict has been for principles to which she clings, as to the last vital drop that visits the heart.... She is the well-wisher to the freedom and independence of all. She is the champion and vindicator only of her own.... She might become the dictatress of the world: she would be no longer the ruler of her own spirit.[7]

In my view, Adams was right in both his prescription and his prognosis. We would be far better off, were we to return to the course he advocated. This is an appropriate time to ponder that possibility. Like it or not, the United States cannot avoid changing course in the Middle East.

We are at an unsustainable dead end with Iran. We are increasingly at cross purposes with Turkey. Our relations with Lebanon are strained. Ties with Syria are stalemated. We are leaving the shambles we made of Iraq without having crafted an approach to Persian Gulf security that deals with the consequences of either our intervention or our withdrawal. We are arming our friends in the Gulf Cooperation Council but have yet to find strategic consensus with them.

Our efforts to promote a "two-state solution" in Palestine—such as they were—have lost all credibility. They cannot continue on the same basis. Israel is more isolated regionally and globally than ever before. Our relations with it are increasingly turbulent. I have spoken elsewhere about the imperative of an Israeli-Palestinian peace. I will not repeat myself today.

Most Americans now want out of Afghanistan. They yearn for an Afghan solution to Afghan problems that will allow us to exit gracefully

---

7. John Quincy Adams, speech to the U.S. House of Representatives, July 4, 1821, http://bit.ly/1Q6demo.

from our frustratingly unsuccessful military intervention there. We do not know what to do about Pakistan's surging anti-Americanism or its continuing use as a haven for terrorists with global reach.

In addition, looming over all of our foreign policies—and our exceedingly expensive reliance on the use of force rather than measures short of war for their execution—is the possibility of an American fiscal heart attack. Our fiscal difficulties promise—among other things—to force major retrenchment in the American military presence and operations abroad. The only question is whether this will happen abruptly or with all deliberate speed. The cause of the forthcoming U.S. pullback from military adventurism abroad is illustrated by some simple math.

Our federal government's revenue from all sources—like income, corporate, excise, Social Security, and Medicare taxes—will total $2.2 trillion this year. Outlays for transfer payments to individuals for unemployment, Social Security, Medicare, and the like will come to $2.4 trillion. We must borrow the $200 billion necessary to make up the shortfall. This is before we pay for all the other functions of government, none of which is now funded by tax revenue. We will borrow another $1.3 trillion to keep our government in business. We take in $2.2 trillion. We spend $3.9 trillion. We are running our government entirely on credit rollovers.

The roughly $1 trillion we spend on military and related activities in the budgets for defense, veterans' affairs, intelligence, military assistance programs, homeland security, nuclear weapons and propulsion, and the like is the major part of government operations. It is all borrowed from future taxpayers and current foreign trading partners. A lot of this escalating military debt is attributable to the Middle East. Even if our military operations were achieving their objectives—which they are not—they are fiscally unsustainable in the long term. As Herb Stein's mother famously observed, "If something can't go on forever, sooner or later it will stop."

One way or another, therefore, change is coming to U.S. policies in the greater Middle East. If properly anticipated and correctly managed, change represents an opportunity, not a setback.

An end to military intervention abroad except for decisive action for precise purposes and a limited time would go a long way toward curbing the further growth of the terrorist threat to our country. A serious effort by our government and public intellectuals to counter and reverse the bigotry of current discourse about Islam and the Arabs in this country could lay a basis for enhanced cooperation with Arab and Muslim governments against Islamist extremists who practice violent politics. After all, they are the enemies of Americans and Muslims alike.

Peace in the Holy Land is essential to secure the security and prosperity of both Israelis and Palestinians. It is equally essential to the United States. It would eliminate a key driver of anti-American terrorism throughout the Muslim world. Measures short of war to mitigate or eliminate other points of tension between the United States and the peoples of the Middle East region would further reduce this threat. A serious dialogue with our partners in the Persian Gulf region as well as Egypt and Turkey could help to identify more effective ways of dealing with the challenges Iran poses to regional security and stability.

In a less fearful atmosphere, Americans could restore civil liberties based on renewed respect for our constitutional traditions and the rule of law. This is the prerequisite for recovery of our status and reputation as a uniquely tolerant society, open to people and their ideas. It is the key to regaining the prestige and influence the United States formerly enjoyed in the Middle East and elsewhere. It is the essential condition for rebuilding relations of mutual trust and confidence with our Arab and Muslim allies and friends. It is the way to make America once again "the ruler of her own spirit."

Israel-Palestine: The Consequences of the Conflict
May 4, 2011[8]

The saga of the Holy Land, ancient and modern, reminds someone with no personal connection to it of nothing so much as the Book of Job in the Hebrew Bible. There seems to be something about Palestine that afflicts the innocent, tests the righteous, and causes incomprehensible suffering to past and present inhabitants. Israeli Jews and Palestinians both claim descent from the ancient peoples of the lands they now contest. Their competing narratives are at the heart of the perverse drama there. In this drama, the spiritual descendants of Jews who left Palestine assert a religious duty to dispossess the biological descendants of those who chose to remain.

Over the course of centuries, the Jews of the Diaspora were grievously persecuted by Christians. This experience helped to inspire Zionism. It culminated in the horrors of the Nazi Holocaust. Meanwhile, under Byzantium and the Caliphate, all but a few of the Jews of Palestine sought refuge in conversion to Judaism's successor faiths: Christianity and Islam. As an ironic result, the homegrown descendants of Palestine's original Jewish population—the Palestinians—now suffer because newcomers proclaim them to be interlopers in lands they have inhabited from time immemorial. Yet another Jewish-descended Diaspora—this time, Christian and Muslim—has been ejected from Palestine to suffer in exile. Not even the most imaginative writer of fiction could have composed an account of traumatic suffering and human tragedy comparable to that which Zionists and Palestinians have undergone and continue to inflict on each other.

The moral harm that these distant cousins continue to do to each other is huge. So is the damage they are doing to their sympathizers and supporters abroad. Resorting to terrorist acts, especially suicide bombings in crowded public places, has caused Palestinians to forfeit much of the international sympathy their cause would otherwise enjoy. The massacre of civilians in the West by Arabs enraged by Western support for Israeli mistreatment of the Palestinians and other affronts has generated intense European and American suspicion of all Arabs. The diffusion of Arab rage to non-Arab regions of the realm of Islam has aroused global antipathy to Islam even as it has inspired acts of terrorism among Muslims.

---

8. The Hisham B. Sharabi Memorial Lecture, Palestine Center, Washington, D.C.

Similarly, the cruelties of Israelis to their Arab captives and neighbors, especially in the ongoing siege of Gaza and repeated attacks on the people of Lebanon, have cost the Jewish state much of the global sympathy that the Holocaust previously conferred on it. The racist tyranny of Jewish settlers over West Bank Arabs and the progressive emergence of a version of apartheid in Israel itself are deeply troubling to a growing number of people abroad who have traditionally identified with Israel. Many—perhaps most—of the most disaffected are Jews. They are in the process of dissociating themselves from Israel. They know that, to the extent that Judaism comes to be conflated with racist arrogance (as terrorism is now conflated with Islam), Israeli behavior threatens a rebirth of anti-Semitism in the West. Ironically, Israel—conceived as a refuge and guarantee against European anti-Semitism—has become the sole conceivable stimulus to its revival and globalization. Demonstrably, Israel has been bad for the Palestinians. It is turning out also to be bad for the Jews.

The early Zionists were mostly secular in orientation. So was the Palestine Liberation Organization. But, as the struggle between Jewish settlers and Palestinians proceeded, it became increasingly infused with religious fervor. On both sides, parties espousing sectarian extremism displaced secular nationalist movements. Religious dogmatism transformed what was at first a secular struggle between competing local nationalisms into a Jewish and Muslim holy war for land in Palestine. In holy wars, compromise is equated with heresy. This tragic mutation of the conflict is now reflected in increasing global animosity between Muslims, Jews, and their Christian Zionist supporters. (Christian Zionists perversely support the Jewish state in order to hasten the arrival of Judgment Day, when they expect Israel to be devastated and the world to be purged of its Jews. Such people, however Rube Goldberg–like the theology by which they propose to annihilate the Jews, are strange allies for Zionists to embrace!)

The ongoing conflict between Israelis and Palestinians has killed and wounded many people. It has done even graver damage to the humane principles at the heart of both Judaism and Islam. Among Jews and Muslims in Israel and Palestine the Golden Rule has been largely forgotten. The principle that one should not do to others what one would not wish done to oneself had been integral to both faiths. In the Holy Land, God's love has been replaced with murderous indifference to the rights of others in a sickeningly bloody bilateral contest to terrorize civilian populations. Ethical voices on both sides exist but they are less and less audible. Amoral and unscrupulous zealots have the podium. Their right to speak in their religious community is seldom challenged. Their utterances blacken the reputations of both religions.

Obfuscatory euphemisms are, unfortunately, the norm in the Holy Land. But rhetorical tricks can no longer conceal the protracted moral zero-sum game that is in progress there. A people without rights confronts a settler movement without scruples. A predatory state with cutting-edge military technology battles kids with stones and resistance fighters with belts of nails and explosives. Israel's cabinet openly directs the murder of Palestinian political leaders. (There have been about 850 such extrajudicial executions over the past decade.[9]) Israel is vigorously engaged in the collective punishment and systematic ethnic cleansing of its captive Arab populations.[10] It rails against terrorism while carrying out policies explicitly described as intended to terrorize the peoples of the territories it is attacking or into which it is illegally expanding. Meanwhile, the elected authorities in Palestine—indeed, most Palestinians—associate themselves with suicide bombers and unguided missiles that indiscriminately murder Israeli civilians. Each side has suspended moral constraints in order to cause the other to suffer in the hope that it will capitulate to such coercion. To a distressing extent, moreover, each side has also been able to enlist unreasoning support for its cause and the indiscriminate condemnation of the other by powerful supporters abroad.

As always in such mayhem, truth and the law have been the first to go missing. Israel regularly attributes to others the very things it itself is doing. It has become notorious for its refusal to accept objective scrutiny or criticism. It routinely rebuffs international investigators' examination of allegations against it, even when mandated by the UN Security Council. Instead, it stages self-indulgent acts of self-investigation calculated to produce exculpatory propaganda. As a result, Israeli government spokespeople—who once were presumed to represent the intellectual integrity for which Jewish scholars have always been renowned—now have no credibility at all except among those committed to the Zionist cause. Meanwhile, regional and international respect for the rule of law, especially humanitarian law, has been greatly degraded. This is a special irony.

Humanitarian law and the law of war are arguably the supreme moral artifacts of Atlantic civilization. Jewish lawyers made a disproportionate

---

9. Al-Zaytouna Centre. An additional 354 bystanders were killed in the course of these executions.
10. Over this period, Israel is reported to have razed nearly 11,000 Palestinian homes and confiscated about 110 sq. miles of Palestinian property.

contribution to the crafting of both. The resulting legal principles were intended to deter the kinds of injuries and injustices that European Jews and other minorities had long suffered and to protect occupied populations from persecution by their occupiers. Both objectives are very relevant to contemporary Palestine. It is, however, hard to find any principle of due process, the several Geneva Conventions, or the Nuremberg trials that has not been systematically violated in the Holy Land. Examples of criminal conduct include mass murder, extrajudicial killing, torture, detention without charge, the denial of medical care, the annexation and colonization of occupied territory, the illegal expropriation of land, ethnic cleansing, and the collective punishment of civilians, including the demolition of their homes, the systematic reduction of their infrastructure, and the de-development and impoverishment of entire regions. These crimes have been linked to a concerted effort to rewrite international law to permit actions that it traditionally prohibited, in effect enshrining the principle that might makes right.

As the former head of the Israeli Defense Forces' legal department has argued, "If you do something for long enough the world will accept it. The whole of international law is now based on the notion that an act that is forbidden today becomes permissible if executed by enough countries.... International law progresses through violations."[11] A colleague of his has extended this notion by pointing out that "the more often Western states apply principles that originated in Israel to their own non-traditional conflicts in places like Afghanistan and Iraq, then the greater the chance these principles have of becoming a valuable part of international law."[12]

These references to Iraq and Afghanistan underscore the extent to which the United States, once the principal champion of a rule-bound international order, has followed Israel in replacing legal principles with expediency as the central regulator of its interaction with foreign peoples. The expediently amoral doctrine of preemptive war is such an Israeli transplant in the American neoconservative psyche. Neither it nor other deliberate assaults on the rule of law have been met with concerted resistance from Palestinians, Arabs, or anyone else, including the American Bar Association. The steady displacement of traditional American values— indeed, the core doctrines of Western civilization—with ideas designed to

---

11. Daniel Reisner, cited in Jeff Halper, "The Second Battle of Gaza: Israel's Undermining of International Law," *MRZine*, February 26, 2010, http://bit.ly/1oDCQAz.
12. Asa Kasher, "A Moral Evaluation of the Gaza War—Operation Cast Lead," Jerusalem Center for Public Affairs Brief 9(18), February 4, 2010, http://bit.ly/21lu6wt.

free the state of inconvenient moral constraints has debased the honor and prestige of our country as well as Israel.

American determination to protect Israel from the political and legal consequences of any and all of its actions has also taken its toll, not just on the willingness of others to credit and follow the United States, but also on the authority of international organizations and the integrity of international law. The Security Council was conceived as the ultimate arbiter and enforcer of an international order in which law could protect the weak and vulnerable from the depredations of the strong. The world has occasionally allowed its sympathy for Palestinians, as underdogs, to override its legal judgment, but the United States has routinely exercised its veto to prevent the application of well-established principles of international law to Israel. The Security Council has been transformed from the champion of the global rule of law into the enemy of legality as the standard of global governance. Repeated American vetoes on behalf of Israel have reduced the United Nations and other international fora to impotence on fundamental questions of justice and human dignity. Confidence in these institutions has largely disappeared. Thus, the Israel-Palestine dispute has shaped a world in which both the rule of law and the means by which it might be realized have been deliberately degraded. We are all the worse off for this.

Israel's strength and prosperity depend on American government and private subsidies as well as Washington's political and legal protection. For Israelis, the moral hazard created by such irresponsible indulgence and unsparing American support has been a tragedy. It has enabled Israel to follow its most self-destructive inclinations by relieving it from the requirement to weigh their consequences. It has bred hubris that encourages the Jewish state to pursue short-term advantage without considering the resulting risks to its long-term viability. For the Palestinians, America's slavish support of Israel has meant an unending nightmare, trapping them in a limbo in which the protections of both law and human decency are at best capriciously applied. For the United States, deference to Israel's counterproductive policies and actions has become a debilitating drain on American power to shape events by measures short of war. The United States is now so closely identified with the Jewish state that Americans cannot escape perceived complicity with any and all of its actions, whether we agree or disagree with them. In the eyes of the world, Israel's behavior is a reproach to the American reputation as well as its own.

Perceived American double standards and hypocrisy on matters related to the Israel-Palestine conflict account for much of the recent decline in international admiration and deference to U.S. leadership in the Middle

East and elsewhere. In 2006, when free and fair elections in Palestine produced a government that Israel detested and feared, the United States joined Israel in seeking to isolate and overthrow that government, thus setting aside and discrediting America's long-professed dedication to the spread of democracy in the Middle East and elsewhere. In 2006 and 2008, the United States encouraged Israeli military actions against Lebanese and Palestinian civilians that were both more brutal and sustained than those that Col. Muammar Qaddafi has recently carried out against his fellow Libyans. Far from calling for no-fly zones over Lebanon and Gaza, however, the U.S. government continued to supply Israel with gifts of ammunition, including cluster bombs and white phosphorus, as the IDF expended its stocks of them on Lebanese and Palestinian civilian population centers, facilities, and infrastructure.

U.S. sponsorship of the late, lamented "peace process" began as a demonstration of American diplomatic power, the indispensable role of the United States in Middle Eastern affairs, and the necessity of all interested in peace to defer to America. The "peace process" has ended by discrediting American power and diplomacy. It has failed to deliver either the self-determination for Palestinians or the acceptance of Israel by its neighbors envisaged in the Camp David accords. Instead, Israel's deepening commitment to "settler Zionism" has uprooted ever greater numbers of Palestinians while alarming and affronting other Arabs and Muslims. Four decades of American diplomacy is now seen in the region as having been an elaborate diplomatic deception, yielding nothing but the continual enlargement of the Jewish state at Palestinian expense.

This failure of the American-led "peace process" is all the more telling because it occurred despite the existence of a compelling, existential interest in the achievement of a formula for cohabitation on the part of both Israelis and Palestinians. This interest is clearly reflected in the eagerness of Palestinian officials to negotiate a basis for peaceful coexistence with Israel that is revealed in the official record of the Israel-Palestine negotiations recently leaked to and by Al Jazeera. The abject pleading of Palestine's negotiators for peace, to which these documents attest, contrasts with the callous determination of their Israeli counterparts not to take yes for an answer. Yet the security and prosperity of Israelis and Palestinians alike is dependent on each accepting the other. Without Palestinian agreement, Israel cannot define its borders or enjoy acceptance by any of its neighbors. Without Israel's agreement, Palestinians cannot achieve self-determination within a defined territory. Without mutual respect and tolerance, neither Israel nor Palestine can hope to live in peace for long. Animosity breeds threats, and no military hegemony is forever.

The inability of the United States to build on the obvious shared interests of Palestinians and Israelis is, at best, damning testimony to the incompetence of those Americans who have made a career of processing peace without ever delivering it. At worst, it is compelling evidence of the extent to which they have functioned as "Israel's lawyers," rather than as mediators sincerely attempting to produce a mutually respectful and therefore durable *modus vivendi* between Israelis, Palestinians, and other Arabs. As such, it is a reflection of the inordinate influence of right-wing Israelis on American policies and the people chosen to implement them. I have had personal experience of this on more than one occasion.

In late November 1988, shortly after the election of George H.W. Bush as president, I was invited to lunch by a senior Israeli official with whom, in pursuance of U.S. policy, I had worked closely to expand Israel's diplomatic and military presence in Africa. I had come to like and respect this official. He wished to thank me, he said, for what I had done for his country. I was pleased. Over lunch, however, he asked me what I planned to do in the new administration, adding, "Tell me what job you want. We can get it for you." The casual arrogance with which this representative of a foreign power claimed to be able to manipulate the staffing of national security positions in the U.S. government was a stunning belittlement of American patriotism. Twenty years later, I was to be reminded that agents of foreign influence who can make appointments to national security positions in the United States can also unmake them.

Under the circumstances, the consistent pro-Israel bias of American officials charged with the management of the Israel-Palestine conundrum and their lack of empathy for the Palestinians are in no way a surprise. A passionate attachment to one side is inconsistent with mediation of its disputes with another. The absence of empathy is fatal to the craft of diplomacy. Such disabilities account, at least in part, for the failure of the decades-long labors of American officials to produce anything but political cover for the ongoing displacement of Palestinians from their homes. The ultimate achievement of American peace processors has been to bring great discredit upon themselves and the United States. American diplomacy on the Israel-Palestine issue is becoming less and less relevant to events in the region and increasingly unacceptable to the world as a whole.

A new milestone in this journey to diplomatic ignominy was reached on February 18, 2011, when the United States vetoed a resolution in the

UN Security Council that had been cobbled together from earlier official American statements. The resolution condemned the expansion of Israeli settlements and called for it to end. In doing so, it echoed numerous previous Security Council resolutions as well as the "Road Map." All fourteen other members of the Council, including America's closest allies, spoke vigorously in favor of the resolution, which had been sponsored by 130 member states. The debate and the vote on that resolution were an unambiguous vote of no confidence in American as well as Israeli policy.

This repudiation of U.S. leadership and Israeli expansionism seems certain to be reiterated even more unmistakably when the General Assembly convenes in September. The international community will then take up the question of whether to underscore its near-unanimous rejection of Israel's claim to any territory beyond its pre-1967 borders by recognizing an independent Palestinian state there and admitting that state to the United Nations. The United States no longer has the political credibility necessary to control the diplomatic context in which Israel operates.

The displacement of the United States from its previously unchallenged primacy in Middle Eastern diplomacy comes amidst other momentous changes in the strategic landscape in the region. The U.S. government's failure to stand by its longtime protégé, Hosni Mubarak, convinced leaders elsewhere who, like Mubarak, had linked their fate to America that Washington is a faithless friend and impotent protector. The decades-long inclination of conservative Arab rulers to curry favor with Washington by acquiescing in American policies has been gravely impaired, perhaps irreparably. But the deep disenchantment with America of the dissidents who overthrew Mubarak was not overcome by the Obama administration's belated abandonment of him. A majority of Egyptians want to annul the Camp David accords. Whether Egypt does so or not, a much larger majority of Egyptians want their country generally to decouple its foreign policy from that of the United States. As goes Egypt, so very likely goes Jordan. Arab deference to American—and hence to Israeli—interests and dictates will manifestly be much less in future than in the past.

There is a great deal of apprehension in Israel over these developments and not a little consternation in Washington's think tanks and belief tanks about them. The storm warnings are up, and for good reason. Had Israel and the United States planned it, we could hardly have contrived a status quo less likely to be accepted as legitimate by a democratized Middle East. If contemporary Israel represents the future, it is certainly problematic. As is so often the case with clouded situations, however, there may be a bright side to the changes in progress.

Given the protracted failure of U.S. diplomacy in the Israel-Palestine arena, Palestinians and others may be forgiven for believing that it is time to entrust peacemaking to other parties who are more objective, less politically constrained, and less emotionally biased. Others in Europe and elsewhere have taken alarmed note of the adverse effects of the unending conflict on Israel, on the Palestinians, on Arab politics, on regional stability, on interreligious relations, on the moral standing of global Jewry and Islam, on Arab and Islamic relations with the West, on international law and organizations, and on world order. Media outside the United States have taken progressively more balanced and nuanced note of the human suffering in the Holy Land. Europeans and others now evidence a considerably greater sense of urgency about these problems than Americans have done. The notion that only Americans have the capacity to manage conflict resolution in the Middle East will no longer withstand scrutiny. One recalls the role of Norway in crafting the Oslo accords. Perhaps, now that the United States has struck out, it's someone else's turn at bat.

A new game is clearly beginning. A self-confident, religiously tolerant but secular Turkey has emerged as a major influence on regional affairs and as an inspiration to its democrats. Arab diplomacy is being invigorated by the aftereffects of the revolutions in Egypt and elsewhere. There is mounting pressure on all Arab governments to accord greater deference to popular opinion in both domestic and foreign policy. The Middle East will no longer allow itself to be the diplomatic playground of great powers outside it. There will, however, be new opportunities for interested outside parties to forge diplomatic partnerships with those in the region. Most are looking for new beginnings, new relationships, and new ideas. All see an urgent need to end the racist oppression and humiliation of Arabs in the Holy Land. These injustices are at the root of regional instability. They empower extremist and terrorist movements in the Middle East and beyond. They threaten the future of the Jewish state.

Diplomatic partnerships between outside powers and Arab governments for the purpose of crafting a durable peace in Palestine—as opposed to stabilizing the iniquitous status quo—have long been conspicuous by their absence. In 2002, the Arab League announced a revolutionary peace proposal in Beirut. Israel and the United States shelved it with minimal acknowledgment. Its potential remains unexplored. It has a limited shelf life but there may still be an opportunity to make use of it.

The Arabs are thinking anew. It is time for Israel to engage in new thinking of its own. Israel has shown great skill at deflecting the peace proposals of others and subjecting them to campaigns of diplomatic attrition. It has never made its own specific proposal of peace to the Palestinians. It has demanded respect for the dignified autonomy of its Jewish identity but has offered no reciprocal recognition of Palestinian identity. Perhaps it is time for Israel to do these things. Its changed strategic environment, the diminished capacity of the United States to protect it from the political and legal consequences of its conduct, and changing attitudes toward it in the Jewish diaspora foretell an end to the moral hazard from which the Jewish state has suffered. For the first time in decades, Israel will have to take into account the risks to its future as it contemplates actions in the present. In the interest of its own survival and prosperity, it may begin to make wiser and more farsighted decisions. We must hope so.

There can, of course, be no peace between Israelis and Palestinians unless there are governments that can commit both sides to terms. Part of the Israeli strategy of deferring peace so as to seize more land for settler Zionists has been a multifaceted effort to ensure that no one has the authority to speak for all Palestinians. The United States has effectively colluded in this strategy of divide and rule, especially since the 2006 elections brought Hamas to power. If Israel is to have peace, however, rather than perpetual rejection by both Palestinians and other Arab and Muslim neighbors, it needs a unified Palestinian leadership with which to strike a deal. Thanks to the skill of Egyptian diplomacy, such a Palestinian government of national unity is now a real prospect. In the interest of peace, the region and the world should welcome and encourage Palestinian unity rather than succumb to Pavlovian impulses to condemn it.

However distasteful they may find it to do so after all that they have suffered at Israeli hands, Palestinians, including Gazans, must collaborate with Israel to achieve peace. But it is equally true that there can and will be no peace for Israel until there is peace for the Palestinians, including those in diaspora. The United States has proven incapable of creating strategic circumstances conducive to serious, as opposed to make-believe, negotiations between the warring parties in the Holy Land. Perhaps, however, such circumstances are nonetheless finally emerging, allowing Palestinians and Israelis to attempt a fresh start at achieving peaceful co-existence. They must look to themselves, to others in the region, and to new, non-American mediators to accomplish this.

That Palestinians and Israelis find a mutually agreeable basis for peaceful coexistence is essential not only to their own well-being but to that of the wider world. Only they can make the decisions necessary to achieve this. But, in our own interest, the rest of us must help them as best we can. The adverse consequences of the Israel-Palestine conflict have penetrated and extended far beyond the two parties to the holy war now raging in Palestine. The benefits of peace there would be equally deep and wide.

Hasbara and the Control of Narrative as an Element of Strategy
December 1, 2012[13]

I would like to put forward some thoughts about the control of narrative and the manipulation of information as an essential element of modern warfare. The Israelis call this *hasbara*. Since they are without doubt the most skilled contemporary practitioners of the art, it seems appropriate to use the Hebrew word for it. Since Israel's most recent war (against the Palestinians in Gaza) sputtered to an end just ten days ago, I'll cite a few examples from that war to illustrate my main points.

Before I get to specifics, let me provide a general description of *hasbara* and its purposes. *Hasbara* is usually translated as "explanation." That does not do the concept justice. *Hasbara* links information warfare to the strategic efforts of the state to bolster the unity of the home front; ensure the support of allies; disrupt efforts to organize hostile coalitions; determine the way issues are defined by the media, the intelligentsia, and social networks; establish the parameters of politically correct discourse; delegitimize both critics and their arguments; and shape the common understanding and interpretation of the results of international negotiations. *Hasbara* is multifaceted and well adapted to the digital age. It embodies a public-private partnership in which the state leads and committed volunteers follow in implementing an information strategy. In its comprehensiveness and complexity, it bears the same relationship to unidimensional public diplomacy as grand strategy does to campaign plans.

Hasbara has its roots in earlier concepts of propaganda, agitprop, and censorship. Like them, it is communication calculated to influence cognition and behavior by manipulating perceptions of a cause or position with one-sided arguments, prejudicial substance, and emotional appeals. Unlike its progenitors, however, *hasbara* does not seek merely to burnish or tarnish national images of concern to it or to supply information favorable to its theses. It also seeks actively to inculcate canons of political correctness in domestic and foreign media and audiences that will promote self-censorship by them. It strives thereby to decrease the willingness of audiences to consider information linked to politically unacceptable viewpoints, individuals, and groups and to inhibit the circulation of adverse information in social networks.

---

13. Remarks to the Jubilee Conference of the Council on Foreign and Defense Policy, Moscow

Past efforts by states to shape domestic and foreign opinion depended on the production of persuasive information and efforts to deprive audiences of access to contradictory information by interrupting its supply through censorship, jamming, and other techniques directed at reducing its flow. By contrast, *hasbara* assumes the free flow of information within an open marketplace of opinion. In that context, it seeks to promote selective listening. The purpose is to constrict the *demand* for information, not its flow. Although *hasbara* includes efforts to impede access to information through a wide variety of techniques adapted to new information technologies, it focuses on limiting audiences' receptivity to information.

In this context, *hasbara* recognizes the control of narrative as a potent weapon. Narrative is an element of rhetoric. It defines context. When *successfully imposed, it provides a cognitive filter. Narratives offer a com*prehensive framework for connecting and interpreting events. They substantiate "groupthink," establishing baselines for conformity and hence for ostracism.

In politics, perception is reality. Narratives legitimize some perceptions and delegitimize others.

Narratives can be drawn upon to reinforce stereotypes by imposing favorable or pejorative labels on information and its sources. Such labels predispose recipients of information to accept some things as credible, to disbelieve others, and to regard still others as so tainted or implausible that they can and should be ruled out of order and ignored. (Not incidentally, adherence to narratives is the usual cause of intelligence failure—the inability to accept or even consider evidence that something outside the established frame of reference is in the process of occurring.)

As the recent fighting in Gaza illustrates, the modern state has at its disposal a wide variety of means of creating and sustaining narratives. Israel announced the war on Twitter. Sources controlled or guided by Israel then saturated American media outlets with talking points that went unchallenged by previously conditioned anchors and journalists. In addition to traditional techniques of agitprop, disinformation, and propaganda in conventional media, the Israeli *hasbara* apparatus made heavy use of more focused channels of communication, like Facebook, Twitter, and YouTube. It inundated audiences with information favorable to its cause and squeezed out information that contradicted its theses. This reflected careful contingency planning and preparation.

Public opinion is increasingly shaped by social media. The state of Israel has organized civilian government and military units to exploit this, including creating websites, social-media accounts, and messages attributed to false identities. It has learned how to manipulate browser functions, search-engine algorithms, and other automated mechanisms that control what information is presented to Internet users. Such manipulation can ensure that certain commentary and information will or will not appear in response to searches. It can assign greater prominence to old material critical of sources or analyses than to new entries favorable to them. It can arrange for searches to find only positive or negative commentary and information on a topic.

In some countries, like the United States, Israel can rely upon a "fifth column" of activist sympathizers to amplify its messages, to rebut and discredit statements that contradict its arguments, facts, and fabrications, and to impugn the moral standing of those who make such statements. Israel makes intelligent use of the possibilities this creates for public-private partnership in propaganda. As one pertinent example, the Jewish Agency for Israel has sponsored an online *Hasbara Handbook* for students around the world to use as advocates of Israel and its policies.[14]

The *Hasbara Handbook* explains many standard techniques of propaganda and deceptive rhetoric. It rehearses specific arguments and counterarguments and outlines a program of training for advocacy and rebuttal. It also stresses the importance of labeling or "name-calling"—linking a person or idea to a negative symbol. The handbook places itself in a larger context. It commends the work of CAMERA—the Committee for Accuracy in Middle East Reporting in America—an organization notorious for the viciousness of its efforts to blacken the reputations of those who criticize Israel or advance accounts of events that deviate from the official Israeli narrative by branding them as "anti-Semitic" or "self-hating Jews." It notes that CAMERA provides a free monthly magazine full of timely *hasbara* materials for Jewish students in the United States. A myriad of Israel-oriented think tanks provide similar guidance online, as do numerous websites based in Israel itself.

In addition, many American rabbis see it as their duty to rally their congregations to Israel's defense. One typical example was a rabbi who, as the Gaza fighting began, stressed to his New York congregants that

> [M]aking yourself well informed and able to articulate Israel's case clearly and compellingly is...important.... No slanted print media article or editorial or electronic report that is...unbalanced and unfair can be allowed to go unchallenged.... Those media organs

---

14. World Union of Jewish Students, *Hasbara Handbook: Promoting Israel on Campus*, March 2002, http://bit.ly/20QMnzQ.

that are habitually anti-Israel should be flooded with letters and e-mails when their stories and pictures paint a...portrait of what we know to be other. Conversations at the water cooler, in health clubs, and particularly at holiday parties and gatherings so common at this time of year...all of these are our challenge. Get informed, stay informed, and let your voice be heard.[15]

Other countries lack Israel's unique foreign network of religious leaders and study sessions dedicated to indoctrinating advocates with its positions and to organizing swarms of them to smother opponents. Still, convenient as it may be, a committed religious community abroad is not necessary to generate "flash mob" attacks to silence those with whom a state disagrees. There is now a wide variety of telecommunication and social-media techniques for organizing such campaigns from halfway around the world.

During the Gaza fighting, Israel sought, as always, to portray itself as the innocent victim of irrationally hate-filled Arab attacks. At least in the United States, it was quite successful in this effort. Despite the fact that Israel initiated the escalation that produced the war, dropped one thousand times as many tons of munitions on Gaza as Gazans fired at Israel, faced a foe with no air defenses with one of the world's most advanced air forces while demonstrating a sophisticated defense against homemade missiles fired at it from Gaza, and killed thirty-two times as many Gazans as Gazans killed Israelis, most Americans continued to cast the issue in terms of Israel's right to defend itself against rocket attack. Almost no one mentioned the fact that Gaza had been under siege by Israel for eight years before this latest outbreak of fighting.[16]

As soon as Egyptian president Mohammed Morsi arranged a truce between Israel and the Hamas authorities in Gaza, Israeli "hasbaristas" moved to recast the Gaza war in terms of previously unmentioned (and entirely fictitious) connections to Iran, which *hasbara* had previously demonized. Aware that the implementation of peace agreements constitutes the war after the war, they also began a quiet campaign to ensure that the multiple ambiguities in the truce would be resolved to Israel's advantage.

---

15. Gerald C. Skolnik, "Ayin L'Tzion Tzofia: Feeling Israel's Pain," *Jewish Week*, November 20, 2012, http://bit.ly/1SNNlNU.

16. An extreme example of *hasbara* narrative reinforcing these points was provided by *Washington Post* editorial writer Charles Krauthammer a few days after the fighting ended: "Why Was There War in Gaza?" *Washington Post*, November 23, 2012, http://wapo.st/1SNNr87.

Israel is a small country, surrounded by enemies and dependent on continuing subsidies and military support from the United States. However one evaluates the wisdom of Israel's policies or the lack of it, it is hardly surprising in this context that Israel has led the way in understanding the importance of information warfare and developing new concepts of how to conduct it. Where Israel has led, others can be expected to follow.

Aeschylus said that "in war, truth is the first casualty." But what if truth is both malleable and, as resculpted and digitized, a full participant in war? In modern warfare, command of the information environment can be as important as control of the battlefield. The Israeli concept of *hasbara* presents a model of how this can be done in the digital age. It is worth further study.

Grand Waffle in the Middle East

January 16, 2013[17]

Over the past half-century or so, the United States has pursued two main but disconnected objectives in West Asia and North Africa: on the one hand, strategic and economic advantage in the Arabian Peninsula, Persian Gulf, and Egypt; on the other, support for the consolidation of the Jewish settler state in Palestine. These two objectives of U.S. policy in the Middle East have consistently taken precedence over the frequently professed American preference for democracy.

These objectives are politically contradictory. They also draw their rationales from distinct moral universes. U.S. relations with the Arab countries and Iran have been grounded almost entirely in unsentimental calculations of interest. The American relationship with Israel, by contrast, has rested almost entirely on religious and emotional bonds. This disconnect has precluded any grand strategy.

Rather than seek an integrated policy framework, America has balanced the contradictions between the imperatives of its domestic politics and its interests. For many years, Washington succeeded in having its waffle in the Middle East and eating it too—avoiding having to choose between competing objectives. With wiser U.S. policies and more judicious responses to them by Arabs and Israelis, Arab-Israeli reconciliation might by now have obviated the ultimate necessity for America to prioritize its purposes in the region. But the situation has evolved to the point that choice is becoming almost impossible to avoid.

The Middle East matters. It is where Africa, Asia, and Europe converge. In addition to harboring the greater part of the world's conventionally recoverable energy supplies, it is a key passageway between Asia and Europe. No nation can hope to project its power throughout the globe without access to and through the Middle East. Nor can any ignore the role of the Persian Gulf countries in fueling the world's armed forces, powering its economies, and setting its energy prices. This is why the United States has acted consistently to maintain a position of preeminent influence in the Middle East and to deny to any strategically hostile nation or coalition of nations the opportunity to contest its politico-military dominance of the region.

---

17. Middle East Policy Council, Washington, D.C.

The American pursuit of access, transit, and strategic denial has made building strategic partnerships with Iran, Saudi Arabia, and Egypt a major focus of U.S. policy. The partnership with Iran broke down over three decades ago. It has been succeeded by antagonism, low-intensity conflict, and the near-constant threat of war. The U.S. relationships with Egypt and Saudi Arabia are now evolving in uncertain directions. Arab governments have learned the hard way that they must defer to public opinion. This opinion is increasingly Islamist. Meanwhile, popular antipathies to the widening American war on Islamism are deepening. These factors alone make it unlikely that relations with the United States can retain their centrality for Cairo and Riyadh much longer.

The definitive failure of the decades-long American-sponsored "peace process" between Israelis, Palestinians, and other Arabs adds greatly to the uncertainty. Whether it yielded peace or not, the "peace process" made the United States the apparently indispensable partner for both Israel and the Arabs. It served dual political purposes. It enabled Arab governments to persuade their publics that maintaining good relations with the United States did not imply selling out Arab or Islamic interests in Palestine, and it supported the U.S. strategic objective of achieving acceptance for a Jewish state by the other states and peoples of the Middle East. Washington's abandonment of this diplomacy was a boon to Israeli territorial expansion but a disaster for American influence in the region, including in Israel.

Over the years, America protected Israel from international rebuke and punishment. Its stated purpose was the preservation of prospects for a negotiated "two-state solution" that could bring security and peace to Israelis and Palestinians alike. A decade ago, every member of both the Arab League and the Organisation of Islamic Cooperation endorsed this objective and pledged normalization with Israel if Israeli-Palestinian negotiations succeeded. In response, Israel spun out its talks with the Palestinians while working hard to preclude their self-determination. It has now succeeded in doing so.

There has been no American-led peace process worthy of the name for nearly two decades. There is no prospect of such a process resuming. No one in the international community now accepts the pretense of a "peace process" as an excuse for American protection of Israel. Eleven years on, the Arab and Islamic peace offer has exceeded its shelf life. On the Israel-Palestine issue, American diplomacy has been running on fumes for some time. It is now totally out of gas and universally perceived to be going nowhere.

Sadly, barring fundamental changes in Israeli politics, policies, and behavior, the longstanding American strategic objective of achieving acceptance for the state of Israel to stabilize the region where British colonialism and Jewish nationalism implanted it is now infeasible. In practice, the United States has abandoned the effort. U.S. policy currently consists of ad hoc actions to fortify Israel against Palestinian resistance and military threats from its neighbors, while shielding it from increasingly adverse international reaction to its worsening deportment. In essence, the United States now has no objective with respect to Israel beyond sheltering it from the need to deal with the unpalatable realities its own choices have created.

The key to regional acknowledgment of Israel as a legitimate part of the Middle East was the "two-state solution." The Camp David accords laid out a program for Palestinian self-determination and Israeli withdrawal from the territories it had seized and occupied in 1967. Israel has had more than forty-five years to trade land for peace, implement its Camp David commitments, and comply with international law. It has consistently demonstrated that it craves land more than peace, international reputation, good will, or legitimacy. As a result, Israel remains isolated from its neighbors, with no prospect of reversing this. It is now rapidly forfeiting international acceptability. There is nothing the United States can do to cure either situation despite the adverse consequences of both for American standing in the region and the world.

In the seventeenth century, English settlers in America found inspiration for a theology of ethnic cleansing and racism in the Old Testament. In the twentieth and twenty-first centuries, Jewish settlers in Palestine have invoked the same scripture to craft a parallel theology. The increasingly blatant racism and Islamophobia of Israeli politics, the Kafkaesque tyranny of Israel's checkpoint army in the occupied territories, and Israel's cruel and unusual collective punishment of Gaza have bred hateful resentment of the Jewish state in its region and throughout the Muslim world. One has to look to north Korea to find another polity so detested and distrusted by its neighbors and with so few supporters among the world's great powers.

The United States has affirmed that, regardless of how Israel behaves, it will allow no political distance between itself and the Jewish state. In the eyes of the world there is none. Israel's ill repute corrodes U.S. prestige and credibility not just in the Middle East but in the world at large.

Israel does not seem to care what its neighbors or the world think of it. Despite its geographical location, it prefers to see itself as its neighbors do: as a Hebrew-speaking politico-economic extension of Europe rather than part of the Middle East. Nor does Israel appear concerned about the extent to which its policies have undermined America's ability to protect it from concerted international punishment for its actions. The United States and Israel's handful of other international supporters continue to have strong domestic political reasons to stand by it, yet they are far less likely to be able to hold back the global movement to ostracize Israel than in the case of apartheid South Africa. America may "have Israel's back," but—on this—no one now has America's back.

For a considerable time to come, Israel can rely on its U.S.-provided "qualitative edge" to sustain its military hegemony over others in its region. But, as the "crusader states" established and sustained by previous Western interventions in the region illustrate, such supremacy, especially when dependent on external support, is inevitably ephemeral—and those who live exclusively by the sword are more likely than others to perish by it. Meanwhile, as the struggle for Palestinian Arab rights becomes a struggle for human and civil rights within the de facto single sovereignty that Israel has imposed on Palestine, Israel's internal evolution is rapidly alienating Jews of conscience both there and abroad. Israelis do not have to live in Palestine; they can and do increasingly withdraw from it to live in diaspora. Jews outside contemporary Israel are coming to see it less as a sanctuary or guarantor of Jewish security and well-being than as a menace to both.

The United States has made an enormous commitment to the success of the Jewish state. Yet it has no strategy to cope with the tragic existential challenges Zionist hubris and overweening territorial ambition have now forged for Israel. The hammerlock the Israeli right has on American discourse about the Middle East assures that, despite the huge U.S. political and economic investment in Israel, Washington will not discuss or develop effective policy options for sustaining the Jewish state over the long term. The outlook is therefore for continuing deterioration in Israel's international moral standing and the concomitant isolation of the United States in the region and around the globe.

This brings me back to the other main objective of U.S. policy in the Middle East: the nurturing of strategic partnerships with the largest and most influential Muslim states in the region. Iran and Syria have proven to be lost causes in this regard. Iraq is now more aligned with them than with America. Turkey is still an important U.S. ally on many matters but, with the exception of some aspects of relations with Syria, Ankara is following policies toward the Middle East that are almost entirely uncoordinated with those of the United States. The two pillars of the U.S. position in the Middle East beyond Israel are Egypt and Saudi Arabia. Neither can now be taken for granted.

Egypt is in the midst of a transition from American-aligned autocracy to self-determination under Islamist populism. It is not clear what sort of domestic political order this populism will shape but it seems certain that future Egyptian governments will listen less to the United States and demand more of Israel. The diversion to Egypt of a portion of the U.S. government's generous annual subsidies to Israel long sufficed to secure Cairo's acquiescence in the Camp David framework. This enabled Israel to pretend that it had achieved a measure of acceptance among its Arab neighbors, despite its default on its obligations to the Palestinians and its escalating mistreatment of them. More importantly, it gave Israel the strategic security from Egyptian attack it had been unable to obtain by force of arms.

Populist Egypt's passivity is very unlikely to be procurable on similar terms. Enough has changed to put the Camp David framework at severe risk. (This is true for Jordan as well. Jordan made peace with Israel in response to the Oslo accords, which the ruling right wing in Israel systematically undermined and finally undid.)

Since 1979, the U.S. relationship with Israel has been both a raison d'être and essential underpinning for U.S.-Egyptian cooperation. It is now reemerging as a point of division, irritation, and contention between Americans and Egyptians. Egypt is once again an independent Arab actor in the affairs of its region, including Israel and Iran. It is no longer a reliable agent of American influence. It reacts to Israeli actions and policies calculatedly, with much less deference to U.S. views than in the past.

Islamist parties now dominate Egyptian politics as they do politics in Tunisia and among Palestinians. It is very unlikely that post-Assad Syria will be democratic but it is virtually certain that it will be Salafist. The so-called Arab awakening has turned out really to be a Salafist awakening. There is a struggle for the soul of Islam underway between *takfiri* Salafists and conservative modernizers. In the traditionally Islamist states of Saudi Arabia and Qatar, this struggle is being won by the forces of tolerance, reform, and opening up. Elsewhere, as in Egypt, the outcome remains in doubt, but nowhere are Muslim conservatives, still less Salafists, at ease with expansionist Zionism or the sort of aggressive anti-Islamism that the United States has institutionalized in its "drone wars."

The U.S.-Saudi relationship, once an example of broad-based strategic partnership, has markedly weakened in the wake of Washington's abandonment of the effort to broker peace between Israel and the Palestinians, the impact of 9/11, the U.S. invasion and occupation of Iraq, and the transformation of a punitive raid in Afghanistan into a long-term attempt to preclude an Islamist regime there. American Islamophobia has erased much of the previous mutual regard between the two countries. The United States continues to be the ultimate guarantor of the Saudi state against intervention from foreign enemies other than Israel. There is no alternative to America in this role. Nor, even when it regains energy self-sufficiency, will the United States be able to ignore Saudi Arabia's decisive influence on global energy supplies and prices. But U.S.-Saudi cooperation is no longer instinctual and automatic. It has become cynically transactional, with cooperation taking place on a case-by-case basis as specific interests dictate.

Policy convergence between Washington and Riyadh continues, but sometimes conceals major differences. This is clearly the case with Iran, where Washington's interest in nonproliferation and desire to preserve Israel's nuclear monopoly in the Middle East overlap but do not coincide with Riyadh's concerns. If Tehran does go nuclear, U.S.-Saudi disharmony will be glaringly apparent in very short order. Similarly, in Syria, the common desire of Americans and Saudis to see Syrians overthrow the Assad government masks very different visions about what sort of regime should succeed it and what the stance of that regime should be toward Israel, Lebanon, or Iraq.

The bottom line is this: U.S. policies of unconditional support for Israel, opposition to Islamism, and the use of drones to slaughter suspected Islamist militants and their families and friends have created an atmosphere that precludes broad strategic partnerships with major Arab and Muslim countries, though it does not yet preclude limited cooperation for limited purposes. The acceptance of Israel as a legitimate presence in the Middle East cannot now be achieved without basic changes in Israeli attitudes and behavior that are not in the offing.

U.S. policies designed, respectively, to pursue strategic partnerships with Arab and Muslim powers and to secure the state of Israel have each separately failed. The Middle East itself is in flux. America's interests in the region now demand fundamental rethinking, not just of U.S. policies, but of the strategic objectives those policies should be designed to achieve.

Israel's Fraying Image and Its Implications
May 22, 2013[18]

I t is a privilege to have been asked to join this discussion of Jacob Heilbrunn's account of Israel's fraying image.[19] His article seems to me implicitly to raise two grim questions.

The first question is how long Israel can survive as a democracy—or at all. The Jewish state has left the humane vision of early Zionism and its own beginnings far behind it. Israel now rules over a disenfranchised Muslim and Christian majority whom it would like to expel and a significant minority of disrespected secular and progressive Jews who are stealing away to the safer and more tolerant environs of the United States and other Western countries. Israel has befriended none of its Arab neighbors. It has spurned or subverted all their offers to accept and make peace with it except when compelled to address these by American diplomacy. The Jewish state has now largely alienated its former friends and supporters in Europe. Its all-important patron and protector, the United States, suffers from budgetary bloat, political constipation, diplomatic enervation, and strategic myopia.

The second question is what difference Israel's increasing international isolation or withering away might make to Americans, including but not limited to Jewish Americans.

Let me very briefly speak to some of the issues that create these questions.

For a large majority of those over whom the Israeli state rules directly or indirectly, Israel is already *not* a democracy. It consists of four categories of residents: Jewish Israelis, who, as the ruling caste, are full participants in its political economy; Palestinian Arab Israelis, who are citizens with restricted rights and reduced benefits; Palestinian Arabs in the West Bank, who are treated as stateless prisoners in their own land; and Palestinian Arabs in the Gaza ghetto, who are an urban proletariat besieged and tormented at will by the Israeli armed forces. The operational demands of this multilayered, militarily enforced system of ethno-religious separation have resulted in the steady contraction of freedoms in Israel proper.

Judaism is a religion distinguished by its emphasis on justice and humanity. American Jews, in particular, have a well-deserved reputation as

---

18. Remarks to a seminar convened by the *National Interest*, Washington, D.C.
19. The original article discussed here is Jacob Heilbrunn, "Israel's Fraying Image," *National Interest* (May–June 2013), http://bit.ly/1Qco79C.

reliable champions of the oppressed, opponents of racial discrimination, and advocates of the rule of law. But far from exhibiting these tradition-al Jewish values—which are also those of contemporary America—Israel increasingly exemplifies their opposites. Israel is now known around the world for the Kafkaesque tyranny of its checkpoint army in the occupied territories, its periodic maiming and slaughter of Lebanese and Gazan ci-vilians, its blatant racial and religious bigotry, the zealotry and scofflaw behavior of its settlers, its theology of ethnic cleansing, and its exclusion-ary religious dogmatism.

Despite an ever more extensive effort at *hasbara*—the very sophis-ticated Israeli art of narrative control and propaganda—it is hardly sur-prising that Israel's formerly positive image is, as Mr. Heilbrunn reports, badly "fraying." The gap between Israel's realities and the image project-ed by *hasbara* has grown beyond the capacity of hypocrisy to bridge it. Israel's self-destructive approach to the existential issues it faces challeng-es the consciences of growing numbers of Americans—both Jewish and non-Jewish—and raises serious questions about the extent to which Israel supports, ignores, or undermines American interests in its region. Many have come to see the United States less as the protector of the Jewish state than as the enabler of its most self-injurious behavior and the endower of the many forms of moral hazard from which it has come to suffer.

The United States has assumed the role of protecting power for Israel, which depends heavily on the ability of American Jews to mobilize subsi-dies, diplomatic and legal protection, weapons transfers, and other forms of material support in Washington. This task is made easier by the sym-pathy for Zionism of a large but silent and mostly passive evangelical Christian minority, as well as lingering American admiration for Israelis as the pioneers of a vibrant new society in the Holy Land. It is noteworthy, however, that those actually lobbying for Israel are, almost without excep-tion, Jewish. Their efforts exploit the unscrupulous venality and appease-ment of politically powerful donors that are essential to political survival in modern America to assure reflexive fealty to Israel's right wing and its policies. When it's not denying its own existence, the Israel lobby boasts that it is the most effective special-interest advocate in the country. Official America's passionate attachment to Israel has become a very salient part of U.S. political pathology. It epitomizes the ability of a small but determined minority to extract tax resources for its cause while blocking efforts to question these exactions.

Americans tend to resent aggressively manipulative behavior and have little patience with sycophancy. The ostentatious obsequiousness in evidence during Prime Minister Netanyahu's address to Congress two years ago and the pledges of fealty to Israel of last year's presidential campaign were a major turn-off for many. Mr. Netanyahu has openly expressed his arrogant presumption that he can manipulate America at will. Still, thoughtful Israelis and Zionists of conscience in the United States are now justifiably concerned about declining empathy with Israel in the United States, including especially among American Jews. In most European countries, despite rising Islamophobia, sympathy for Israel has already fallen well below that for the Palestinians. Elsewhere outside North America, it has all but vanished. An international campaign of boycott, disinvestment, and sanctions along the lines of that mounted against apartheid South Africa is gathering force.

Those who have lost the support of more than a passionate minority are often driven to defame and vilify those who disagree with them. Intimidation is necessary only when one cannot make a persuasive case for one's position. As the case for the coincidence of American interests and values with those of Israel has lost credibility, the lengths to which Israel's partisans go to denounce those who raise questions about Israel's behavior have reached levels that invite ridicule, parody, melancholy, and disgust. The Hagel confirmation hearings evoked all four among many, plus widespread foreign derision and contempt.[20] Mr. Hagel's "rope-a-dope" defense may not have been elegant, but it was as effective against bullying assault as nonviolent resistance usually is in the presence of observers with a commitment to decency. The American people have such a commitment and reacted as might be expected to their senators' overwrought busking for political payoffs.

Outside the United States, where narratives made in Israel do not rule the airwaves, the Jewish state has lost favor and is now widely denigrated. Israel's bellicosity and contempt for international law evoke particular apprehension. Every war that Israel has engaged in since its creation has been initiated by it with the single exception of the Yom Kippur/Ramadan War of 1973, which was begun by Egypt. Israel is currently threatening to launch an unprovoked attack on Iran that it admits cannot succeed unless it can manipulate America into yet another Middle Eastern war. Many, if not most outside the United States see

---

20. See Philip Weiss, "Hagel Offers Himself as Secretary of Israel's Defense," *Mondoweiss*, January 31, 2013, http://bit.ly/1L6siDu.

Israel as a major source of regional instability and—through the terrorism this generates—a threat to the domestic tranquility of any country that aligns with it.

To survive over the long term, Israel needs internationally recognized borders and peace with its neighbors, including the Palestinians. Achieving this has for decades been the major objective of U.S. diplomacy in the Middle East. But no effort to convince Israel to do what it must to make peace goes unpunished. Jimmy Carter's tough brokering of normal relations between Israel, Egypt, and, ultimately, Jordan led to his disavowal by his own party. Barack Obama's attempt to secure Israel's acceptance in the Middle East led to his humiliation by Israel's prime minister and his U.S. yahoos and flacks. The Jewish state loses no opportunity to demonstrate that it wants land more than it wants peace. As a result, there has been no American-led "peace process" worthy of the name in this century. Israel continues to ignore the oft-reiterated Arab and Islamic offer to normalize relations with it if it just does what it promised in the Camp David accords: withdraw from the occupied territories and facilitate Palestinian self-determination.

Israel has clearly chosen to stake its future on its ability to maintain perpetual military supremacy in its region, with the support of the United States. Yet this is a formula with a convincing record of prior failure in the Middle East. It is preposterous to imagine that American military power can indefinitely offset Israel's lack of diplomatic survival strategy or willingness to accommodate the Arabs who permeate and surround it. Successive externally supported crusader kingdoms, having failed to achieve the acceptance of their Muslim neighbors, were eventually overrun by these neighbors. The power and influence of the United States, while still great, are declining at least as rapidly as American enthusiasm for following Israel into the endless warfare it sees as necessary to sustain a Jewish state in the Middle East.

The United States has made and continues to make an enormous commitment to the defense and welfare of the Jewish state. Yet it has no strategy to cope with the tragic existential challenges that Zionist hubris and overweening territorial ambition have now forged for Israel. It is the nature of tragedy for the chorus to look on helplessly as a heroic figure with many admirable qualities is overwhelmed by faulty self-perception and judgment. The hammerlock that the Israeli right has on American discourse about the Middle East assures that America will remain an onlooker rather than an effective actor on matters affecting Israel, unable to protect Israel's long-term interests or its own.

The outlook is therefore for continuing deterioration in Israel's image and moral standing. This promises to catalyze discord in the United States as well as the progressive enfeeblement of American influence in the region and around the globe. Image problems are often symptoms of deeper existential challenges. By the time Israel recognizes the need to make compromises for peace in the interest of its own survival, it may well be too late to bring this off. It would not be the first time in history that Jewish zealotry and suspicion of the bona fides of non-Jews resulted in the disappearance of a Jewish state in the Middle East. The collateral damage to the United States and to world Jewry from such a failure is hard to overstate. That is why the question of the United States enabling Israel's shortsightedly self-destructive behavior needs public debate, not suppression by self-proclaimed defenders of Israel operating as thought police. It is also why Mr. Heilbrunn's essay needs to be taken seriously, not just as an investigation of an unpalatable reality but as a harbinger of very serious problems before both Israel and the United States.

2

After the Arab Uprisings: Regression and Anarchy

One of the risks of making predictions on the record is that some of them are bound to be wrong. This is always humbling, but it shouldn't deter one from trying to understand the future on the basis of what's happening now and speaking out about it. As the texts that follow show, I told it as I saw it while the Arab uprisings and related confusions unfolded in the Middle East.

Unlike most others, I was careful to avoid confusing the objectives of the mobs in the streets of Tunis, Cairo, Sana'a, Manama, and Damascus with the westernized democracy evoked by the term "Arab Spring." Despite caveats, however, I was still much too optimistic about the liberalization of Arab politics. This took hold in Tunisia, where the uprisings began, but nowhere else.

In Egypt, maladroit politics and inept governance by an elected Islamist democratic movement (the Muslim Brotherhood) soon led to its overthrow in a military coup, putting the secular and antidemocratic "deep" (garrison) state back in power. I correctly predicted a protracted struggle in Bahrain and Iranian meddling there and elsewhere. In Yemen and Syria, though, I did not foresee that, with a lot of help from foreign intervention of various kinds from multiple quarters, Iraqi-style anarchy, religious strife, and proxy wars would replace autocratic order. Because politics did not liberalize in Egypt and elsewhere, Turkish influence atrophied and, instead of going into remission, the Salafi-jihadi threat metastasized.

Still, I got the geopolitical significance of what was under way for U.S. interests broadly right. I anticipated rising regional disillusionment with the United States and the decline of American influence as nationalism became more assertive and Arabs shucked off the vestiges of past deference to colonialism. To support this trend, Arab states continued their drive to diversify their foreign relationships beyond the United States and the former colonial powers in the region to include China, India, Russia, and new partners in Europe. What happens in the Middle East is now decided in the Middle East.

Part of what is happening in the region is the invention and export of new systems of Islamic governance. But these are not the liberal systems based on *shura* (inclusive consultation) that many in the region and I anticipated. They are tyrannical theocracies in the form of Islamic "emirates," including an especially brutal, self-proclaimed "caliphate" or "Islamic state." Meanwhile, the effort begun by Saudi Arabia's King Abdullah ibn Abdulaziz al-Saud to co-opt the Salafi narrative and retell it in terms of the tolerant traditions of early Islam appears to have been abandoned by his successor as custodian of the two holy mosques, King Salman ibn Abdulaziz al-Saud.

The section that follows chronicles the unhappy story of the collapse of the old order in the Middle East.

The Arab Reawakening and Its Strategic Implications
March 26, 2011[1]

The year 2011 is 1432 in the Hijri calendar, which measures the life of Islamic civilization. However one numbers it, this year will be long remembered. It has begun with uprisings in Tunis and Cairo, a popular revolt and civil war in Libya, and the disturbance of domestic tranquility by demands for reform in many other parts of the Arab world. After long acquiescence in a regional order fixed by European colonialism and sustained by American dominance, the Arabs are standing up for themselves. The governed in this region have discovered that they can, if necessary, take back their consent to be governed and thereby compel regime change. A reawakening of the Arabs by the Arabs is occurring in country after country across the wide expanse of West Asia and North Africa. The age of foreign protectorates in this region has passed. With its demise come major uncertainties about the future.

The short-term effects of these uncertainties will include higher and more volatile oil and gas prices, slower recovery from the Great Recession in America and to a lesser extent in Europe and Japan, and an accelerated shift of global wealth to rising powers in East and South Asia as well as to energy producers in West Asia. I note that Citibank has just projected that, in 2050, Saudi Arabia will have the sixth-highest GDP per capita in the world.[2] Recent events make that outcome more rather than less probable. That aside, the long-term effects of current events are less easy to forecast. They seem likely to include:

- Liberalized and more assertively nationalistic politics in Arab countries, coupled with greater self-reliance and autonomy in their management of regional affairs.
- A major reduction in the ability of outsiders—notably, the United States—to shape trends and events in West Asia and North Africa.
- The further isolation of Israel.
- The revival of Cairo, Baghdad, and Damascus as leading actors in the affairs of the Arab East, rejoining Riyadh in that role.

---

1. Remarks to the Asia Business Council, Riyadh, Saudi Arabia;
2. Press Trust of India, "Saudi Arabia to Have 6th Highest Per Capita GDP by 2050: Report," *Economic Times (Times of India)*, March 8, 2011, http://bit.ly/1RXnDFI.

- A concomitant setback for recent Iranian gains in prestige and influence in a revivified Arab world.
- Opportunities for Turkey to strengthen its newly prominent regional leadership.
- Accelerated development of Arab ties to East and South Asia (and possibly to Russia) to offset and balance past dependence on the United States, Britain, and France.
- The displacement of the jihadi threat to Arab societies as milder forms of Islamism assume a larger role in governance.
- If new models of consultative governance arise in the Arab world, the spread of these models to non-Arab parts of the Muslim world.

In short, the peoples of this region—long in a state of foreign-supported political torpor—must now expect interesting times. So, then, must the rest of the world. The Middle East is, after all, where Africa, Asia, and Europe intersect, where Judaism and Christianity began, where Islam is centered, and where the world's energy resources are concentrated. It is also where an abiding absence of peaceful remedies for injustice inspires local unrest and stimulates terrorists with global reach to attack the West. A single tremor in such a place can trigger a political-economic tsunami.

I will discuss each of these issues briefly. Before I do, however, I should make it clear why much of what I have to say applies to the former colonies of Europe in West Asia and North Africa but not to Saudi Arabia. It matters greatly in this context that Saudi Arabia is the only society on the planet never to have experienced coercive intrusion by Western militaries, missionaries, or merchants. The Kingdom has never compromised its independence. When the West finally came here, it came not as a conqueror, spiritual tutor, or mercantile exploiter, but *as hired help*. Saudis therefore display none of the angst, almost none of the self-doubt, and—apart from a few people who went to college in Beirut and Cairo—very little of the chip on the shoulder that other Arabs have about their largely humiliating encounter with the West. Saudis seem in many ways to see the world as composed of two classes of people: themselves and potential employees. They do not lack confidence in their values, faith in their political traditions, or respect for their ruler and his family.

It matters, in short, that Saudi Arabia is a society in which modernity and the institutions that support it have been imported by Saudis themselves, not imposed by outsiders. This is a country with a system of government derived from purely native models, with a compact of governance that mirrors that of its constituent tribes, and with borders that it, not colonial bureaucrats in London or Paris, established for itself. In this uniquely Arabian polity, the task of the ruler has been to discover, shape, and proclaim a consensus that is consistent with the dictates of faith, not to impose foreign-inspired policies upon an unconsulted people.

In Saudi Arabia, moreover, those who make decisions have never been able to avoid close interaction with those whom their decisions affect. Rulers and ruled meet in frequent open sessions—*majlises*—at which both personal and policy matters can be and are discussed. Within this context, Saudis have sought to ensure that economic progress reinforces rather than erodes the values imparted by religious faith and tradition. The Saudi compact of governance dictates that a primary duty of government is to ensure that the less fortunate benefit from the prosperity of society as a whole. Accordingly, Saudi Arabia has invested its public funds mainly in infrastructure and the construction of a welfare state for its people, not in foreign capital markets. There are numerous policy differences among the inhabitants of this Kingdom, but there is no crisis of legitimacy.

Saudi Arabia is not, of course, immune to popular discontent. Rightly or wrongly, for example, there is widespread resentment of the employment of foreigners rather than Saudis in key jobs throughout the economy. Despite much progress in recent years, the Kingdom's Shiite minority remains politically and economically disadvantaged. The history of Saudi Arabia is one of top-down reform. The people look to the king to guide and regulate change. Some Saudis criticize King Abdullah for promoting too little change too slowly. Others accuse him of trying to change too much too fast. But everyone acknowledges the king as a reformer who is skillfully engaged in opening up this kingdom to the outside world while balancing competing political pressures at home.

This king is popular among his people, if not with those abroad who disparage Islam and the Arabs out of ignorance or for their own purposes. At home, the authority of the Saudi monarchy is accepted by almost all but a dwindling band of discredited extremists. Al-Qaeda's charge that the Kingdom tolerates and cooperates with the non-Muslim world rather than treating it with hostility has little resonance here and even less appeal abroad.

Saudis are very conscious that, as His Royal Highness Prince Turki Al-Faisal recently put it, their country is "the heart of the Muslim World and the cradle of Arab identity." Given its pivotal position, it is fortunate that the Kingdom's distinctive character makes it relatively immune to contagion from the instability now sweeping the rest of the Arab world. The uprisings there have sought to replace despots perceived to be under foreign protection with regimes that more authentically reflect the aspirations and opinions of their peoples. Disputes about public policy issues in Saudi Arabia are sometimes serious, but their context does not resemble that in Tunisia, Egypt, Libya, or other parts of the Arab world.

Saudi youth, like Arab youth elsewhere, are now networked into a transnational Arab community that knows no borders. But the spreading anarchy in other countries has little if any appeal in this nation of strong families, strong tribal affiliations, and strong individual commitments to the peaceful practice of Islam. That's just as well for the world, given the dependence of the global economy on this Kingdom's energy and petrochemical exports. To Saudi Arabia's south, Yemen is now in turmoil. To Saudi Arabia's north, Jordan, Iraq, and now Syria are all under varying degrees of stress. Saudi Arabia itself is quiet.

The one plausible source of contagion for Saudi Arabia is the civil strife in its much smaller sister kingdom of Bahrain, just twenty-five kilometers off its coast. There, discontent with longstanding discriminatory treatment has once again erupted into confrontation between disparate elements of the disadvantaged Shiite majority and the privileged Sunni minority. The Saudi Arabian government is understandably concerned that escalating protests in Bahrain could spread across the causeway to its own largely Shiite and oil-rich Eastern Province.

The close association of religious tendencies with class differences in Bahrain is distinctive. It is hard to find analogies to it elsewhere in the Arab world, now that the Shiite majority rules in Iraq. Despite Bahrain's uniqueness, however, the ouster of its royal family, as some protesters have demanded, could incite instability in the other small city-states that, with Saudi Arabia, make up the Gulf Cooperation Council. Beyond this concern, GCC members fear that majority Shiite rule in Bahrain would draw the island into the Iranian orbit, handing Iran a strategic base of influence in their midst. None of these risks is acceptable to them. Under Saudi leadership, they have now intervened to restore order on the island.

The GCC's members are aware that, by using force to suppress Shiite unrest in Bahrain, they may have given Iran an opening for subversion there. At various moments in ancient times, Bahrain was controlled by Persia. The temptation is strong for Iran to support its fellow Shiites in a struggle against their Sunni rulers. The U.S. Fifth Fleet headquarters is ashore in Bahrain, and it would be a tempting target in such a campaign.

Then, too, the GCC intervention gives Iraq, newly dominated by Shiites with close ties to Iran, an excuse to make common cause with Iran in supporting Shiite insurrection in Bahrain. Outright alliance between Baghdad and Tehran to this end would have far-reaching adverse impli cations for Gulf security. The strategic stakes in Bahrain are higher than many outside the region appreciate.

Events in Bahrain have also sharpened the differences between Saudi Arabia and the United States. While Washington in no way obstructed the Saudi intervention there, it publicly counseled the king of Bahrain to answer the protesters' demands with offers of reform. In the view of Saudi Arabia and other GCC members, however, offering concessions to an un-ruly mob is more likely to feed its frenzy than to pacify it. Riots in the streets that challenge government control of them are not conducive to considered judgments about reform. From the GCC perspective, the res-toration of peace in Bahrain is the prerequisite for peaceful change there.

The core demand of Bahrain's demonstrators is an end to the discrim-ination that has kept the Shiite standard of living significantly below that of Sunnis on the island. The GCC has just offered substantial economic assistance to help Bahrain close this economic gap. This addresses some symptoms of the problem in Bahrain but will not, in itself, resolve it.

Bahrain is a regional financial center and entrepôt. Confidence in its banks and businesses depends on the maintenance of social harmony and stability on its streets. The religious divide in Bahrain is now a matter of vivid record in the Arab blogosphere and stimulates furious dissension between Sunnis and Shiites across the region. Without reforms to cure the underlying causes of unrest, further outbreaks of instability will remain an ever-present danger.

Julius Nyerere once remarked that "small countries are like indecent-ly dressed women; they tempt the evil-minded." This is all the more the case when they expose their soft spots to those who might have designs on them. Once order has been restored, therefore, the earliest possible civil dialogue and implementation of reform are very much in the interest of the GCC as a whole, not to mention the world. In their own self-interest, the various classes of Bahrainis must now compose their differences. GCC leaders know that the status quo in that small but strategically important kingdom is no longer sustainable. Once their intervention to restore order has succeeded, they may be expected to work with Bahrain's government and people to contrive a new basis for socioeconomic integration and po-litical harmony there.

Elsewhere in the Arab world, the most surprising element of the spreading revolutions to many has been the extent to which they have avoided religious, class, or foreign-policy agendas. To Iran's and al-Qaeda's dismay, there has been no significant Islamist or jihadi element to these rebellions. Pan-Arabism too has been notably absent. Many protesters have criticized the leaders they are seeking to overthrow as satraps of America or collaborators with Israel's anti-Arab pogroms. With a few exceptions, however, they have not directed their fury at the United States or Israel as such.

These revolutions have been made by people seeking greater liberty in their own societies under governments that reflect their will rather than that of despots or foreign powers. Those who have rebelled have not done so to install foreign models or mores. They hope for new constitutional dispensations that will give them a voice in determining public policy and that assure them security in their persons and their homes.

The aspirations of those who made these revolutions are rooted in their domestic experiences. It is clearer what they are against than what they are for. It is still too early to say whether their expressed desire for some form of democracy will be fully respected by the military authorities who are now in charge. Nor is it yet clear what future balance will be struck between secular and Islamist politics. The Islamic concept of *shura*—government by consultation—accords with democracy but is distinct from it. Countries determined on constitutional reform that is consistent with Islam have a wide range of democratic models between which to choose, with Turkey at one extreme and Hamas-ruled Palestine at the other.

Whether they adopt democracy or not, Arab governments—even those that escape or survive the current turmoil—will now be much more deferential to the will of their peoples. Islamism, in one or more of its many forms, will surely advance as a result. For many Muslims, the legitimacy of rulers is measured by the extent to which they exemplify moral standards as they lead the *umma*, or community of the faithful. In the new circumstances, this perspective will have a larger voice than before.

There are already many efforts under way to achieve a reformation of public morality in the Islamic world and to restore Arab civilization to a position of global leadership. Some of the most noteworthy initiatives in this regard are taking place in Saudi Arabia. They aim to restore Islam to the exemplary state of tolerance, open-mindedness, and scientific leadership it enjoyed in its earliest centuries. King Abdullah's initiatives to promote intra-Muslim and interfaith dialogue are part of this effort. The newly established King Abdullah University of Science and Technology is another. This graduate-level university is not just an attempt to lay the basis for a knowledge-based economy in Saudi Arabia. It is conceived as a new *Bait al-Hikma*, or House of Wisdom, like the one in Baghdad during the Golden Age of Islam. That ancient House of Wisdom was where many of the extraordinary contributions of Islamic culture to the world's science, mathematics, and technology were made. Of special interest in this time of ongoing financial crisis, the Islamic world also invented much of the basis for the world's banking practices and institutions. Islamic bankers in this region are once again creating innovative ways of financing trade and investment.

Elsewhere in the Arab world, new Muslim democratic parties are in prospect, paralleling the Christian democratic parties that arose in Europe twelve decades ago. The emergence of such parties should be welcomed. It will further marginalize al-Qaeda, which, I note, has been a pathetically isolated onlooker as the Arab revolutions have unfolded. Terrorism against Arab governments is likely to subside. Unfortunately, however, politically motivated violence against Israeli and American targets may well increase. Israel's occupation and colonization efforts in the West Bank as well as its brutal siege of Gaza have left Palestinians with no peaceful path to self-determination and Arabs as a whole with no incentive to accept a Jewish state in their midst.

Arab youth remain loyal citizens of particular countries, but they have also become netizens of a virtualized Arab commonwealth. They are very much aware of the state of political and economic affairs, as well as public morality, in countries other than their own. Arab leaders can no longer safely ignore the imperative of reform or the examples set by others in the community of Arab states who pursue it. A year or two from now, no country in this region is likely to have the same domestic and foreign policies as it does now.

Egypt, in particular, has been jolted from the senile repose in which it slumbered for almost two decades. Egypt has reawakened. If Egyptians go on to choose effective leaders, they will resume a central role in the affairs of this region. They could develop an ideology with broad appeal throughout the Arab world and beyond. Egyptian diplomacy is almost certain to be reinvigorated. It will now reflect Egyptian opinion and values rather than what a single leader regards as expedient. As a result, neither the United States nor Israel will be able to count on Egyptian cooperation or support of policies that are anathema to the Arab street.

A reanimated Egypt will also balance and thereby diminish the regional influence of Iran. Without the burden of close association with American foreign policy, Cairo is likely to be more effective at this than in the last decade or more, when American blundering, Egypt's listlessness, and the sidelining of Arab powers other than Saudi Arabia helped Iran make major inroads in influence in Iraq, Lebanon, and Palestine. Egypt now seems certain to reemerge as a formidable competitor for leadership of the Arab world and the broader realm of Islam. Realignments in intra-Arab relations and politics are sure to follow.

These changes are occurring as the United States withdraws from Iraq, leaving behind a ruined country under heavy Iranian influence. Iraq is incapable, at least for now, of resuming its historic role as part of an Arab coalition to check Persian aspirations for hegemony in West Asia. If one accepts the need to counter Iran as a given, this makes a continuing American military presence in the Persian Gulf essential to guarantee regional balance. But recent events have cost the United States the little credibility in the Arab world it had retained, following its introduction of a bloody anarchy to Iraq, its transformation of a punitive raid against al-Qaeda and its Taliban hosts into an attempt at foreign pacification of Afghanistan, its close association with hateful Israeli policies toward Israel's neighbors, and its recent abandonment of its decades-long attempt to halt the Jewish holy war for Palestinian Arab land.

Washington's tardy, ambivalent, and ineffectual official approval of regime change in Tunisia and Egypt has done little to persuade those on the Arab street of American sincerity in supporting their demands for democracy. They will not easily forget decades of U.S. embrace of dictatorial regimes. Meanwhile, belated American demands that longstanding protégés of the United States take leave of power has convinced the region's rulers that Washington is undependable—neither faithful to those it befriends nor reliable as their protector. As a result, Arabs, Turks, and even Israelis are no longer convinced—if they ever were—of the wisdom, trustworthiness, and reliability of the United States and its policies. Even the belated American acceptance of GCC and Arab League demands for a "no-fly zone" in Libya has perversely backfired. The air attacks on Libya have done more to reinforce the U.S. reputation for heartless brutality to Muslim civilians than to convince Arabs that America is on their side.

Past confidence in American guarantees of West Asia's peace, well-being, energy exports, and strategic transport routes has taken some hard knocks over the years. But there is no apparent alternative to the United States as the guarantor of these public goods. The world cannot afford instability in this region. But if either popular antipathy to America in the Gulf Arab states or the fiscal crisis in the United States were to result in a significant reduction in the U.S. presence and perceived level of commitment in the Gulf, this would be enormously destabilizing. Unless Iraq stepped forward once again to balance Iran, an American drawdown would face the Gulf Arabs with a choice between accommodating Tehran and building some sort of innovative coalition to balance and contain it. I don't think that anyone can now count on Iraq not to side with rather than against Iran. I also doubt that there is much prospect of an end to the millennial rivalry between Persians and Arabs.

There is no distant great power other than the United States able to project forces into the Persian Gulf region. It is unlikely that there will be another power with such capabilities for decades, if ever. Despite the glib salesmanship of its multiple defense ministers, Europe lacks the coherence or conviction to substitute for America. Russia's ability to respond to Arab requests for support is limited by its unresolved relationship with Europe and its fixation on its own problems. India is developing the capability to play an important politico-military role in this region, but it is both far from ready to do so and greatly distracted by its strategic rivalries with China and Pakistan. In the long run, countries like China and others to the east of India may have to share the burden of protecting their own as well as global interests in West Asia. But I do not see much possibility that they will soon muster either the will or the capabilities to do so.

So, in the absence of the United States, any coalition to secure this region would have willy-nilly to draw on the strength of mid-level powers nearer by. This suggests a combination of Turkey, Egypt, and Pakistan with the GCC—but such a coalition would be expensive, difficult, and time-consuming to concoct. It would have too many moving parts to substitute reliably for the United States. Pakistan could be particularly useful in providing an extended nuclear deterrent against Iran as well as Israel, if either task becomes necessary. But Pakistan will always have its eye more on India, Kashmir, and Afghanistan than on the Gulf. Depending on the course of events in occupied Palestine, Egypt's current cold peace with Israel may well give way to something more like a cold war, riveting the attention of Egyptians on their own immediate defense needs. Turkey, at least for now, seems more inclined to accommodate Iran than to join others in countering it.

In practice, therefore, much as they may doubt the reliability of the United States, West Asians have no realistic possibility of separating themselves from a measure of dependence on America. In this context, it is ironic that the dreadful fiscal condition of the United States will probably not permit it to sustain military capabilities in this region at anything like recent levels. The American imperative of budgetary retrenchment and the Gulf Arab effort to reduce dependence on the United States to the greatest extent possible will thus reinforce each other. In the decade to come, the states of this region will seek reassurance in new security partnerships. East and South Asian countries with an interest in this region's energy resources must expect to have to begin sharing the burden of supporting their interests here much sooner than they now realize.

All in all, it seems very likely that Arab countries will achieve—indeed, they will be unable to avoid—the greater self-reliance and autonomy in managing their affairs to which the current revolutions aspire. This region plays a central role in the global economy. Having decided to seize control of their own destiny, Arabs must now determine it themselves. They will. What they decide and what they do will make a difference to all the world.

Revolutionary change has already come to some Arab countries. Evolutionary change is underway in the countries of the Arabian Peninsula. Change of any kind entails unpredictability, which is another word for an unexpected series of problems for the unprepared and opportunities for the alert. As they meet the challenges of change, the Arabs will not abandon their ties to the United States or Europe. They will, however, seek to supplement and offset them with expanded relationships with East and South Asia.

Viewed from afar, the Arab world, even this peaceful and prosperous part of it, may appear at present to be a zone of strife. Viewed from up close, even in these turbulent times, this country and this region can be seen to present many more opportunities for transnational cooperation than they do for conflict.

After Abbottabad: Islam and the West
May 16, 2011[3]

I t's an honor to open this conference on dialogue between Islam and the West. It is entirely fitting that such a discussion take place in Abu Dhabi. This emirate and the federal state of which it is part have long exemplified the coexistence of Muslim piety with tolerance for other faiths and ways of life. The United Arab Emirates preserves a precious heritage from the Islam of bygone days that facilitates the dialogue of civilizations. The spirit of tolerance exhibited here is all too rare today. As a non-Muslim, I admire it.

I once heard a story about the late ruler of Abu Dhabi and father of the UAE, Sheikh Zayed Al-Nahyan (may he rest in peace), that seemed to me to encapsulate this spirit. If it isn't true, it ought to be.

Apparently, Sheikh Zayed took an intense personal interest in the landscaping of Abu Dhabi's lovely waterfront promenade. The Corniche was shaped by his hands and watered with his sweat, as well as that of other notables of this city. It got so that his friends were afraid to drive by the construction site for fear that he would pop out of a hole he was digging and hand them a shovel. Shortly after the Corniche was finished, the story goes, Sheikh Zayed received a visit from a group of religious elders. They said to him, "Your Highness, we hardly know how to tell you this, but at the hotels on your Corniche, they are serving alcohol." Abu Dhabi's ruler thought for a moment and replied, "Well, then, I guess you better not go there."

The Emirates remain a place in which, out of respect, non-Muslims do not drink while they dine with their Muslim friends, but in which, out of respect for their non-Muslim friends, Muslims would be silently forgiving if they did. Piety—even the piety of a faith one does not share—is truly admirable when it is married to respect for the moral autonomy of others and the rules they obey.

By contrast with the Torah and many Christian texts, which reject the standing of other faiths, the notion of tolerance and respectful interfaith dialogue is completely integral to the message of Islam. The sixty-seventh and sixty-eighth *ayat* of the Surat al-Hajj (Sura 22:67–68) in the Holy Qur'an advise:

---

3. Remarks at the Emirates Center for Strategic Studies and Research Conference on Civilized Dialogue, Abu Dhabi

To every people have We appointed ceremonial rites [of prayer] which they observe; therefore, let them not wrangle over this matter with you, but bid them to turn to your Lord [since that is the main objective of religion]. You indeed are rightly guided. But if they still dispute you in this matter, [then say,] "God best knows [the value of] what you do."

Likewise, the forty-first verse of the Surat al-Zumar (39:41) says:

Whoever guides himself by [the message of Islam] does so to his own advantage, and whoever turns away from it does so at his own loss. You [Muslims] certainly are not their keepers.

Thanks mainly to the late Osama bin Laden and his co-conspirators, the detractors of Islam in the West are now legion. They have spilled a lot of ink and vitriol to demonstrate the obvious: that Muslims and Muslim societies often belie these messages of tolerance as well as the sacred instruction to avoid "compulsion in religion." In places in America where no Muslim has ever trod, good folk fear the imposition of Shariah law—the Islamic Talmud. Their fear is all the greater since they have absolutely no idea what either the Shariah or the Talmud is. Western Islamophobia is one of Osama's most loathsome legacies, if far from his only one.

By any standard of righteousness, Osama bin Laden deserved to die. His life dishonored Islam. His death in Abbottabad dishonored no one but himself. He was condemned by his own actions, which violated the moral principles of every religion. He personally incarnated the exception to the rule against the killing of human beings that is recounted in the Holy Qur'an. It recalls (5:32) that God "decreed for the Children of Israel that to kill any person who has not committed murder or horrendous crimes is like murdering all of humankind."

Osama was that very murderer who directed the commission of horrendous crimes. He leaves behind him many monuments to the evil in his heart. He does not deserve them, but these monuments are both numerous and large. It will take a long time to pull them down, but this must now be done.

Osama expected to die by violence, as he did. Sadly, he probably died a satisfied man. In addition to alienating Muslims and the West from each other, as was his aim, he achieved so many other transformations of the order he sought to overthrow. Everyone who walks shoeless through a metal detector in an airport pays grudging tribute to him. His legacies include hatred and suspicion that have erected barriers to travel to and within the West and that impede the sort of dialogue you in this gathering are about to begin. He catalyzed two wars. He bears responsibility for the death of thousands in the West and hundreds of thousands in this region. The unfunded financial burden of the conflicts he ignited has come close to bankrupting the United States. Indirectly, it is upending the international monetary system. It has produced recession in the West. Osama will have been pleased.

The mass murders Osama contrived inflamed passions that spurred American political leaders to set aside the constraints of the U. S. constitution and laws. There has been serious erosion in American civil liberties amid popular disdain for the rule of law both at home and abroad. This is what paved the way for the horrors of Abu Ghraib, "extraordinary rendition," and "enhanced interrogation techniques"—otherwise known as "cruel and unusual punishment," "kidnapping," and "torture."

Ironically, the manner of Osama's death confirmed his success at having swept away much of the traditional American deference to due process of law. He was subjected to an extrajudicial execution carried out in violation of the sovereignty of another nation. This was as lawless as it was emotionally fulfilling. Few objected. For most, the end fully justified the means. Not many have taken the time to ponder the implications of the precedent his ruthless slaying may have established for the targeted killing of American and other leaders by their foreign enemies.

In short, Osama left the world a far worse place than it had been when he entered it. It is up to those of us who have outlived him to carry out the patient work of undoing as much as possible of the harm he and others of his kind have done. This will take time and much effort.

I think of the initiative of King Abdullah ibn Abdulaziz of Saudi Arabia to convoke a conversation among the many schools of Islam at Mecca. In June 2008, that gathering prepared the way for a historic meeting of leading figures from all the world's religions a month later at Madrid. The Madrid conference reconvened under UN sponsorship in November 2008 in New York. King Abdullah is now engaged with others in establishing a permanent center for continuing interfaith dialogue in Vienna.

I think also of Abu Dhabi's crown prince, Sheikh Mohammed bin Zayed, who has encouraged a week-long seminar among Muslim, Christian, and Jewish scholars who specialize in conflict resolution. This is to convene at the Yale Divinity School in New Haven, Connecticut, four weeks from today. I could cite other examples. Extremists on all sides have sought to prevent respectful discourse between the world's Muslims and those of other faiths. They have done much damage, but they have not prevailed. Despite zealous apostles of bigotry on all sides, a hopeful process of mutual discovery is underway.

This is vitally important. The West (of which Israel counts itself part) and Islam have much to learn from each other and much to unlearn. The core values of all three Abrahamic faiths are the same. All are rooted in the ancient Jewish experience and consciousness. In many ways, Judaism and Islam are closer to each other both doctrinally and in their approach to dispute resolution than either is to Christianity. The invention of irreconcilable conflicts between Jews and Muslims since time immemorial is a willful distortion of history. Zionist propagandists have imposed this false narrative of age-old religious victimization on Israel's battle with Palestinian nationalism. That is as prejudicial to peace as it is sinful.

No relationship between differing religious communities is without its tensions and its bad moments. In retrospect, however, societies like Muslim Spain and the Ottoman Empire were remarkable exemplars of tolerance. Their experience offers hope for the peaceful coexistence of moral communities in our times, not evidence of its impossibility.

The Ottoman Empire was brought down by contagion from European nationalism, followed by vivisection by European imperialists. Its violent disintegration amid genocide and ethnic cleansing was a function of newly aroused passions for ethnic self-determination, not religious schism. Still, religion was an ideological weapon to which all sides in that mayhem resorted. One ironic result was that the religious tolerance that had distinguished Ottoman Turkey was succeeded by an extreme form of secularism that was hostile to expressions of religious identity.

The gradual reemergence in today's Turkey of a tolerant secularism that respects liberty of religious conscience is a reminder that the best elements of the past can sometimes be reborn. The evolution of Turkey offers hope for the coexistence of Islam with other religious heritages. It is an example not just to Arab countries reawakening from the darkness of Islam's eclipse by Western imperialism but also to Europe. In their treatment of Muslim and other minorities, Europeans are once again demonstrating a dismaying inability to coexist with religious and cultural traditions other than those of Christianity. Islamophobia is the ugly successor to anti-Semitism.

Centuries of anti-Semitism are a despicable feature of European history. This tradition of religious persecution and racism culminated in the attempted annihilation of Europe's Jews. The lesson of that Holocaust is that religious hatred is never innocent; it is the precursor and progenitor of unspeakable crimes, and it must not be tolerated.

Neither America nor the Muslim world was complicit in Europe's horrors, but distance from events cannot excuse denying them. If it is wrong to distort history to justify hatred and suspicion of other communities, it is equally wrong to withhold compassion from those who have suffered. Without empathy, there is no possibility of reconciliation. Anti-Semitism was evil when it was Western; it is evil when it infects Arabs and Muslims.

Too many of today's conflicts have taken on the characteristics of "holy war," in which revenge and viciousness are seen as vindications of faith and acts of kindness are despised as heresy. The degeneration of the struggle between competing nationalisms in Palestine into one between gangster Zionism and terrorist Islamism is but one example. The inhumanity of each side to the other has brought discredit on both Judaism and Islam. In the eyes of the world's Muslims, Christianity is also disgraced by its followers' abetment of Israeli misdeeds. The New Testament teaches that "love worketh no ill to his neighbor: therefore love is the fulfilling of the law" (Romans 13:10). Not much love or law is in evidence in the West's treatment of the Israel-Palestine issue.

In America's and NATO's several wars in the region, many Muslims see a rebirth of the Crusades—violent incursions and lethal interventions in Muslim societies by Christian warriors. They call in response for jihad against the West. Some Americans join them in the view that U.S. military operations in Afghanistan and Iraq are sacred wars of religion.

The antidotes to such ignorant enmity and cruelty are to be found in the core beliefs of all three Abrahamic faiths, which are in accord: the prerequisite for peace is respect and compassion for others. Mutual understanding and empathy can only be found through considerate dialogue between minds ready to abandon prejudice, to change behavior, and to work toward policies that promote harmony rather than confrontation.

As Father Hans Küng once famously remarked, "There will be no peace among the nations without peace among the religions. There will be no peace among the religions without dialogue among the religions."[4] He was right. Many Muslims are now working to promote such peace through dialogue. So too are many Christians, not a few Jews, and the sizable Muslim community in the United States. This gives me hope.

But, in the end, hope is only vindicated by the results of the efforts it inspires. Arabs and Americans face challenges that cannot be met without mutual trust and confidence that only intimate reacquaintance can

4. Hans Küng, "The World's Religions: Common Ethical Values," speech delivered at Santa Clara University, Santa Clara, CA, March 31, 2005, http://bit.ly/1T20wvb.

establish. So, too, the Jewish, Christian, and Muslim peoples of the Middle East. How, otherwise, shall we deal with the bleeding ulcer that is now the Holy Land? What shall we do about fitting a post-occupation Iraq back into its region? How shall we manage an assertive but internally divided Iran? What can we do to help Pakistan step onto a more promising path? What roles shall we play in a free Afghanistan? How may we benefit from the diplomatic invigoration of Egypt? How should we help the Arab Spring of North Africa not become an Arab winter elsewhere?

So many questions, so many common interests, and so little common understanding on which to base effective responses. Asked, on his arrival in London, what he thought of Western civilization, Mahatma Gandhi replied that he thought "it would be a good idea." Civilized dialogue among peoples with mutually misunderstood heritages is an even better idea.

The Mess in the Middle East
October 27, 2011[5]

A famous expert on the Middle East was, many years ago, asked to describe U.S. policy there. He replied, "We don't *have* a policy in the Middle East; but that's just as well because, if we did, it would be the *wrong* one."

Recent events suggest that this was a major and memorable insight. The more that "change we can believe in" unfolds in the Middle East, the more things stay the same or retrogress. The more policy we have, the more perverse the results it seems to produce for our country.

Over the year since we last met here in this hall, there have been momentous events in West Asia and North Africa. Some Arab regimes have fallen to popular uprisings. Others appear to be at risk of doing so. Throughout the broad expanse of the Arab world, incumbent governments of all kinds must now be much more deferential than before to the will of their people on both domestic and foreign affairs. This is good news for those who favor more accountable government, as I'm sure everyone here does—at least for foreigners. Americans concerned with the capacity of the United States to shape events in the Middle East should, however, hold the elation. Self-determination is, by definition, a rejection of subservience. This means, among other things, that Arab rulers are considerably less inclined to do America's bidding than in the past. They are starting to do things they see as in their interests even when these things are not in ours.

This is especially the case with regard to the Israel-Palestine issue, which remains central to our relations with the region. Given our unbreakable bonds with Israel, it is not at all helpful that that country has now—as some of us feared it might—alienated those few of its neighbors with which it once enjoyed normal ties. American policies have long put sustaining Israel's military dominance of the region ahead of encouraging it to make peace with Palestinians and other Arabs. Shielded militarily from the need to deal respectfully with its neighbors and those over whom it rules, the Zionist state has progressively segregated itself both morally and politically from the region and most of the international community, including a growing number of Jews here and elsewhere in the West.

---

5. Remarks to the 20th Annual Arab-U.S. Policymakers Conference National Council on U.S.-Arab Relations, Washington, D.C.

Israel has nonetheless also demonstrated that its hold on domestic U.S. politics remains unbroken. This past year, it was able to compel our president to swear allegiance to expansive Zionism and to repudiate policies endorsed by his own and previous administrations as well as the international community. By contemptuously overriding the views and interests of the United States in this way, Israel and its American claque debased and discredited American international prestige and regional credibility. As a consequence, the world has come together in a series of ever firmer votes of no confidence in U.S. leadership and diplomacy on the Israel-Palestine dispute. American military might remains unchallengeable, but the power of the United States to protect Israel from the political and legal consequences of its policies, statements, and actions has been gravely impaired. This is a perverse result for an Israeli government and its supporters to have engineered.

For their part, the Palestinians, after decades of bitter frustration with a feckless, fraudulent, and ultimately fruitless American-led "peace process," have concluded that they cannot count on the United States. They have ended their deference to what they (and most of the world) now see as America's meretricious manipulation of their affairs to their occupier's advantage. They have taken the initiative to rally regional and global support for their self-determination and independence from Israel. They hope in this way to transform the struggle for Palestinian independence into a more equal contest. Theirs will no longer be a bilateral struggle between a strong, U.S.-backed Israel and a Palestine with no leverage. It will, they hope, become a contest between Israel and the world's conscience.

Ironically, political reactions here to these developments promise not only to isolate the United States in international organizations but to deprive us of our residual influence with the Palestinians. The end of U.S. subsidies to the Palestinian Authority will force Israel to assume responsibility for security and other services in the occupied territories that it had successfully unloaded on Palestinian collaborators funded by American and other foreign taxpayers. Instead of facilitating the occupation by paying Palestinians to police it, Americans and Europeans are now likely to face demands to pay Israel directly to conduct it. Europeans, at least, are unlikely to take up this burden.

The perceived need to counter Israeli and American policies is already throwing together some strange diplomatic bedfellows. It is also marginalizing American influence on other issues of concern in West Asia and North Africa. The regional clout of non-Western powers like China, India, and Russia will surely grow concomitantly.

If this sounds grim, I apologize. I cannot promise that, as is the case on Saudi Arabia's Channel One, amusing cartoons will follow the sermon. I must leave it to those who follow me to provide comic relief. I'm happy to do that. Years ago, Ronald Reagan told me, "You know, they say that hard work never killed anybody. But why take a chance?" He delegated as much as he could to experts who were smarter than he was. He set a good example I plan to follow.

This conference has been convened to weigh the implications of the trends and developments I've outlined. As I look at the agenda, I see that it will also consider other legacies of past and present U.S. policies in the region, like Iran's resentful anti-Americanism and assertive search for regional hegemony, the cancerous growth of sectarianism in the Arab world, the deepening Iraqi strategic alignment with Iran, the proliferation of vengeful anti-American radicalism, and the likely fallout from the failing U.S.-led pacification effort in Afghanistan. In the past, denying the urgency of these problems may have sufficed to evade uncomfortable but necessary dialogue. Neither silence nor inaction is now a viable option for Americans, Arabs, Iranians, Israelis, or others with a stake in the future of the Middle East.

Three decades after Iran's revolution, some or all of the world's 340 million Arabs are following Persians into a repudiation of foreign tutelage. The upheaval of 1979 marked the end of any notion of Iran as the political or cultural ward of Britain, Russia, or the United States. Country by country, whether under new or existing governments, Arabs too are now asserting the right to their own self-determined national identities and policies. Arabs are not Persians; Sunni political culture is not that of Shiism; the histories of the diverse parts of the Arab world differ significantly from those of Iran. It's unlikely that any Arab country will follow Iran into uncompromisingly theocratic forms of governance that derive their legitimacy from broad confrontation with the West and its values. Still, the Arab uprisings of 2011 have made it politically impossible for rulers to put the agendas of Western patrons ahead of the views, interests, and religious traditions of their own publics.

This shift in mindset and popular expectations has huge strategic implications. It foretells Arab governments and policies that seek the authenticity that only the consent of the governed and respect for their values and views can provide. The colonial era was over elsewhere five or six decades ago. As the Arabs insist on independence under popular sovereignty, whether exercised through one ruler or many, the last vestiges of neocolonialism are vanishing in West Asia and North Africa as well. In the new era, relations between Middle Eastern states will be determined by local judgments about what is right, proper, and to the national advantage, not what is ordained, championed, or paid for by an outside power, patron, or overlord. That has been the case for Israel. It will now be the case for Israel's Arab neighbors as well.

Arab rulers have just had it driven home to them that they cannot rely on Americans to protect them from domestic backlash to unpopular policies. They've also learned that they cannot look to America to constrain Israel. The strategic utility of the United States to Arab governments has been correspondingly devalued. As a result, Israel can no longer count on U.S. alliances, aid programs, or patron-client allegiances to exempt it from the consequences of its dysfunctional relationships with its neighbors.

Israelis played a major role in creating the adverse circumstances in which they now find themselves. They must now make their own peace with Turkey, sustain their own relations with Egypt and Jordan, and find their own basis for coexistence with Iran, Iraq, and Saudi Arabia, among others. They must craft their own *modus vivendi* and achieve their own reconciliation with Palestinians and Lebanese, whom they have heretofore treated with contemptuous cruelty and disrespect.

The spectacle of members of Congress bouncing up and down like so many obsequious yo-yos as Prime Minister Netanyahu spoke to them last May was irrefutable evidence of Israel's hammerlock on U.S. policy. But U.S. policy no longer decides what happens politically or economically in the Middle East. This has created a new and less certain political environment in West Asia and North Africa. For the first time in decades, Israel must manage its regional and international relationships on its own. Judging from Israel's recent handling of incidents with the UAE, Turkey, and Egypt, neither its current government nor its political elite understands the new environment or is mentally prepared to cope with it.

Israel would be in difficulty even if American prestige in the Middle East had not imploded. But it has. Our previous reputation was so strong that Americans had to work really hard to do it in. With a little help from our friends, we proved we were up to the task.

The factors that went into destroying our appeal and authority are many. They begin with the disingenuous diplomacy of the now defunct "peace process." The major result of three decades of American mediation has been to discredit American diplomacy. In effect, the United States facilitated Israel's ongoing seizure of territory at the expense of a just settlement of differences between Israelis and Palestinians and of Palestinian self-determination.

The reputation of the United States for wisdom, truthfulness, and competence was also gravely damaged by the invasions of Afghanistan and Iraq. The course of events in both countries convincingly demonstrated the limitations of U.S. military power. The strategic fallout continues to spread. In Iraq, the United States ravaged a proud Arab society. The resulting anarchy set off a widening firestorm of sectarian violence in the Arab world. It also catalyzed a major—and so far uncountered—extension of Iranian influence in the region.

Washington's eager connivance in the maiming of Lebanon in 2006 and of Gaza just before the Obama administration took office added to the perception of the United States as indifferent to, if not sadistically happy about, the suffering of Arab or Muslim populations. By conservative estimate, U.S. policies and military actions in the post–Cold War period have directly or indirectly caused the deaths of between 250,000 and a million Muslims and displaced at least 10 million from their homes. One does not need an advanced degree to understand the origins of Muslim rage against America.

America's ideological appeal has also faded. The abuses at Kandahar, Bagram, Abu Ghraib, and Guantánamo erased the international image of America as a champion of freedom, fair play, the rule of law, and human rights. Inconsistencies in the U.S. response to the popular uprisings in various Arab countries seriously undercut the credibility of American support for democracy. So has Washington's willingness to attempt the overthrow of freely elected governments it and Israel dislike, like the Hamas-led government elected in Palestine in 2006. There is little sympathy for Hamas in most of the Arab world, but there is now universal outrage at U.S. collusion in the ongoing Israeli effort to terrorize Palestinians in Gaza and permanently ghettoize them. The blatant hate speech against Arabs and Muslims that now pervades American political discourse further reduces the willingness of people in the region to give a sympathetic hearing to American perspectives on events.

So too, I am sorry to say, does the mounting global perception of the United States as a country that can't get its act together. In the first few years of this century, many abroad came to see us as a military bully. More recently, they have viewed our national leadership as terminally uncivil, unable to set priorities or otherwise address urgent national and international problems, economically illiterate and fiscally incompetent, ignorant and indifferent to foreign realities, and committed to the view that threats, sanctions, and military intervention are the answer to most foreign-policy problems.

Of course, we're not a bully. We're just a superpower with attitude. A friend of mine who works on Capitol Hill assures me that foreigners seriously "misunderestimate" our politicians. Seen up close, he says, they are without doubt the finest decision-makers that political contributions can lease. If "that government is best which governs least," he boasts, the United States has now achieved a rare perfection. We have attained a level of political gridlock in which the people's representatives celebrate their faith in God by leaving it to Him to solve the problems their own previous misbehavior created. We should be happy to be so thoroughly ungoverned, my friend believes. But even he, a well-traveled French intellectual, admits that, from afar, we don't look as good as we once did.

The fact is that, even without the strategic albatross of all-out support for self-destructive Israeli policies, the United States now has less going for it than ever before to help it shape the strategic contours of a changing Middle East. Yet it is in this highly adverse context that we Americans must protect our interests. To do this, we must acknowledge the multiple failures of our policies to achieve their declared objectives.

We have not persuaded Israel to accept the recognition and reconciliation that all twenty-two Arab countries and thirty-five additional Muslim states have offered. There has been no Israeli offer of peace to the Palestinians or anyone else in the region, only demands for unconditional acceptance of Israel as a Jewish state. Yet contemporary Israel is a transplant in the region that needs mutually respectful relations with its other peoples to assure long-term survival. It is now clear beyond a reasonable doubt that we Americans do not have the will or the self-confidence to help Israel achieve this. Nor do we have the bona fides necessary to conduct the sort of shuttle diplomacy we once did. Anyone who watched the U.S. Congress clap, curtsy, and kowtow to Mr. Netanyahu understands why we now have no credibility as a mediator.

We have not been able to end the increasingly brutal Israeli occupation and siege in the West Bank and Gaza. Neither is compatible with international law, Security Council decisions, Israel's undertakings in the Camp David accords, the spirit of the Oslo agreement, the terms of the "Road Map," or other relevant doctrines and decisions. We routinely deplore Israel's policies and actions without ceasing to fund them and prevent anyone else from halting them. No one takes what we say about Israeli or Palestinian behavior seriously anymore.

We are now trying to scuttle our own longstanding approach to the achievement of Palestinian self-determination and independence from

Israel. The only answer we have to others' objections to this is the power of the veto, but there is no reason to expect the Palestinians or the vast majority of the international community that is now aligned with them against us to restrict their challenges to the Security Council or other arenas where we can block them. They are pretty clearly ready to exclude and bypass us.

We do not know how to douse the spreading wildfire of sectarian violence in the Muslim world that we inadvertently ignited by thrusting Iraq into anarchy. We have no coherent answer to uprisings and unrest in places as disparate as Bahrain, Syria, and Yemen or to the success of rebellion in Libya. We do not know how to deal with democratic Islamists. We have not come up with a way to counter Islamist terrorists with global reach. Our current approach simply intensifies their fervor, strengthens their base among the Muslim faithful, and multiplies their supporters and copycats.

We have no strategy for countering Iranian inroads in the Arab world or causing Tehran to abandon its presumed nuclear ambitions. Iraq is aligned with Iran on issues from Syria and Lebanon to Bahrain. We are about to withdraw from Iraq without reaching any strategically advantageous understanding with Baghdad. We are conducting our relations with Pakistan and Afghanistan in ways that maximize the risk of protracted terrorist reprisal for our slaughter of civilians and alienation of religious and tribal elements in both. We don't know what to do about the situations we have helped create in either or both countries.

That's a lot of "known unknowns." It would be easy to become depressed.

On the other hand, over the past year, like all right-thinking Americans, I have learned to be happy and love national credit rollovers. I count it a triumph that we have so far avoided a government shutdown. And I'm confident that the "Super Committee" has our fiscal situation in hand. According to my French intellectual friend on Capitol Hill, the Supers are about to produce a comprehensive, nonpartisan resolution of our fiscal dilemmas. This will contract the economy while creating jobs and slash budgetary outlays while upping defense spending to produce the best of all possible worlds. I really want to believe this, even if it's clearly nuts. After all, if voodoo economics could get us into this mess, why can't it get us out of it?

In the absence of fiscal sorcery and some serious changes in policy, however, some or all of the following is very likely in our future.

Israel will be increasingly ostracized, boycotted, and prosecuted internationally for its scofflaw behavior, racist policies, daily violence, and intermittent pogroms against Palestinians. The United States will suffer correspondingly from guilt by our continuing close association with Israel. Over our objections, Turks, Egyptians, Saudis, and other Gulf Arabs will make common cause on matters relating to Palestine. The good news is that the Ayatollah Khamenei is aligned with Prime Minister Netanyahu and other yahoos in seeking to block a viable two-state solution in Palestine. Iran will therefore not make common cause with Arab countries. It doesn't share their current and our former belief that the way to bring peace to the Middle East is through the implementation of United Nations Security Council Resolution 242 by recognizing the division of the Holy Land between Israel and a much smaller state of Palestine.

The Palestinian issue will move from meeting rooms where we are present to conference rooms where we are not—or where our objections to measures against Israel are opposed or ignored by large, unsympathetic majorities. The defunded Palestinian Authority will likely cease to function. Instead of being able to rely on continuing Palestinian collaboration on intelligence and security matters, Israel will try to deal with those parts of the occupied territories still inhabited by Palestinians the same way it does with Gaza. Palestinian and Arab politics will be further radicalized.

Some Palestinian factions, long quiescent, will resume operations against Israelis in Israel as well as the occupied territories. Others will return to terrorism against the soft targets represented by Israel's supporters abroad. Not a few Israelis will conclude that the United States, not Israel, is the only secure domicile for the world's Jews. Jewish emigration from Israel will accelerate. The United States will gain many desirable new citizens as a result.

The visible presence of U.S. troops on Arab soil will attract escalating local protests as well as terrorist attacks. The United States will step up assassinations of alleged proponents, planners, and perpetrators of such attacks. Collateral damage will mount. So will popular rage against the United States and pressure on Arab governments to deny U.S. forces access to facilities and installations in the region. Eventually, one or more Arab governments will decide that having an American military presence on its territory or facilitating transit or overflight by the U.S. armed forces is too provocative to local opinion. Other Arab governments will follow. The United States' ability to rely on strategic lines of communication in the Gulf to link Asia to Europe and to project power around the world will take a big hit.

The Gulf Arabs, Iran, and Turkey will compete for the support of previously uncommitted external powers, like Brazil, China, India, and Russia. Gulf Arab governments will find it easy to buy arms from these countries but impossible to persuade them to replace weakening U.S. defense commitments with their own. GCC member countries will be driven toward greater self-reliance and stronger cooperation with each other. Some will ally with Turkey, Pakistan, and Egypt. Others will make their peace with Iran. Military training in the United States and the ease of cooperation and habits of coordination that it fosters will decline as U.S. budgets contract, military ties to the Gulf attenuate, and the region's military relationships diversify.

Now that I've cheered you up, let me turn briefly to what might be done to avoid or mitigate developments like these. The writing may be on the wall, but nothing is certain until the ink dries. Other speakers will have creative ideas about what is to be done. We need some new ideas to end our current wars and to restore our domestic security and tranquility. Before other speakers step up to this challenge, let me venture a few thoughts.

In the Holy Land, it's about time we recalled the Hippocratic Oath. This advises those with the power to intervene to "abstain from doing harm." To put it more realistically, we should abstain from doing more harm than we already have. Foolishly encouraging Israelis to indulge in a belief that they can enjoy security through eternal reliance on American subsidies and protection and through sustaining a perpetual state of war with neighboring peoples not only does them no favors, it does Israel, the United States, and the Arabs great harm.

For a long time, we have enabled Israel's self-injurious behavior. This has made it possible for Israel to choose land over peace, to corrupt its democracy, to deviate from the core values of its official religion as understood by Jews abroad, to empower racism and bigotry among its Jewish majority, and, most recently, to humiliate the president of the United States while extracting twenty-nine kowtows from Congress.

No one now harbors any real hope that America can either deliver peace or help Israelis, Palestinians, and those with whom they share their region to achieve it. We have shown convincingly that bilateral negotiations between grossly unequal parties cannot produce an equitable and sustainable result unless outside parties are willing to intervene to redress the imbalances in power. Yet an equitable and sustainable result is an imperative not only for Israelis and Arabs but for Americans as well. The costs of no peace are becoming too great to be sustained.

The essential objective of stated U.S. policy has always been to achieve acceptance for Israel in its region through self-determination for the Palestinians in their own state. This is what the Arab peace initiative of 2002 offered. Americans need to get out of the way and let the international community work with the Arabs to help Israel embrace peace.

The last American with a valid claim to the status of peacemaker in the Middle East is the much-maligned Jimmy Carter. He put the squeeze on Menachem Begin to accept the peace that Anwar Sadat had bravely offered. There is no prospect that any elected or appointed American official could now act toward an Israeli leader with the determination that President Carter showed in September 1978 at Camp David. Conversely, as long as the United States fawns on Israel and uses drones and hit teams to carry out extrajudicial executions in an expanding list of Arab and Muslim countries, no president will have any credibility with Palestinians, other Arabs, or the broader Islamic community. The American-led "peace process" is over. We blew it.

The United States must now let the international community do for Binyamin Netanyahu what Jimmy Carter did for Menachem Begin—make Israel an offer of peace it will not let its prime minister refuse. This means ceasing to block the diplomatic tough love for Israel that only non-Americans can provide, and it means withdrawing U.S. funding and other support for Israeli policies and programs that harm U.S. interests or constitute obstacles to peace. The combination of international pressure and diminishing U.S. support is necessary to concentrate Israeli minds on the long-term choices before their country.

Peace has long been available if Israel would only trade sufficient land for it. The vast majority of Israelis favor swapping land for peace. A succession of right-wing Israeli governments has worked to obviate this possibility by creating adverse "facts on the ground." It is time instead to create circumstances that will empower the Israeli majority to push their country's recalcitrant politicians into peaceful coexistence with the other peoples of the Middle East.

Most Americans would rather forget Iraq now that we're leaving it. But Iraq isn't going away as an issue. Our invasion of Iraq left Iran without a credible military challenger in the region. Our withdrawal from Iraq leaves us with no strategy for countering Iranian aspirations for hegemony in the Middle East other than keeping a large part of our armed forces in the Arab countries of the Gulf. Such a presence is a stimulus to terrorism. Sustaining it is also almost certainly beyond our future fiscal capacity. Our usual response in such situations is to ask for host nation support. Given the loathing our policies in the Holy Land now inspire and the hatred our drone and other attacks are stoking, it is uncertain how Gulf Arab governments would respond to such a request. Subsidies to an American military presence are likely to be highly unpopular, even where exceptional levels of citizen affluence prevail.

A better approach would be to adopt a more economical and less fatiguing strategy, like backstopping security arrangements that the GCC might contract with Turkey, Egypt, and Pakistan as well, possibly, with others, like a Syria that is no longer in the Iranian political orbit. Among other benefits, this would share the burden of guaranteeing Gulf Arab security between the United States and other countries with an interest in the security of energy supplies, regional stability, and a global oil patch undominated by a single supplier. Such countries include all the great powers of Europe and Asia. Why should those who benefit from global order not share the burden of sustaining it by supporting the GCC?

In this context, the situation in Bahrain has much broader strategic implications than many seem to realize. Bahrain is a fundamentally decent society but there are serious injustices there, as many in the Bahraini ruling family will admit. The Bahraini opposition is now infected with the revolutionary Iranian ideology of *wilayat al faqih*, a self-serving and self-righteous clericalism that rejects accommodation with secular authority.

The issues are complex. Negotiation is difficult for both sides. Yet, if there is no meeting of the minds, the disharmony in Bahrain, already an ulcer on GCC security, will afflict more than just Bahrainis. It will become an open wound that neither Iran nor Shiite Iraq will be able to resist probing.

It is hard to see how the U.S. Fifth Fleet could remain ashore in Bahrain under such circumstances. The island kingdom has become a crucial arena for the widening sectarian struggle in the Gulf as well as the contest for regional influence between Saudi Arabia and Iran. A measure of order has now been restored in Bahrain. Substantial reform must follow if domestic tranquility is to be sustained and opportunities for external mischief-making contained.

The situation in Bahrain is an example of the strategic dangers posed by injustice that is contaminated by sectarian division. In this and other contexts, I have to say, it's hard to understand what's in it for Saudi Arabia to continue to attempt to define itself by its Islam rather than by its character as the heartland of the Arabs. Where Saudi Arabia differs from Iran and resembles the Iranian-penetrated states and societies of Bahrain, Lebanon, and Iraq is in its "Arabness," not its adherence to one or another school of Islam. The assertion of an Islamic rather than an Arab identity was a rational response to the challenge of secular Arab nationalism half a century ago. It makes little sense today, when the threat emanates from within *Dar al-Islam* and the objective must be to discourage other Arab states from aligning with a non-Arab state against the Kingdom.

Religious ideology is Iran's battleground of choice. One should never allow one's adversary to pick the field of battle. Only Saudis can decide who they are, but in terms of Saudi prospects for victory in the struggle for the soul of the Arab world, Arab identity and tradition would seem to be a more promising choice of terrain on which to make a stand than religion. There is nothing Arab about the concept of rule by mullahs as embodied in the recent theological innovation of *wilayat al faqih*. It is not a doctrine that Arab Shiites should find appealing, any more than Arab Sunnis do. The need to ensure that Shiite Arabs do not embrace it is an argument for expanded religious dialogue and tolerance.

Iran's hegemonic ambitions are a serious problem for its neighbors. There is no magic bullet to put an end to this problem. Military action is more likely to create new problems than to solve this one. Dealing with Iran requires a comprehensive strategy and engagement linked to a long-term effort by the GCC that is backed by the United States and others. No such strategy or effort is in place. The current cascade of sanctions, threats of air attack, and covert actions against nuclear facilities does not add up to a strategy. The sanctions impoverish ordinary Iranians and rally them against foreign enemies. The threats emphasize to them how much safer they would be if only they had a nuclear deterrent. The cyberattacks and other covert actions against Iran retard its nuclear program but do not address its motivations for the program or halt it.

There is no unity of purpose among those concerned about the various dimensions of Iranian behavior. The GCC does not have anything useful to say to Iran about its nuclear programs. Those in the region, like Turkey, who have tried to speak to Iran on this issue have been undercut rather than supported by the West. Iran's roles in Iraq, Syria, Lebanon, Palestine, Afghanistan, and elsewhere are unaddressed by American diplomacy, which is entirely focused on eliminating the presumed Iranian threat to Israel's regional nuclear monopoly. It is clearly time for all concerned about the diverse challenges Iran presents to confer, to deconflict their disparate policy priorities, and to cooperate.

Osama bin Laden was finally apprehended through classic intelligence and law enforcement work. He was killed by Navy SEALs, but it is hard to argue that a military hit team was essential to arresting or executing him. America seems wedded to a militarized approach to combating terrorism, despite the fact that this is widening our struggle to an expanding list of Muslim countries—not narrowing it—while deepening existing Muslim animosity toward the United States. We need to rethink our approach. Decimating leadership structures can demoralize and disorient armies—but we are not dealing with armies. We are dealing with an enraged global community and an ideology that tells individuals within it what targets are legitimate objects of retribution and reprisal and that motivates them to act on their own or to seek others of like mind to join them in acts of terrorism.

Unless the causes of Muslim indignation are mitigated and the deviant ideology of those who exploit it is refuted, anti-American terrorism will continue to flourish. The apprehension and execution of Osama bin Laden or other prominent terrorists punishes their crimes against us but we should be under no illusion that it shakes either the motivation or the rationale of those they inspire. To accomplish that, we need the help of Muslim allies. We Americans are good at killing our enemies. We are unqualified to refute Islamic heresies and unsuited to persuading those who have embraced these heresies to step aside from the path to terror. We need Muslim help to accomplish both.

I want to close by affirming my faith in the adaptability and resilience of the United States. With all the problems we have made for ourselves and our friends in the Middle East, we have just about run out of alternatives to doing the right things. Now we may get around to actually doing them, *insha'Allah.*

About Syria
April 23, 2014[6]

I'm honored to share a very brief moment with you tonight. I crossed the Atlantic to be here for two reasons.

First, the work of the Al Madad Foundation is crucial. An entire generation of young people in the Levant is being crippled by the combination of trauma and educational deprivation. The organizers and supporters of the foundation are people I admire and respect for their humane generosity. Their cause is timely and just. It deserves all the help we can give it.

Second, the foundation is now very appropriately focused on Syria, which is where civilization began and where it has now collapsed. Syrians have always been a people of great charm, sophistication, and ability. For much of their history, they have suffered from bad governance. The horrors they are now enduring are without precedent.

Governments are part of the cause of the persistent chaos in Syria. So far, they are not part of the solution. If you care about what is happening in Syria, you must take action on your own. You can do so through civil society organizations like the Al Madad Foundation and its partners in Syria, Lebanon, and neighboring countries. Syria and Syrians matter.

The first time I visited Syria, I was living in Saudi Arabia; I asked a Saudi-Syrian friend what I needed to know before visiting Damascus. This was back when there was still a Soviet Union. To my surprise, my friend responded by asking me whether I had followed "the most recent Special Forces Olympics."

He explained that every four years, the best commandos in the world compete in a world martial arts championship. The last such contest, he said, had ended up in a playoff between the United States, the USSR, and Syria. Each team was asked to select one soldier to go into the forest alone, bare-handed, and bring out a rabbit.

So an American, a Russian, and a Syrian commando each went into the forest. After a while, the Russian came out, holding a rabbit by the ears. The American soon followed with another rabbit. But the Syrian officer did not appear.

The sun began to go down. People became concerned. They went looking for the missing Syrian. After a while, they found him. He was holding

---

6. Remarks to the Al Madad Foundation, London

a donkey by the ears, beating it, and hissing, "Confess you are a rabbit! Confess you are a rabbit!"

Over the last three years of sectarian violence in Syria, the great powers of the world and the region have behaved more like rabbits than like men. Surely, W.B. Yeats anticipated today's Syria when he declaimed:

> The blood-dimmed tide is loosed, and everywhere
> The ceremony of innocence is drowned;
> The best lack all conviction, while the worst
> Are full of passionate intensity.[7]

Two decades ago, reflecting on the savagery in Bosnia, a British general formulated three principles for intervention in civil wars: "(1) Don't. (2) If you do, pick the side that will win. And, (3) help that side win fast." His point was that sometimes the resolution of a conflict, any resolution at all, is better than the interminable continuation of violence. Whether he was right or wrong, in Syria the world has violated all of his rules. The outcome has been and remains hideous.

As you all know, the statistics are horrifying. Nine and a half million Syrians are now in desperate need. There are 2.5 million Syrian refugees in neighboring countries and 7 million displaced internally. At least 150,000 Syrians are thought to have died by violence over the last three years. By conservative estimate, about 600,000 have been wounded. More than 10,000 children have been killed and another 40,000 injured. Altogether, 5.5 million Syrian children have been affected by the conflict. At least 1.2 million of them have fled to neighboring countries, including 425,000 under the age of five. One in five Syrian girls is being forced into early marriage rather than going to school. There is no way to measure the degree of trauma all this has inflicted on the generation that must eventually rebuild Syria.

In February, the UN Security Council finally adopted a resolution demanding that Syria's government and other combatants provide immediate access to relief workers. Nothing was said or proposed to be done about access to education, yet 4,000 Syrian schools have closed. Thousands of teachers are displaced and out of work. An entire generation of Syrians is being denied the experience of a normal childhood and deprived of access to education. Meanwhile, relief is not getting through to those who need

---

7. William Butler Yeats, "The Second Coming," *Collected Poems of W.B. Yeats* (1989), republished by the Poetry Foundation, http://bit.ly/1g8iJAd.

it in Syria. Refugees in camps in neighboring countries are safer, but not much better off.

The unrest in Syria began amidst the wave of Arab uprisings that wishful thinkers in the West called the "Arab Spring." Tunisia's president Zine El Abidine Ben Ali and Egypt's Hosni Mubarak were rapidly deposed by demonstrators; Yemen's Ali Abdullah Saleh faced a similar ouster. Bashar al-Assad panicked. His government's brutal suppression of demonstrators in southern Syria ignited an insurrection against him.

Arab and Western governments alike already loathed Assad It was all too easy for Washington, Riyadh, Doha, Ankara, and other capitals to imagine that, with a little help from outsiders, rebellious Syrians could overthrow Assad's government. This was, and remains, a tragic misjudgment. After seeing what followed Saddam Hussein's removal from power in Iraq, a lot of Syrians with no love for Mr. Assad had formed a well-founded fear of who and what might succeed him. Iranians, Russians, and Hezbollah proved willing to fight to the last Syrian for their own interests in Syria. They believe these interests are best served by Mr. Assad's survival. No one has really made the case to them that they should have an urgent interest in ending the suffering of the Syrian people. As the chemical-weapons deal with the Assad government illustrates, this is an age in which diplomacy, not the use of force, is the last resort.

The Assad government's contempt for its own citizens has collided with sectarian tensions and the fanaticism of religious zealots to make life in much of Syria ever more "nasty, brutish, and short." The struggle almost immediately ceased to be purely between Syrians. It quickly expanded to a set of zero-sum contests that pits Iran against Saudi Arabia, Russia against the United States, and Hezbollah against *takfiri* jihadists. None of these parties has any incentive to compromise. Some may be genuinely anguished by what is happening in Syria—or, at least, to those Syrians with whom they sympathize—but, in practice, each prefers continued combat to any outcome favoring an opponent. So concerned governments have blocked all efforts at promoting either a diplomatic solution or an effective humanitarian response to the situation. When they have not been funneling weapons to the various parties in Syria or training them to kill each other, they have wrung their hands while sitting on them.

No one has clean hands in Syria. It is not clear who is responsible for what, but it is clear who is suffering from it. At some point, the mayhem in Syria will end. Whether it will do so before it catalyzes the dismemberment of Lebanon and Iraq or the destabilization of Jordan is an open question. But the strife in Syria *will* end. Who will then pick up the pieces and reconstruct a civilized society for Syrians and their neighbors? Will there be educated Syrians to do this? Will enough of the humane values of Syria's ancient culture have survived to flower again?

UNICEF reports that at present about half of Syria's school-age population, "nearly 3 million children in Syria and in neighboring countries are unable to go to school on a regular basis."[8] There is no point in waiting for foreign governments and organizations to do what must be done to save the next generation of Syrians from illiteracy, ignorance, and incompetence. In one form or another, the three Abrahamic religions all counsel, in the words of God in the Holy Qur'an, that "to kill any person who has not committed murder or horrendous crimes is like murdering all of mankind, but to save a life is like saving all of humanity." That is a call to action not to be refused.

Ladies and gentlemen, the vision of the Al Madad Foundation is a Middle East "where basic education and literacy are accessible to all, where young minds are cultivated, and where children are given the tools to build positive futures for themselves and for those around them." The foundation needs help to save the lives of the children of the Levant and rescue them from abuse and neglect. Every child that the foundation reaches is a potential contributor to a reborn society once the current madness is past us. Educating as many of the next generation of Syrians as possible to be able to meet the challenges before them is, I submit, an urgent cause that is worthy of our support. It has mine. Does it have yours?

8. UNICEF, quoted in Louis Charbonneau, "Syria Among 'Most Dangerous Places on Earth' for Children: UNICEF," Reuters, March 10, 2014, http://reut.rs/1keT37J.

The Collapse of Order in the Middle East
October 28, 2014[9]

Will Rogers once observed that "when you get into trouble 5,000 miles from home, you've got to have been looking for it." It's a good deal more than 5,000 miles to Baghdad or Damascus from here. And, boy, have we gotten into trouble!

We are trying to cope with the cumulative consequences of multiple failures. Just about every American project in the Middle East has now come a cropper. There is a new Velcro-backed military-campaign morale patch commemorating this. It is available through Amazon.com for $7.45. The patch bears an escutcheon with a logo that, in the interest of decorum, I will not read out. It sounds like Operation Enduring FlusterCluck.

If you're a Middle East groupie, which your presence here suggests you may be, you need one of these patches for your jacket. It describes what is now the characteristic within-the-Beltway approach to problem-solving: If at first we don't succeed, we do the same thing again harder, with better technology, and at greater expense. The patch provides a cogent—if uncouth—summary of the results of this approach so far this century.

We're once again down to the wire in our decade-long negotiations with Iran to cap its nuclear program in return for sanctions relief. There is no evidence that sanctions have had any effect at all on Iran's policies. Maybe that's because it doesn't have the nuclear weapons program our politicians say it has. Our intelligence agencies tell us there's no evidence it does. No matter. Iran's mastery of the full nuclear fuel cycle and its development of missiles could give it "nuclear latency"—the future capacity to weaponize nuclear materials on short notice. The deadline for the latest and likely final round of negotiations is now only thirty-one days away. The failure to reach agreement could drive Iran to decide to build a bomb sooner rather than later. Still, those in the region against whom such weapons would be deployed seem to want the talks to fail. Agreement with Iran would, after all, open an ominous path to better relations between it and the West.

The half-century-long U.S.-managed effort to achieve acceptance for the Jewish state in its region has meanwhile died of a fatal build-up of glib hypocrisy, sometimes called Netanyahu Syndrome. Despite decades of trying,

9. Remarks to the Twenty-Third Annual Arab-U.S. Policymakers Conference, Washington, D.C.

American diplomacy has also definitely failed to reconcile Palestinians to indefinite existence as disenfranchised captives of Israel's Jewish democracy. The so-called "peace process" will be missed. Eventually there will be an exhibit about it in the museum of diplomatic debacles. In the meantime, politicians will visit its grave at opportune moments. There they will pray, piously, for peace, by which they mean entirely unclear and incompatible things.

The region's leaders were long worried that Israel's abuse of its captive Arab Muslim population would radicalize their own citizens and destabilize their societies. Now that this radicalization has actually occurred, Israel's cruelty to the Palestinians has become just another outrage that Muslim extremists cite to justify terrorist reprisals against the West. Fixing the Israel-Palestine conflict would no longer call off the anti-American terrorism and wars of religion it helped catalyze. This does not remove the Israel-Palestine issue as a motivator for anti-American terrorism but, in the years to come, you'll hear a lot about why curing injustices in the Holy Land need no longer be a concern for American diplomacy.

A not entirely unrelated discovery is that, in the contemporary Middle East, elections—at least the first round of them—invariably empower Islamists. This has dialed down the American passion for free elections in Arab societies. Think Palestine and Egypt. The revelation that anarchy also empowers Islamists is now cutting into American enthusiasm for regime removal. Think Iraq, Libya, and Syria. But as Americans trim our ideological ambitions, the so-called "Islamic State"—which is as Islamic as the Ku Klux Klan is Christian, so I'll call them Da'esh—is demonstrating the enduring potential of religious fanaticism to kill men, maim children, and enslave women in the name of God.

The United States and many NATO countries are now engaged against Da'esh from the air, with a bit of help from a few Arab air forces. So far, however, the Shiite coalition of Iran, Hezbollah, and the Iraqi and Syrian governments has been and remains the main force arrayed against Da'esh on the ground outside the Kurdish domains. This has exposed the awkward fact that Iran has the same enemies as the United States, if not the same friends. In the region that coined the adage, "my enemy's enemy is my friend," everyone is waiting to see what—if anything—this might mean. For now at least, Da'esh is a uniquely brutal force blessed with an enemy divided into antagonistic and adamantly uncooperative coalitions.

Da'esh has been out to make itself an irresistibly attractive nuisance by committing dramatic atrocities and publicizing them to an easily vexed

Western world. It is battling to energize the disaffected among the Islamic faithful against the West and to cleanse the Arab world of Western influences. It wants to erase the states that Western colonialism imposed after the collapse of the Ottoman Empire. It regards them as illegitimate entities that could not survive without continuing support from the West.

Da'esh judges that both its policies and its narrative have been validated by the American and European response to its provocations. The major contributors to the U.S.-led military coalition opposing Da'esh are the former colonial powers. These are Western, predominantly Christian nations, some of them with reputations in the region for recent sacrilegious mocking of Muslim piety. Token participation in the U.S.-led bombing campaign in Syria by the air forces of Jordan and some Gulf Arab states fits easily into the Da'esh narrative. Da'esh portrays those arrayed against it as a new crusader army with Arab lackeys attempting to restore the broken framework of Sykes-Picot.

In this context, Western-led military intervention is not just an inadequate response to the threat from Da'esh. It is a preposterously counterproductive response. It is as if the Ottoman Sultanate had attempted to deal with Europe's Thirty Years' War by condemning Christian atrocities and treating them as a military problem to be resolved by the intervention of Muslim janissaries.

Admittedly, the United States cannot escape responsibility for policies that helped birth Da'esh in Iraq and mature its fighting forces in Syria. The U.S. invasion of Iraq kicked off an orgy of intolerance and sectarian killing that has now taken at least 700,000 lives in Iraq and Syria and traumatized both, while threatening the existence of the other states created by Sykes-Picot a century ago. The rise of Da'esh is a consequence of the anarchy brought on by Western attempts at regime change, but it is ultimately a deviant cult within Islam. Its immediate objective is to destroy the existing order in the Muslim world in the name of Islam. Its doctrines cannot be credibly rebutted by non-Muslims. The threat it poses requires a Muslim-led politico-military response. A U.S.-dominated bombing campaign with token allied participation cannot kill it. The United States is well supplied with F-15s, F-16s, and drones, but it lacks the religious credentials to refute Da'esh as a moral perversion of Islam. Arab air forces are helpful. Arab religious engagement and moral leadership are essential to contain and defeat Da'esh.

Da'esh and the 15,000 foreign jihadis it has attracted are an existential threat to Arab societies and a potential menace to Muslim societies everywhere. Da'esh poses no comparable threat to the United States. Some

Americans argue therefore that Da'esh doesn't matter. A few suggest that, because tight oil and shale gas production is making North America energy self-sufficient, what happens in the Middle East as a whole should also no longer matter much to Americans. But the Persian Gulf is where international oil prices are set. If you doubt this, ask an American tight oil producer what's happening in today's energy markets and why. Without stability in West Asia, the global economy is also unstable.

Da'esh aspires not only to destroy the states of the Mashriq—the Arab East—but to conquer their territories and use their resources to mount attacks on the United States, European countries, Russia, and China. It wants to get its hands on the world's major energy reserves. Its depredations are a current threat only to stability in West Asia, but its recruitment efforts are as global as its aspirations. Quite aside from the responsibility the United States bears for creating the conditions in which this dangerous cult could be born and flourish, Da'esh threatens American interests abroad today. It promises to threaten American domestic tranquility tomorrow. It sees inflicting harm on the West as a central element of its mission.

For all these reasons, the United States and other nations outside the Middle East cannot ignore Da'esh. It requires a response from us. But Da'esh must be actively countered first and foremost by those it targets within the region, not by the United States and its Western allies. This means that our response must be measured, limited, and calculated to avoid relieving regional players of the primary responsibility for protecting themselves from the menace that Da'esh represents.

Muslims—whether Shiite or Sunni or Arab, Kurd, Persian, or Turk—now have an expanding piece of hell in their part of the Earth, a growing foulness near the center of Islam. It is almost certainly a greater threat to all of them than they have ever posed to each other. Da'esh will not be contained and defeated unless the nations and sects on its regional target list—Shia and Sunni alike—all do their part. We should not delude ourselves. The obstacles to this happening are formidable.

Virtually every group now fighting or being victimized in Iraq, Syria, and Lebanon has engaged in or been accused of terrorism by the others. Sectarian violence continues to stoke hatred in the region. The religious animosities between Shiites and Sunnis are more intense than ever. The geopolitical rivalry between Iran and the Gulf Arabs remains acute. The political resentments between Turks, Kurds, and Arabs and between Arabs and Persians are entrenched. Each describes the other as part of the problem, not part of the solution.

Unity of command, discipline, and morale are the keys to both military and political success. Da'esh has all three. Its opponents do not. Some are dedicated to the defense of Shiite privilege. Others assign priority to dislodging Shiite or secular authority. Some insist on regime change. Others seek to prevent it. A few support Islamist democratic movements. Others seek to suppress and eradicate them. Some fear terrorism from the victims and enemies of Da'esh more than they fear Da'esh itself. Most treat opposing Da'esh as a secondary strategic objective or a means of enlisting American and other foreign support in the achievement of other priorities, not as their primary aim.

With few exceptions, the states of the region have habitually looked to outside powers for leadership as well as firepower and manpower with which to respond to major security challenges. Despite vast imports of foreign weapons systems, confidence in outside backing has enabled the countries in the region to assume that they could avoid ultimate responsibility for their own defense, relying instead on their ability to summon their American and European security partners in times of crisis. But only a coalition with a strong Muslim identity can hope to contain and shrink Da'esh.

There is no such coalition at present. Every actor in the region has an agenda that is only partially congruent with the Da'esh-related agendas of others. Every actor focuses on the reasons it cannot abide or work with some or all of the others, not on exploring the points it has in common with them.

The United States has the power-projection and war-fighting capabilities to back a Muslim-led effort against Da'esh, but lacks the political credibility, leadership credentials, and diplomatic connections to organize one. Since this century began, America has administered multiple disappointments to its allies and friends in the Middle East, while empowering their and our adversaries. Unlike the Gulf Arabs, Egypt, and Turkey, Washington does not have diplomatic relations with Tehran. Given its non-Muslim identity, solidarity with Israel, and recent history in the Fertile Crescent, the United States cannot hope to unite the region's Muslims against Da'esh. Da'esh is a Muslim insurgency. A coalition led by inhibited foreign forces, built on papered-over differences, and embodying hedged commitments will not defeat such an insurgency, with or without boots on the ground.

There is an ineluctable requirement for Muslim leadership and strategic vision from within the region. Without it, the existing political geography of the Arab world—not just the map drawn by the Sykes-Picot Agreement—faces progressive erosion and ultimate collapse. States will be pulled down to be succeeded by warlords, as is already happening in Iraq and Syria. Degenerate and perverted forms of Islam will threaten the prevailing Sunni and Shiite religious dispensations, as Da'esh now does.

Where is regional leadership with acceptable credentials to come from? The Sunni Arab states of the Gulf will not accept guidance from Iran, nor will Iran accept it from them. The alternatives are Egypt and Turkey. Both are partially estranged American allies. Their relations with each other are strained, but any strategy that accepts the need for leadership from within the region must focus on them. They are the only plausible candidates for the role. Both are problematic.

Egypt is internally stressed and dependent on support from Gulf Arab partners whose main objectives are to carry out regime change in Damascus, push back Shiite dominance in Iraq, and contain Iran. The Egyptians themselves put suppressing the Muslim Brotherhood and Hamas ahead of dislodging Mr. Assad or defeating Da'esh. Turkey is more eager to remove Assad and roll back the Kurdish factions associated with its longstanding domestic-terrorism problem than it is to contain Da'esh. It does not want problems with Iran. Until the governments in Cairo and Ankara conclude that containing and defeating Da'esh deserves priority over other foreign-policy objectives, neither will assume a leadership role in the struggle against it. In time, they may come to that conclusion. In the meantime, the fact that none of our major security partners in the region agrees with American priorities suggests that we are right to proceed with caution.

To be effective, any American strategy for dealing with the menace of Islamist terrorism of the sort Da'esh represents must not only find regional partners to support, it must address the pernicious legacies of past U.S. policies. These include the legacy of the botched "peace process" in the Holy Land and the more general problems inherent in moral hazard, the confusion of values with interests, and the illusion that military power is a substitute for diplomacy.

The Israel-Palestine issue remains a substantial burden on the effectiveness of U.S. diplomacy in the Middle East. As far as I know, the United States has never killed a single Palestinian. Americans have just given Israel the arms, money, and political protection it has needed to oppress and massacre Palestinians. In the region, we are not seen as having much of an alibi for our role in fostering Palestinian suffering. Willingness to give us the benefit of the doubt and time to produce justice for the Palestinians expired forever along with the U.S.-led "peace process" we claimed for decades was going to accomplish this and cited as a reason for the world to leave Palestinian self-determination to the Israelis.

The next nonviolent phase of the struggle for Palestinian liberation from Israeli occupation and dispossession is likely to take place not at the negotiating table but in the courts of international law and opinion, as well as other venues the United States cannot control. Given the intimacy of American political, economic, cultural, and military relationships with the Jewish settler state in Palestine, there is a strong prospect that the mounting international effort to boycott, sanction, and disinvest from Israel—including, especially, the Arab lands it seized in 1967—will directly affect American companies and individuals in ways it has not since the Oslo accords brought about the suspension of the Arab boycott of Israel.

More to the point, the Palestinian cause seems certain to prove irresistible to Da'esh as it consolidates and expands its hold on the region, as there is currently every reason to believe it will. After all, Palestine combines the perfect mix of issues for Da'esh—foreign occupation, suppression of Muslims, and interference with worship at important Islamic holy sites. With diplomacy having definitively failed, the Palestinians believe they face a choice between capitulation and violent resistance. Da'esh is reported to be gaining ground as an alternative to more moderate movements, like Hamas. To a majority in the region, Israel's continuing cruelty to Palestinians justifies reprisal not just against Israel but the United States.

Palestinian refugee communities provide a deep reservoir of recruits for terrorist attacks on Israeli and American targets. The growing sympathy for the Palestinian plight in Europe, Latin America, Africa, and Asia offers opportunities to recruit Western cohorts. Assaults on Israel and its American supporters meet every criterion of political constituency-building Da'esh could hope to find.

Israel's right-wing government has inadvertently been doing everything it can to incite Da'esh to focus on the Jewish state. During Israel's recent rubbling of Gaza, its deputy minister of defense threatened Palestinians there with a "holocaust." Not to be outdone, a senior figure in the HaBayit HaYehudi party, which is part of the governing coalition in Israel, called for the destruction of "the entire Palestinian people...including its elderly and its women, its cities and its villages, its property and its infrastructure."[10] Meanwhile, a deputy speaker of the Knesset called for the forced depopulation of Gaza.[11]

This brings me to a core issue in U.S. policies in the Middle East: the moral hazard inherent in U.S. unilateralism. Moral hazard is the condition that obtains when one party is emboldened to take risks it would not otherwise take because it knows that another party will shoulder the consequences and bear the costs of failure. U.S.-Israel relations exemplify this problem. American political and legal protection plus subsidies and subventions enable Israel to do whatever it feels like to its Arab neighbors with no concern for the consequences. But the same phenomenon has been at work in Arab approaches to the nuclear disarmament of Iran. If America can be induced to take the lead in handling the Iranian threat, why should anyone in the region try to do anything about it themselves? Similarly, why should any Muslim country rearrange its priorities to deal with Da'esh when it can count on America to act for it? If America thinks it must lead, why not let it do so? But responsible foreign and defense policies begin with self-help, not outsourcing military risks.

U.S. policy should encourage the nations of the Middle East to develop effective political, economic, and military strategies to defend and advance their own interests, not rush to assume responsibility for doing this for them. Part of such a policy adjustment toward emphasizing the primary responsibility of the countries of the region for their own security would involve weighing the opinions of our partners in the region much more heavily in our decisions than they have been since 9/11. Had we listened to our Gulf Arab friends, we would not have invaded Iraq in 2003. Iraq would still be balancing Iran. It would not be in chaos and it would still have a border with Syria. The United States needs to return to respecting the views of regional powers about the appropriate response to regional threats, resisting the impulse to substitute military campaign plans made in Washington for strategies conceived by those with the greatest stake in their success.

The need for restraint extends to refraining from expansive rhetoric about our values or attempting to compel others to conform to them. In practice, we have insisted on democratization only in countries we have

---

10. Ayelet Shaked, Facebook post dated June 30, 2014; screencaps and translation in Ali Abunimah, "Israeli lawmaker's call for genocide of Palestinians gets thousands of Facebook likes," *Electronic Intifada*, July 7, 2015, http://bit.ly/1Im9sDz.

11. Moshe Feiglin, quoted in Jill Reilly, "Israeli Official Calls for Concentration Camps in Gaza and 'the Conquest of the Entire Gaza Strip, and Annihilation of All Fighting Forces and Their Supporters,'" *Daily Mail*, August 4, 2014, http://dailym.ai/1XIE4WR.

invaded or that were otherwise falling apart, as Egypt was during the first of the two "non-coups" it suffered. When elections have yielded governments whose policies we oppose, we have not hesitated to conspire with their opponents to overthrow them. But the results of our efforts to coerce political change in the Middle East are not just failure, but catastrophic failure. Our policies have nowhere produced democracy. They have instead contrived the destabilization of societies, the kindling of religious warfare, and the installation of dictatorships contemptuous of the rights of religious and ethnic minorities.

Americans used to believe that we could best lead by example. We and those in the Middle East seeking nonviolent change would all be better off if America returned to that tradition and foreswore ideologically motivated intervention. Despite our unparalleled ability to use force against foreigners, the best way to inspire them to emulate us remains showing them that we have our act together. At the moment, we do not.

Finally, we should have learned by now that military might, no matter how impressive, is not in itself transformative. American military power has never been as dominant in the Middle East as in this century. Yet its application has repeatedly proved counterproductive and its influence limited. It shattered rather than reshaped Iraq. It has failed to bring the Taliban to heel in Afghanistan or Pakistan. It did not save Mubarak or the elected government that followed him from being overthrown by coups d'état. It does not intimidate either Bashar al-Assad or Da'esh. It has not shifted Iran's nuclear policy. It does not obviate military actions by Israel against its neighbors. It has had no impact on the political kaleidoscope in Lebanon. It does not assure tranquility in Bahrain. It did not produce satisfying results in Libya. Its newest incarnation—drone warfare—has not decapitated anti-American terrorism so much as metastasized it.

War is an extension of policy by other means. If the policy is incoherent, the use of force to further it will be purposeless, military action in support of it will be feckless, and the results it produces will be contradictory. Bombing first and developing a strategy later does not work. But that's what our political establishment stampeded us into doing with Da'esh. President Obama was right to insist that we take the time to develop a strategy before resorting to the use of force. Unfortunately, he did not have the courage of his convictions.

Where this leaves us is in an unfortunate position. Without a strategy that addresses the sociopolitical factors and grievances that have empowered Da'esh and its predecessors, we are going to lose this war.

We have a military campaign plan but lack a political program. We are bombing Da'esh to contain it. There is little reason to believe this will prove effective. Based on past experience, there is no reason to believe it will evolve into a strategy.

We and our European allies are, in many ways, the wrong leaders of the struggle against Da'esh. It can only be defeated by a coalition with credible Islamic credentials. Our armed forces and intelligence services could provide decisive support to such a coalition, but none is now in prospect.

Da'esh displays unity of command, strong discipline, and elevated morale. The coalition we have assemble to oppose it has no agreed objectives. It is divided, disjointed, and demoralized.

Da'esh is taking territory and seizing strategic positions. We are using air power tactically for mainly humanitarian and propaganda purposes. This has led us to defend areas that are of little or no strategic importance. We are not blocking Da'esh from expanding its territory, population, and resource base.

There is no concerted effort outside the Kingdom of Saudi Arabia to refute and discredit the deviant theology that inspires Da'esh and its sympathizers. It has gobbled up large parts of Iraq and Syria. Lebanon, Jordan, and Palestine could well be next.

Even if Da'esh can somehow be eliminated, Arab backlash to the distress of foreign attack from the air, sectarian violence, and civil strife ensures the birth of successor movements. Adding yet another factional force to this mix is not going to alter this reality. It may exacerbate it.

The approach we are using to deal with Da'esh is a variant of the bomb-first-develop-a-strategy-later approach we have used over the past decade and more. This has helped to spread Islamist terrorism across an ever wider swath of territory, from Mali to Kashmir. There is no reason to believe that air force and drone attacks will produce a different result now.

If we cannot correct these deficiencies, we are very likely to see widening multinational and Palestinian terrorist activity against Americans and Israelis, coordinated by Da'esh or something like it. No Arab or Muslim country will be immune to disruption. If there were ever a moment for Arabs and Americans to work together, it is now. If there were ever a moment for the United States to insist on Arab commitment and leadership of such a joint effort, this is it.

3

The Middle East and the World Beyond It

The "Middle East," meaning West Asia and adjacent areas of North Africa, got its name from the great American naval strategist Alfred Thayer Mahan. He saw that, from the American perspective, the "near East" is Europe, while the "far East" is India. The zone in the middle is West Asia. So Mahan thought the name "Middle East" appropriate for Americans to use in describing it. As American power and influence in world affairs grew, even the peoples of West Asia and the Arabian Peninsula adopted the term to describe their region.

The Middle East has always been a crossroads. It is the epicenter of the three Abrahamic religions. Islam links it to South, Southeast, and Central Asia, where two-thirds of the world's Muslims live. History—including lost Greek, Roman, Islamic, Turkish, and European Christian empires—has often connected the peoples of the Middle East and Europe. The prevalence of Islam in the Sahel and East Africa ties these regions to the Middle East as well.

In the age of Western European imperialism and colonialism, inaugurated by Napoleon's invasion of Egypt in 1800 and ended by World War II and the start of the Cold War, Western nations suppressed the Middle East's links with Asia and Africa or rendered them irrelevant. Europeans drew the borders and called the shots in the Middle East. During the Cold War, Americans and Russians competed to dominate the region. After Russia defaulted in its contest with the United States for global supremacy, America alone briefly held sway in the Middle East.

Unchecked by any strategic rival, the United States felt free to intervene in Iraq. This American intervention inadvertently overthrew the secular order imposed by European imperialism in the Middle East. Many of the states that embodied that order are now in various stages of disintegration.

The "Pax Americana" is over in the Middle East and receding elsewhere. The region is in chaos. After oil, its greatest export has become political violence in the name of its religions.

This is the context within which connections between the Middle East and other regions that were dormant for two centuries are now being revived and renewed. New relationships with rising powers in Asia like China and India are forming. The rapid growth in these ties is driven mainly by trade and investment, but it is aided and abetted by the desire of longtime American protectorates in the Middle East to seek added security from the anarchy in their region by diversifying their international relationships.

As interregional connections thicken, the Middle East is looking beyond its traditional focus on the Mediterranean world, Europe, and America. It is increasingly linked to parts of Asia once remote from it. "Asia," meanwhile, has evolved from an abstraction imposed by non-Asian cartographers to a concept with resonance and roots in every people of the continent. China's $1.4 trillion "one belt, one road" project now promises in coming decades to create a single Eurasian economic space, in which all of Asia as well as Europe and the Arabian Peninsula will be included. The wealthy Arab societies of the Gulf are becoming financial centers with global reach.

Thus the societies of the Middle East are ever more engaged—politically, economically, militarily, and culturally—with the lands and peoples beyond its borders. The United States no longer has a monopoly on power in the region. Non-American players are increasingly engaged in the games of power and intrigue that are driving the progressive collapse of the long-stagnant order in the Middle East.

The Challenge of Asia
February 17, 2011[1]

The Greeks are to blame for many things. Not least of these is the somewhat preposterous idea of "Asia." For thousands of years after strategists in Greece came up with this Eurocentric notion, the many non-European peoples who inhabited the Eurasian landmass were blissfully unaware that they were supposed to share an identity as "Asians." After all, except during the near-unification of Asia under the Mongols, they had little to do with each other. Arabs and Chinese, like Indians, Japanese, Malays, Persians, Russians, Turks, and others, had different histories, cultures, languages, religious heritages, and political traditions. Their economies were only tenuously connected by the gossamer strands of the Silk Road and its maritime counterpart.

But all this is now changing. "Asia" is leaving the realm of Greek myth and becoming a reality. Asians are drawing together as they rise in wealth and power. Their companies and their influence now extend throughout their own continent and beyond. In the twentieth century, the world had to adapt to American domination of its global political economy. Americans must now adapt to a political economy increasingly centered on Asia.

In much of Asia, as late as the last decades of the past century, post-colonial hangovers deranged politics with love-hate relationships that distorted attitudes toward the West. This is easy to understand. After all, Western colonialism had humbled the armies, crushed the self-esteem, and suppressed the values and political traditions of societies from Turkey to China.

In West Asia, Turks, Arabs, and Persians bit by bit yielded their autonomy, territory, and national dignity to predatory Europeans. In India, the British overthrew Muslim rule, imposed a single sovereignty, and embroiled the once-isolated subcontinent in the quarrels of Europe. States in South Asia that had for long contributed about one-fifth of the global economy were subordinated to British mercantilism and subjected to British rule.

The East Indies and Indochina also fell to European imperialism. In East Asia, only Thailand and Japan embraced key elements of westernization with sufficient alacrity to keep the West more or less at bay. Japan did this with such drive and discipline that it soon imposed its own colonial

---

1. Remarks to the Camden Conference, Camden, Maine

rule in Korea and parts of China. In the Russo-Japanese War and World War II, Japan went on to demonstrate that, when allied to modern technology, its martial traditions would let it punch far above its nominal military and economic weight.

Russia gobbled up Central Asia. It gnawed away at China from the north as Western powers nibbled at it from the south and east. Foreigners carved China into spheres of influence, annexed parts of its territory, and placed bits and pieces of it under their extraterritorial jurisdiction. Europeans and Americans had to do this, we said, to be able to exercise our right to peddle narcotics and proselytize an alien religious ideology to the Chinese people over the outlandish objections of their rulers.

The colonial order in Asia collapsed in the wake of World War II. As the rest of Asia rejected a reassertion of foreign control, America occupied Japan and placed it under our tutelage and protection. China defiantly "stood up," expelling foreigners and their influence from its soil. Southeast Asia revolted against its various colonial masters and their American allies. India hived off Pakistan as both took their freedom from the British. Iran reemerged as an aspirant to regional power. Turkey took its place as the stalwart eastern bulwark of Europe's defenses against an expanded Soviet empire. A new era began.

Only in West Asia—where Africa, Asia, and Europe intersect, where Judaism and Christianity began, where Islam is centered, and where the world's energy resources are concentrated—did major elements of the pre–World War II order persist. In the last days of colonialism, European Jews conquered and colonized four-fifths of the Holy Land, displacing many of its inhabitants. Palestinian Arabs and others in the region reacted with shock and horror at this unexpected culmination of both European anti-Semitism and the age of imperialism. Neither the shock nor the horror has yet been cured by Israeli or Western diplomacy.

During the Cold War, the states of the Middle East sank into uneasy dependence on the contending superpowers, which handled conflicts among them as proxy wars. Israel aside, leaders in the region became noted for their fatalistic deference to powerful foreign patrons and their feckless accommodation of European, Soviet, and American insults to the sovereignty, independence, and cultural identities of the peoples over whom they ruled. The first rip in the fabric of this neocolonial order came in the Islamic Revolution of 1979 in Iran. That ended Iran's role as "America's gendarme" in the Middle East and forced the United States to switch to military reliance on Saudi Arabia and Egypt. Nearly simultaneously,

Egypt's American-brokered peace with Israel made the preservation of the autocratic status quo in the region an overriding priority of U.S. policy.

Even a cursory reading of the Camp David accords is a poignant reminder that they were explicitly premised on Israel's undertaking to end its occupation of the West Bank and Gaza and to facilitate self-determination for Palestinians. Failure to do either ensured that the peace between Israel and Egypt was a cold one that could not warm. The Palestinians gained no relief from humiliation and injustice. Instead they saw both intensify. Peace with Israel lost any chance to gain legitimacy in Egypt or elsewhere. In large measure due to this, Israel and the United States have become thoroughly detested in Egypt, by other Arabs, and in the Islamic world as a whole.

America's willingness to underwrite the Mubarak dictatorship and the Hashemite monarchy in Jordan with cash, weapons, and moral support bought the Camp David framework at least the appearance of durability. But the ability of the United States to substitute conflict avoidance for a real effort to make peace has probably expired along with the Mubarak regime. Since Israel continues adamantly to prefer the expansion of its borders to peace with either the Palestinians or its neighbors and since there has not been a serious "peace process" for more than a decade, it is now unclear how America will continue to stabilize and contain the Israel-Palestine conflict. It is in fact unclear how much influence, if any, we Americans will now exercise in the region as a whole.

The recent uprisings of Arab citizens against their rulers have cast aside the fatalistic sense of impotence and obsequious deference to foreign power with which Arabs long hobbled themselves. They see the United States as having cynically supported despotism over democracy to keep Israel safe from Arab reactions to its behavior. Neither Israeli nor American interests have been the immediate target of these revolutions, but the decisions of Egyptians and other Arabs to seize control of their own future will affect both Israelis and Americans. Thirty years after the Iranian upheaval, the postcolonial order in the Middle East is at last collapsing.

The spreading disorder in West Asia comes after American policies in the opening decade of this century have thoroughly discredited the United States, devalued its military power, and cemented Iran's influence in Iraq, Lebanon, Gaza, and Syria. Regionwide political change is occurring as America withdraws from Iraq, leaving behind a ruined country riven by secular passions and with no sure strategic orientation. Meanwhile, the United States' armed forces are generating more terrorists than they are killing in Afghanistan and Pakistan. This is the context in which western Asia's ties to other parts of the continent are thickening. Some might consider it ominous.

The Arabs, Turks, and others in West Asia were trying to reduce their dependence on the United States even before current events illustrated how much contempt they feel for our perceived hypocrisy and how little weight the American word now has among them. They are, of course, well aware that they cannot avoid a measure of reliance on America. The United States is still the only military world power; it is able to invade, if not impose its will on every corner of the globe. Americans account for over one-fifth of global consumption and are the world's greatest debtors. The United States may no longer be the global source of new ideas for managing world and regional affairs it once was, but it has the ability to block reform initiatives from others. So, like other Asians, Middle Easterners are locked in a Catholic marriage with America. Much as some of them—the Iranians, for example—might wish to send the United States packing, no divorce is possible. But they, of course, are mostly Muslim and untroubled by polygamy, so they are busily contracting new relationships to offset their still substantial ties to America.

China and India, in particular, are happy to oblige. They are not only the fastest-growing large economies in the world, but the fastest-growing markets for Persian Gulf oil and gas. Over the decade to come, China and India are expected to account for over half the growth in global energy demand. The spectacular rise of Asia's industrious East and South has fueled a boom in its energy-rich West. Chinese construction companies, having proven their capabilities in vast infrastructure projects at home, are building big things from Mecca to Tehran. If the current emblems of the United States in the region are bombers, boots on the ground, and lethally armed drones, China increasingly evokes images of tower and gantry cranes, engineers, and containers full of consumer goods.

The Chinese are succeeding in establishing an influential presence in the region for the same reasons Americans once did. They pay cash, deliver value for money, and make no demands on business partners or hosts to conform to their values, endorse their political preferences, or help them advance an imperial agenda. In these respects, America has met a rival—and it is us, as we used to be. If China is admired for its apparent modesty and competence, though, no one in the region, still less elsewhere in Asia, sees it as an exemplar of relevant political ideals, as many if not most once saw America.

This underscores a key feature of Asia's integration. It is driven by economic and financial factors, not politics or ideology. Trade between the Persian Gulf region, China, and India has been growing at 30 to 40 percent each year for the past decade. (Over that same period, China grew from 10 percent of the size of the U.S. economy to 40 percent. By 2050, only forty years from now, China's economy may be twice the size of America's and India's economy will match our own in size. We are talking serious economic growth in Asia, with serious geostrategic consequences.

Oil, engineers, and consumer goods are not the only factors drawing West Asia toward the East. Arab investors are flush with cash. They once had a very strong preference for putting their money to work in the United States. American Islamophobia and the reawakening of ancient Islamic ties to China, as well as Central and Southeast Asia, are well along in curing them of this preference. Meanwhile, both public and private Arab investment in China's petrochemical industries, services, banks, telecommunications, and real estate have surged. The same trend is setting in with India, though it is hampered by corruption scandals and the apparent inability of Indian politicians, like ours, to resist the opportunity to grandstand on specific transactions.

Asia's newfound integration is not limited to trade and investment. Islamic banking, with its now very appealing avoidance of leverage and derivatives, is as much a feature of finance in Malaysia as in the Persian Gulf. It is being taken up in China and elsewhere. Tourism, religious pilgrimages, student exchanges, and language learning are all on a rapid upswing. A few years ago, some were stunned to see China's president, Hu Jintao, shown around the world's largest oil company, Saudi Aramco, by a series of Chinese-speaking Saudi graduates of China's best engineering schools. In China, dozens of universities and institutes now teach Arabic. Hundreds of Chinese are enrolled in Arab universities. In a few trading centers in China, like the city of Yiwu in Zhejiang Province, Arabic now rivals English as the second language of Chinese merchants. Chinese Central Television has a twenty-four-hour Arabic-language service.

The appearance of Chinese officials who speak fluent Arabic on satellite news services like Al Jazeera has long since ceased to be a novelty. The success of Chinese oil companies in acquiring exploration and production rights in Iraq owes much to the proficiency in Arabic of Chinese officials and businessmen. Similarly, fluency in Russian—the *lingua franca* of Central Asia—has been key to China's ability to secure widening access to energy supplies there. Overall, the foreign student population in

China has been growing by 20 percent per year. The largest numbers of such students come from other East Asian societies, like south Korea, but there are now also thousands of Indians studying in China. In an effort to boost competitiveness, India is adding the study of Chinese to the national primary-school curriculum.

This development reflects the astonishing advance of Sino-Indian ties—despite India's view of itself as China's strategic rival in Asia. Sino-Indian trade grew from $200 million in 1989 to about $60 billion last year. China surpassed the United States to become India's largest trading partner in 2007. The target for Sino-Indian trade in 2015 is $100 billion. Prospects for Sino-Indian economic cooperation are particularly promising. The two countries' economies are broadly complementary in ways that invite cross-investment, with India disproportionately strong in services and China in industrial production. Investment had lagged until late last year, but Premier Wen Jiabao's year-end visit to South Asia was the occasion for new Chinese investment commitments to India and Pakistan of almost $16 billion each.

Both China and India depend on growing levels of raw-material imports from Africa and Latin America and energy shipments from Africa and the Middle East. Despite their obvious common interests in securing sea lines of communication, there is, however, real reason to doubt whether they will be able to cooperate militarily. The Sino-Indian frontier is about as long as the U.S. border with Mexico, but a lot less peaceful. It is now the only land boundary that China has been unable to settle through peaceful negotiations. China and India fought a brief war along it in 1962, and there are still frequent clashes between their military patrols. Indian apprehensions about growing Chinese military power now play as large a part in driving its defense modernization as do its hostile relationship with Pakistan and the related conflict in Kashmir.

India's concerns about China have pushed it to strengthen military ties with the United States. They have also led it to open security dialogue with similarly apprehensive countries to its east like Vietnam and Japan. Since the Meiji Restoration of 1868, Japan has been accustomed to being "number one" in Asia, but last year China's economy displaced Japan's as the world's second largest. The rise of China has pushed Japan off balance psychologically and left it strategically perplexed, unsure about how to cope with its changing place in the Asian pecking order. Some in Tokyo see a defense relationship with India as a useful hedge against China, as the American political and economic global leadership on which Japan long relied continues to erode.

Last September's collision between a Chinese fishing boat with a drunken captain and Japanese coast guard vessels off the disputed Senkaku (or Diaoyu) Islands alarmed many in Japan. It pushed Tokyo closer, at least for a time, to Washington. It catalyzed the redeployment of Japanese self-defense forces away from Russia and toward the perceived threat of China. It also stimulated Japan to explore prospects for military cooperation with south Korea, something that deeply rooted antipathies on both sides had long made politically impossible. Still, many factors—including rising dependence on growth in the Chinese economy for its future prosperity—continue to draw Japan ever closer to China. A full 20 percent of Japan's trade is now with China, which surpassed the United States as Japan's top economic partner some years ago. At over 25 percent, south Korea's dependence on the China market is even greater.

All of eastern Asia (including Japanese and Korean companies, as well as those in China and Southeast Asia) is now inseparably connected through supply-chain relationships. India is beginning to be drawn into these as well as other relationships with eastern Asia. Its choice of Indonesia's president as its chief guest at this year's Republic Day celebrations in New Delhi is a big straw in this wind.

The importance of Southeast Asia as a crucible for Asian economic integration is hard to overstate. Chinese communities there played a key role in the creation of cadre capitalism in China, which incorporates many elements of overseas Chinese commercial and financial culture. The pan-Chinese consensus is that "the business of China and its people is business"—to paraphrase Calvin Coolidge's trenchant description of early-twentieth-century America. This has facilitated the setting aside of territorial claims and other potential conflicts so that everyone can get on with making money, not war.

As he hoped it would, Deng Xiaoping's notion that "to get rich is glorious" has birthed a Greater China. It is healing the rift between Chinese on either side of the Taiwan Strait. Greater China includes the systemically distinctive political economies of the China mainland, Hong Kong, Macau, and Taiwan. Its ideology, to the extent it has one, is best expressed in the orderly meritocracy and pragmatic use of industrial policy seen in Singapore. The economies of greater China, the members of the Association of Southeast Asian Nations, and—to a lesser extent—traditionally protectionist Japan and south Korea, are now well along in forming a huge free-trade area, with which India and other South Asian countries are interested in associating themselves.

Asia's remaining great power—Russia—stands somewhat apart from these processes of integration, but not entirely. It remains a primary source of weapons systems and technology for both India and China. It is becoming a significant energy supplier to China as well as Europe. The beaches of Hainan Island, Vietnam, and India are now the winter playground of the Russian middle class. Lots of Russians are studying and working in China and other countries throughout Asia.

Moscow joined with Beijing and Central Asian nations to form the Shanghai Cooperation Organization (SCO). The SCO seeks to deny the region to great-power rivalries, Islamic extremism, and Chinese ethnic separatists, but Russia seems more focused on relationships with Europe than with Asia. Chinese linkages to Central Asia's energy supplies and transportation corridors are eroding Russia's traditional dominance there. Its sparsely populated but natural resource-rich far eastern regions are being drawn into the Chinese, Japanese, and Korean economic orbits. Siberian agriculture is increasingly reliant on Chinese migrant labor. Russia's future relationship with the rest of Asia remains a bit of a wild card—as ill-defined and undetermined as the Russian identity, political system, or role in Europe and the Middle East.

The implications of Asia's emergence as a much more integrated set of economies and societies are only beginning to become apparent, but they promise to be vast. Asianization is likely to join globalization as a defining phenomenon of this century. We are already seeing this in the emergence of Asian supply-chain economics as both the heart and circulatory system of global trade. Most financial analysts expect that Asian currencies, like the Chinese yuan, will in time dilute the now dominant role of the dollar as the denominator of trade and international monetary reserves. The human and natural resource diversity of an ever more integrated Asia provides a firm basis for continued economic expansion amidst rapidly rising productivity.

In 2050—only forty years from now—our best bankers and economists say that China should have a GDP of over $70 trillion in current dollars. (By way of comparison, U.S. GDP is now about $14 trillion; by 2050 it might be as large as $35 trillion.) That same year, India's GDP should, we are told, be the same or even bigger than that of the United States. Other Asian economies, like that of Indonesia, should have grown proportionately. The figures may be disputable but there is little reason to doubt that, by midcentury, the world's economic center of gravity will be in Asia, somewhere between Beijing and New Delhi. Arabs and Indonesians,

Turks and Japanese, Indians and Americans, Europeans, Africans, Latin Americans, and others will be there alongside Chinese. A rising China and India now lift all Asians. Asia has begun to lift the world.

Three centuries ago, Europe, followed by America, displaced Asia from its longstanding preeminence in scientific and technological innovation. (Think of the invention of the zero, the compass, the rocket, paper money, movable type, chemistry, the beauty parlor, and the bank check, for example. These are, respectively, Indian, Chinese, Korean, Arab, and Islamic contributions to human civilization.) But the ranks of the Asian educated are swelling and institutions that can translate ideas into products—like research universities and venture capitalism—have already taken root on the continent. As this century proceeds, no one should be surprised to see Asia resume a seat at the head of the class.

The prestige and influence of Asian culture can also be expected to grow. We seldom reflect on the extent to which Asian ways have already infiltrated our daily lives. A prior generation of Americans would have found our delight in sushi and sashimi unimaginable. ("Seaweed-wrapped rice and raw fish for dinner? You can't be serious!") Indian-style body piercings, studs, and hanging ornaments, once seen as barbarously exotic, now adorn (or—depending on your viewpoint—disfigure) many Americans, young and old. The hookah has come to our cities in the form of sheesha parlors. Sudoku is all the rage. People pay attention to feng shui and our kids study the martial arts. What next from Asia? There will surely be something that now seems improbable. Before long, we will make it too ours, take it for granted, and forget its Asian origins.

Before I close, I want to put forward a few observations on every American's favorite subject—the search for plausible enemies to replace the late Soviet Union. That Russian-dominated empire very irresponsibly dropped out of the race to dominate the world, leaving us to do so but giving us a bad case of enemy-deprivation syndrome. We need an existential threat to rationalize spending more on our military than the rest of the world combined, and to justify exempting defense spending from the budget cuts necessitated by impending national bankruptcy. Russia just isn't up to this anymore. So we have come up with two alternative candidates to do us in, one centered in Asia's West and one in its East—Islam and China. But neither really rises to the role we have assigned it.

Muslims desire to resume a place of dignity in the world's affairs. They have been having an escalating and occasionally violent argument among themselves about how to order their societies. Some strongly oppose the influence of our culture on theirs and want to exclude it. Others, as the examples of Tunisia and Egypt show, embrace elements of the ideals in which modern Western political systems are grounded without wishing to adopt either our model or our mores. All resent our backing Israel against their coreligionists and all but a few are horrified by our armed invasions of Muslim lands and their results. Most want us gone so they can sort out their differences among themselves. Few have any aspiration to convert us to their faith. None has the capacity to conquer us. Islam doesn't meet the existential-threat test. It is a menace to our military domination of the countries that profess it, not a challenge to the independence, values, or security of a secular America.

As for China, we seem most of all to fear that it might become like us—a country animated by armed evangelism, equipped with a military designed for power projection and imbued with an impulse to impose its values on the world. In Chinese, the two ideograms that make up the word "China" mean "central country." In this century, China is very likely once again to live up to the sense of this name in many spheres of human endeavor. But China is in the middle of things in other respects as well. It is hemmed in by militarily powerful neighbors—Russia, India, Japan, Korea, Vietnam, and, of course, the United States, which has a formidable naval presence right up against its twelve-mile territorial sea boundaries and powerful land and air forces in Afghanistan and other places along its western marches. China must manage many challenges to its national security, only a few of which directly concern the United States and none of which is remote from its frontiers.

In short, China faces too many immediate military, social, and economic development problems to be able to follow the United States in attempting to dominate the world—even if it were tempted to do so. The security environment in twenty-first-century Asia will be characterized by shifting coalitions and balances with and against China. In this respect, Asia will resemble nineteenth-century Europe. It too will offer an opportunity for offshore balancing, should the United States wish to draw on the experience of Great Britain then. The British buttressed actors on the continent when and where they needed reinforcement to dissuade the ambitions of neighbors, but seldom intervened directly. Not bad for government work!

As a final illustration of the complexity of emerging Asian military realities, I want briefly to consider their nuclear dimension. Not counting the United States (which has nuclear-capable forces on three sides of it), Asia is already home to six of the world's nine nuclear-armed powers.

In time, many suspect, Iran could make this seven out of ten. Even without Iran, the nuclear geometry in Asia is already pretty complex. China, Russia, and the United States aim at each other. North Korea targets Japan and south Korea and would target the United States if it could. India targets Pakistan and China. Pakistan targets India. So does China. Nobody with nuclear weapons yet targets Israel, but Israel aims its arsenal at everyone around it. Neither India nor Israel nor Pakistan is a party to the Non-Proliferation Treaty, at which north Korea has thumbed its nose. This is one reason that the continuing U.S. focus on preventing proliferation now seems so quaint. The tigers are out of their cages. Asia is where theories of nuclear deterrence face their final exam. In this context, the grotesquely overbuilt nuclear arsenals that Russia and the United States inherited from our Cold War experiment with mutually assured destruction are irrelevant and a huge waste of money.

The same could be said about some, but not all, of the now well-established American hysteria about nuclear attacks by nonstate actors. Every nation that has a bomb made a big investment to build it and has a compelling security problem its bomb is intended to address. No one is going to give such a precious thing away. Concerns about the deliberate transfer of weapons to terrorists seem greatly exaggerated, if not delusional.

There is, however, a possibility that a breakdown of order within a state with nuclear weapons might offer disgruntled elements or murderous extremists in it the chance to pilfer a bomb or two. In this context, at present, Pakistani militants or Israeli settlers come to mind. Over the course of the decades to come, there are likely to be other situations like these to worry about unless the sources of the conflicts that animate fanaticism can be addressed. Vigilance is therefore justified. So is a renewed focus on resolving civilizational conflicts, ending oppression, and building peace, justice, and prosperity in Asia as elsewhere.

To sum up: The challenge to the United States is to harness Asia's progress to our own, not to dominate the continent or retard its advance. Asian prosperity is essential to American wealth and well-being. Asian intellectual excellence and economic productivity should spur us to raise our own performance standards, not seek to lower theirs. Asian innovations must be met by a renewed American commitment to science and technology, not closed minds and protectionism. Intra-Asian dynamics invite agile American diplomacy that can reduce our defense burden while containing conflict, not militaristic lurches into armed intervention there.

We will not succeed if we fail to recognize that, after a couple of bad millennia, the Greek concept of "Asia" is back. A large organism that fits the description is actually emerging. We cannot hope to handle this beast—let's think of it as an elephant—if we have a policy for its hindquarters but not for its trunk, head, legs, or belly. Each part of the Asian anatomy presents its own problems and calls for its own policy tools but, in some respects, the greatest challenge we face may be to see the continent as a whole and to conceive our strategy and act accordingly. Neither the current organization of our academies and government nor past experience will be at all helpful in this regard, but it must be done. Understanding the increasing interconnectedness of Asia is a prerequisite both for restoring American leadership there and for effective global governance in the decades to come. Both are sorely needed.

Change without Progress in the Middle East
October 25, 2012[2]

I t's an honor to have been asked once again to address this important annual conference on US-Arab relations. The theme of this year's discussion is "transition within constancy." I confess I'm still trying to figure out what that means. My best guess is that it's something like "progress without change"—a policy approach that only Saudi Arabia has ever managed to pull off. In many ways, however, "change without progress" would be a more accurate description of most of the conundrums in the Middle East.

In any event, the United States is not in an encouraging position in the Middle East. We are less free of Iraq than we wish we were, groping for the exits without a plan in Afghanistan, uncertain how to deal with the Arab uprisings and their aftermath, dabbling from the sidelines in the Syrian civil war, stalemated with Iran and at odds with a belligerent Israel over it, snookered in the Holy Land, nowhere in the affections of the world's Muslims, and in sometimes deadly peril on the Arab street.

Almost a decade ago, the United States invaded and occupied Iraq. Advocates of the operation assured us that this would be a "cakewalk" that would essentially pay for itself. The ensuing war claimed at least 6,000 American military and civilian lives. It wounded 100,000 U.S. personnel. It displaced 2.8 million Iraqis and—by conservative estimates—killed at least 125,000 of them, while wounding another 350,000. The U.S. invasion and occupation of Iraq will ultimately cost American taxpayers at least $3.4 trillion, of which $1.4 trillion represents money actually spent by the Department of Defense, the Department of State, and intelligence agencies during combat operations; another $1 trillion is the minimal estimate of future interest payments; and the other $1 trillion is future health care, disability, and other payments to the almost 1 million American veterans of the war.

The only way to assess military campaigns is by whether they achieve their objectives. Outcomes—not lofty talk about a tangle of good intentions—are what count. In the case of Iraq, a fog of false narratives about weapons of mass destruction, connections to al-Qaeda, threats to Iraq's neighbors, and so forth left the war's objectives to continuing conjecture. None of the goals implied by these narratives worked out. Instead, the war produced multiple "own goals."

---

2. Remarks to the Twenty-First Annual Arab-U.S. Policymakers Conference, Washington, D.C.

Those who urged America into war claim Iraq was a victory for our country. If so, judging by results, the George W. Bush administration's objective must have been to assure the transfer of power in Iraq to the members of the Supreme Council for the Islamic Revolution in Iraq, all of whom had spent the previous twenty years in the Islamic Republic of Iran. The former "decider" made doubly sure of this outcome when Sunni and Shiite nationalist forces, like those of Sayyid Muqtada al-Sadr, threatened the pro-Iranian politicians the United States had installed in Baghdad. Bush "surged" in additional troops to ensure that these politicians remained in office—and there they abide.

The neoconservative authors of the "surge" claim to have produced an important American victory through it. Certainly, in terms of its immediate objective of tamping down violent opposition to the regime, the surge was a tactical success. Still, one can only wonder about the sanity of people who argue that consolidating ethnic cleansing in Baghdad while entrenching a pro-Iranian government there represented a strategic gain for our country. The very same band of shameless ideologues, militarists, and armchair strategists who brought off that coup now clamor for an assault on Iran. One wonders why anyone in America still listens to them. Anywhere else, they would have been brought to account for the huge damage they have done.

If the United States invaded Iraq to demonstrate the capacity of our supremely lethal armed forces to reshape the region to our advantage, we proved the contrary. We never lost a battle, but we put the limitations of U.S. military power on full display.

If the purpose was to enhance U.S. influence in the Middle East, our invasion and occupation of Iraq helped bring about the opposite. Iraq is now for the most part an adjunct to Iranian power, not the balancer of it that it once was. Baghdad stands with Tehran in opposition to the policies of the United States and its strategic partners toward Bahrain, Lebanon, Palestine, Syria and Iran itself, including Iran's nuclear programs. Iraq's oil is now propping up the Assad regime in Syria. Iraq bought a big package of American weapons and training as we withdrew, but it's already clear that its future arms purchases will come mainly from Russia and other non-American sources.

If the point was to prove that secular democracy is a viable norm in the Middle East, events in Iraq have borne savage witness to the contrary. The neoconservatives asserted with great confidence that the fall of a corrupt and tyrannical regime would pave the way for a liberal democratic government in Iraq. This was a profound misreading of history as well as Iraqi realities. The Salafist awakening and the sectarian conflagration kindled by our attempted rearrangement of Iraqi politics have not abated. Sectarian conflict continues to scorch Iraq and to lick away at the domestic tranquility of its Arab neighbors in both the Levant and the Gulf.

If the aim of our invasion and occupation of Iraq was to eliminate an enemy of Israel and secure the neighborhood for the Jewish state, we did not succeed. Israel's adversaries were strengthened even as it made new enemies—for example, in Turkey—and began petulantly to demand that America launch yet another war to make it safe, this time against Iran. Mr. Netanyahu wants America to set red lines for Iran. Everyone else in the region wishes the United States would set red lines for Israel.

If the idea was to showcase the virtues of the rule of law and American-style civil liberties, then our behavior at Abu Ghraib, our denial of the protections of the Geneva Conventions to our battlefield enemies, and our suspension of habeas corpus (as well as many other elements of the Bill of Rights) at home put paid to that. These lapses from our constitution and the traditions of our republic have left us morally diminished. They have greatly devalued our credibility as international advocates of human freedoms everywhere, not just in the Middle East. We have few ideological admirers in the Arab or broader Islamic worlds these days. Our performance in Iraq is part of the reason for that.

All this helps to explain why most Americans don't want to hear about Iraq anymore. A few weeks ago, the Congress failed to authorize funding for the continuation of the U.S. military training mission in Iraq, forcing the Pentagon to come up with the money internally. Almost no one here noticed.

On one level, the failure to fund a relationship with the Iraqi military through training represents a shockingly casual demonstration of the willingness of American politicians to write off the many sacrifices of our troops and taxpayers in our Iraq war. On another, it is an example of America's most endearing political characteristic: our capacity for nearly instant amnesia. ("Iraq war? What Iraq war? You mean we sacrificed the lives and bodies of over one hundred thousand Americans and took on debt equivalent to one-fourth of our GDP to occupy and refashion Iraq? Really? Why?") They say the test for Alzheimer's is whether you can hide your own Easter eggs. Apparently, we Americans can do that.

Failure is a much better teacher than success, but only if one is willing to reflect on what caused it. Our intervention in Iraq was a disaster for that country as well as for our own. It reshaped the Middle East to our disadvantage, yet we shy away from attempting to understand our fiasco even as those who led us into it urge us to reenact it elsewhere.

The military lessons we took away from Iraq have so far also proved hollow or false. When applied in Afghanistan, where we have now been in combat for more than eleven years, they haven't worked. Analogies from other conflicts are not a sound basis for campaign plans, especially when they are more spin than substance. "In for a billion, in for half a trillion" is no substitute for strategy, let alone grand strategy.

Communities engaged in resistance to the imposition of government control where it has never before intruded do not see themselves as insurgents but as defenders of the established order. Counterinsurgency doctrine is irrelevant when there is no state with acknowledged legitimacy against which to rebel, no competent or credible government to buttress in power, and no politics untainted by venality, nepotism, and the drug trade to uphold. Pacification by foreign forces is never liberating for those who experience it. Foreign militaries cannot inject legitimacy into regimes that lack both roots and appeal in the communities they seek to govern.

One cannot reap the fruits of politico-military victories one has not won. Military reinforcements are not a substitute for policy failure. Surges don't work when there is no regime with a strong, independent power base for the additional troops to prop up. Invading men's homes and shaming them in front of their wives and children does not endear them to new codes of conduct, still less instill feminist values. Nor can one beat a set of ideas—even bad ideas—with targeted killings of militants, especially when the definition of a militant is anyone killed during a drone attack. Drones multiply enemies, fuel rage, and invite indiscriminate reprisal. They ensure that we will never run out of terrorists in Afghanistan, Pakistan, the Horn of Africa, Yemen, and elsewhere.

There is an international consensus that it's time to leave Afghanistan, letting Afghans be Afghans. After eleven years of combat, we're all out of patience and pretty much out of money. So far, the United States alone has spent about $575 billion. Almost 2,000 Americans have died and 16,000 have been seriously wounded in Afghanistan. In the end, the Afghan war is likely to cost us, our children, and our grandchildren about $1.5 trillion—all of it borrowed. That's about $50,000 per person in a country where the per capita income is about $1,000.

In Chicago last May, NATO agreed on an exit plan broadly reminiscent of "Vietnamization." It's only thirty-seven years—less than two generations—since Saigon fell. Did our political elite really forget every-thing we learned in Vietnam? Apparently so. In any event, in Afghanistan, as eventually happened in Vietnam, we're in final fallback mode. The plan this time is to train Afghans to be soldiers for their national government, not just natural warriors committed to the defense of their tribes and clans. But when those being trained are so uncommitted to this cause and so annoyed by the demeanor of their foreign trainers that they kill them, it's hard to take "Afghanization" seriously as an exit strategy.

Al-Qaeda fled Afghanistan during the battle of Tora Bora in December 2001. There has always been a possibility under the Pashtunwali (the ten ethical principles that define honor for the Pashtun people) that the Taliban might join other Afghans in agreeing to deny reentry to anti-American terrorists, including al-Qaeda or other movements like it. It has never been conceivable that religious Afghans would agree to adopt Western norms for their country's governance. No one can say we haven't made a serious effort to transform Afghanistan, but it's time to admit that some designs are beyond reach.

When we entered Afghanistan in 2001, we had no thought of trans-forming the place. Our aim was simply to bar "terrorists with global reach" from using its territory as a sanctuary or training ground in which to prepare further assaults on America and Americans. A deal that sup-ported this essential but limited objective of strategic denial, but not the remodeling of Afghan mores, has long been open to us. Sadly, however, it may now be too late for an agreement with all concerned to deny bases to Islamist terrorists.

How much that actually matters is a question on which reasonable men and women may differ. Whatever they may think of jihadis, there can be few Afghans eager to invite further foreign intervention in their coun-try by once again harboring "terrorists with global reach." But it's still worth a try to formalize an understanding on this. After all, that would vindicate our original purpose in invading the place.

Afghanistan itself has become largely irrelevant to the problem of global terrorism but the unfortunate net effect of our operations there has been to ignite a broader struggle with the Muslim world. The result has been to entrench anti-American terrorists in Pakistan, Yemen, parts of North Africa and the Sahel, and a few places in Europe and Asia, not to exorcise or contain them. Calling off the attempt to pacify Afghanistan would remove it as the potent symbol of American crusade against con-servative Islam that it has become.

This brings us back to the causes of virulent anti-Americanism and its spread. For anyone with an open mind, these causes are not hard to understand. The fanatics who carried out the atrocities of 9/11 went out of their way to describe their motivations and outlined their objectives to anyone who would listen. America turned off its hearing aid. It's still off. The grievances that catalyzed 9/11 remain not simply unaddressed but ignored or denied by Americans.

Al-Qaeda saw 9/11 as a counterattack against American policies that had directly or indirectly killed and maimed large numbers of Muslims. Some of those enraged by our policies were prepared to die to achieve revenge. Still, there were few in the Muslim world in 2001 who sympathized with al-Qaeda's attack on us. There are many more now. It is not our values that they hate. It's what we have done and continue to do. We won't stop terrorists by trying to impose our narrative on them while ignoring theirs, however politically expedient it may be to do so. We can't fight anti-American extremists effectively or otherwise fend off the menace they present if we refuse to consider why they attacked us and why they still want to do so.

The chief planner of 9/11, Khalid Sheikh Mohammed, testified under oath that a primary purpose of al-Qaeda's criminal assault on the United States was to focus "the American people...on the atrocities that America is committing by supporting Israel against the Palestinian people."[3] In so-called fatwas in 1996 and 1998, Osama bin Laden justified al-Qaeda's declaration of war against the United States by reference to the same issue, while levying other charges against America. Specifically, he accused Americans of directly murdering one million Muslims, including 400,000 children, through the U.S. siege and sanctions against Iraq, while "occupying" the Muslim heartland of Saudi Arabia.

Al-Qaeda members have described the war strategy they ultimately adopted as having five stages. Through these, they projected, the Islamic world could rid itself of all forms of aggression against it.

In stage one, al-Qaeda would produce massive American civilian casualties with a spectacular attack on U.S. soil in order to provoke American retaliation in the form of the invasion of one or more Muslim countries. In stage two, al-Qaeda would use the American reaction to its attack to incite, energize, and organize expanding resistance to the American and

---

3. Khalid Sheikh Mohammed, quoted in "Substitution for the Testimony of Khalid Sheikh Mohammed," U.S. District Court, Eastern District of Virginia, posted February 16, 2013, at http://bit.ly/20QP1Wc.

Western presence in Muslim lands. In stage three, the U.S. and its allies would be drawn into a long war of attrition as conflict spread throughout the Muslim world.

By stage four, the struggle would transform itself into a self-sustaining ideology and set of operating principles that could inspire continuing, spontaneously organized attacks against the U.S. and its allies, impose ever-expanding demands on the U.S. military, and divide America's allies from it. In the final stage, the U.S. economy would, like that of the Soviet Union before it, collapse under the strain of unsustainable military spending, taking the dollar-dominated global economy down with it. In the ensuing disorder, al-Qaeda thought, an Islamic caliphate could seize control of Saudi Arabia, Egypt, and the rest of the Middle East.

This fantastic, perverted vision reflected al-Qaeda's belief that if, against all the odds, faith-based struggle could bring down the Soviet Union, it could also break the power of the United States, its Western allies, and Israel. This strategy seemed ridiculous when al-Qaeda first proclaimed it. It is still implausible but, frankly, has come to sound a bit less preposterous than it once did.

The immediate objective of the 9/11 attacks was explicitly to provoke the United States into military overreactions that would enrage and arouse the world's Muslims, estrange Americans from Arabs, stimulate a war of religion between Islam and the West, undermine the close ties between Washington and Riyadh, curtail the commanding influence of the United States in the Middle East, and overthrow the Saudi monarchy. The aftershocks of al-Qaeda's 9/11 terrorist operation against the United States have so far failed to shake the Saudi monarchy but—to one degree or another—it has realized all its other immediate goals. Among other things, it has burdened future generations of Americans with about $5 trillion in debt from the Afghan and Iraq wars, helping to thrust the United States into fiscal crisis.

Mao Zedong observed that "a single spark can start a prairie fire." His point was that, when conditions arise that can be exploited to favor a cause, it can spread with frightening speed and ferocity. The U.S. response to 9/11 has inflamed Islamist anti-Americanism in a widening swath of the Muslim world. By the time he died, Osama bin Laden surely felt entitled to pronounce the first stages of his mission accomplished. Islamist terrorism did not die with him. It lives on. One cannot decapitate a network. Nor can one shrivel an ideology by military means alone.

Islamist terrorists were initially encouraged by the extent to which the Arab uprisings of 2011 and 2012 upended the regional order in North Africa. These uprisings liberated Salafism, the tendency within Islam from which extremists draw their spiritual inspiration, from political repression. Where the uprisings succeeded, however, the changes they set in motion set back the cause of extremism by entangling Salafists in tasks of governance from which they had previously been excluded. By contrast, where the uprisings achieved only limited success or went nowhere, as in Yemen, Syria, and Bahrain, Salafist jihadism has found fertile soil in which to grow.

Overall, the past two years have represented less an Arab than a Salafist awakening. Salafi populism asserts that the failings of contemporary Muslim societies are due to their distance from the most repressive traditions of Islam and that secularism and moderation cannot be reconciled with true Islam. This view has gained major ground in the Arab world. The elected governments in Egypt and Palestine (the Muslim Brotherhood and Hamas) face their most formidable challenges not from the secular left but from the Salafist right.

The U.S. was long antagonistic to the Muslim Brotherhood and proscribed official dialogue with it. America has labeled Hamas a terrorist organization and sought to isolate it and overthrow its rule in Gaza, but the militant Salafist opposition to Muslim Brotherhood rule in Egypt seeks to revise or repudiate the Camp David accords. The opposition to Hamas seeks to end its de facto ceasefire and acceptance of Israel. If U.S. interests are to be protected, U.S. policy must recognize and deal with the emerging political realities in the Middle East, not stick to dead narratives. As Kierkegaard said, "Life can only be understood backwards, but it must be lived forwards."

The NATO approach to Libya assumed that the removal of a tyrant would somehow inevitably lead to a liberal democracy. Indeed, this was the dominant initial interpretation of the "Arab Spring" in the West. Most pundits thought that, as corrupt and tyrannical governments fell, regimes that used social media to implement Western principles of democratic governance would sprout up in their place. Implicit in this was a profound lack of understanding of the political cultures of the countries where the uprisings occurred, the strength of their rulers, the diversity of the opposition in each, and the likely forces that would emerge from the success of that opposition. What actually followed Muammar Qaddafi's regime in Libya has been ongoing warfare between clans, tribes and ideological militias, including some determined to take advantage of any opportunity to strike at the United States. The Libya where Ambassador Chris Stevens died was not the Libya of Washington's imagination.

Wishful thinking and ignorance have nowhere been more in evidence than with respect to Syria, where the demise of the Assad regime has been just around the corner for nineteen months now and early, enthusiastic descriptions of the nature of the opposition to it have not withstood scrutiny. More than 31,000 Syrians have died to date in an escalating civil war. From a humanitarian point of view, this is appalling—but to cynics determined to deprive Iran of Syria as a strategic asset, either regime change or continuing anarchy in Syria can get the job done, so it doesn't really matter if the war never ends. Some dream of post-Assad Syria as a platform from which to mount rollback operations against Iranian influence in Iraq.

Unlike other revolts in the Arab world, the revolt in Syria risks jump-starting interstate conflict. Syria is already, in many respects, a proxy war between Saudi Arabia and Qatar, on the one side, and Iran and Hezbollah on the other. The fighting has begun to spill over Syria's borders into both Turkey and Lebanon. Nearly 700,000 Syrians have sought refuge in Jordan, Lebanon, Turkey, Iraq, and Egypt. As Syrians leave, foreign jihadis arrive.

It has long been clear that the international consensus that permitted so-called "humanitarian intervention" in Libya will not be replicated in Syria. The UN Security Council's authorization of a "no-fly zone" in Libya was blatantly stretched well past its breaking point to rationalize an open campaign of support for rebellion and regime change. This destroyed Qaddafi's regime and killed him. It probably also killed the possibility that the "responsibility to protect" will ever become generally accepted international law.

China now sees what happened in Libya as the deliberate exploitation of a humanitarian crisis by outside forces bent less on relieving suffering than on justifying foreign intervention to engineer regime change. Russia agrees with China on this point and, unlike China, has a substantial investment in the Assad regime to protect. Neither China nor Russia will allow the UN Security Council to repeat the Libyan precedent. In the absence of some new approach that obviates this political reality, all that can be said with assurance is that the fighting in Syria will continue to escalate until some development in Syria brings it to an end.

Syria's neighbors seem more likely to suffer spillover from the turmoil than to enter it directly themselves. Overt foreign intervention in Syria is not impossible to imagine but it is unlikely, given its probable knock-on effects. Russia might well respond to an attempt to establish a "no-fly zone" in Syria behind the back of the UN by equipping the Assad regime with advanced air defenses, thus further internationalizing the conflict. Though neither side wants this, Syria's air and artillery duels with Turkey could progress to the point that NATO feels obliged to act militarily. Syrian Kurdish separatists in league with their fellow Kurds in Iraq and Turkey could draw either or both countries into conflict. Iraq and Iran both support the Assad regime against its opposition, which risks their being dragged into direct participation in the fight. Then, too, as Libya shows, a sudden end to civil war can release warriors with weaponry to destabilize an entire region.

Syria is not just a horrible humanitarian disaster. It is a dangerous international dilemma. So, in its own way, is the state of U.S. relations with Syria's ally, Iran.

U.S.-Iran relations are at their lowest level since the two countries first began to deal with each other officially 137 years ago. There is no serious dialogue between the two governments. People-to-people exchanges between the United States and Iran are nearly nonexistent; media on both sides are biased and inaccurate in their reporting about the other. The United States has effectively outsourced its Iran policy to Israel, with the only difference between the two presidential candidates being whether to do so with or without reservation. The issue Israel cares about is whether Iran acquires nuclear weapons, not Iran's aspirations for hegemony in the Persian Gulf region, its struggle with Saudi Arabia for leadership of the world's Muslims, or its search for strategic advantage in Bahrain. In virtually every respect, the American view of Iran more closely mirrors Israel's than that of the Arabs.

Israel's view combines what can only be described as psychotic fears that Iran might attempt to annihilate the Jews in the Holy Land with entirely rational apprehensions about the impact on Israel's military freedom of action if it loses its nuclear monopoly in the region. Few outside Israel believe that Iran's possession of nuclear weapons would embolden it to attack Israel, given Israel's ability to obliterate Iran in response. No one has suggested that Iran might attack Israel with anything other than nuclear weapons—which it doesn't yet have. But Israel's threats to attack Iran give Iran a very convincing reason to secure itself by developing a nuclear deterrent. Given this logic, Israel's fear of losing its nuclear monopoly in the Middle East seems likely to become a self-fulfilling prophecy.

In this connection, all concerned are playing very duplicitous and dangerous games. Iran claims that, inasmuch as nuclear weapons are immoral, it will not acquire them. Yet it seems in practice to be reenacting Israel's clandestine weapons-development program of five decades ago, developing capabilities to build and deliver nuclear weapons while denying that it intends actually to do any such thing. Israel lacks the capability to eliminate Iran's nuclear programs but keeps threatening quixotic military action to do so. Israel's purpose is clearly to force the United States, which could damage Iran's facilities as Israel could not, into a war with Iran on its behalf. In pursuit of this, the Israeli prime minister has blatantly intervened in the U.S. elections in support of the Republican candidate, who has explicitly committed himself, if elected, to allow Israel to dictate U.S. policy on Iran, Palestine, and other issues in the Middle East.

The United States, joined by some of its allies, has bypassed the UN to impose what it describes as "crippling sanctions" on Iran. American politicians and pundits gloat over the suffering these are causing the Iranian people. Washington has offered Tehran no way to achieve relief from these sanctions other than complete capitulation to U.S. and Israeli demands. Meanwhile, the U.S. Congress has provided generous funding to efforts to overthrow the Iranian regime. America is working with Israel and the Mujahedin-e-Khalq to carry out cyberwarfare and assassinations inside Iran. By any standard, these are acts of war that invite reprisal. There is no negotiating process worthy of the name underway between the United States and Iran.

In these circumstances, instead of bringing Iran to its knees, U.S. sanctions seem far more likely to provide further evidence of the truth of Dean Acheson's assertion that "the idea of using commercial restrictions as a substitute for war...is a mischievous superstition in the conduct of foreign affairs." Politically convenient as they may be, sanctions will not end Iran's nuclear program. To pretend they will is naive or disingenuous.

On the other hand, there are no good military options. An attack by Israel on Iran would thrust the entire region into turmoil and deal a heavy blow to the world economy, while stoking Iran's nuclear ambitions. An attack would not permanently cripple Iran's ability to go nuclear. Air and related attacks on Iran by the United States could set back its nuclear program but not eliminate it. They would, in fact, unite Iranians in demanding that their government develop and field a nuclear deterrent. Any attack by either Israel or the United States would result in Iranian retaliation against Israel and the Arab countries of the Gulf, while creating a far more active, long-term Iranian threat to both than at present. Such a war could deepen the dependence of the GCC countries on American military power for their defense, while simultaneously making the military presence of the United States on their soil politically precarious.

So far our diplomacy toward Iran resembles the approach we have taken with north Korea. In the absence of major adjustments in the U.S. approach to reach a compromise with Tehran, this diplomacy seems likely to yield the same result it has with Pyongyang. The only thing worse than an Iranian nuclear weapon would be an attack on Iran to stop it from developing one. The most likely prospect is that Iran, like north Korea, will eventually get its bomb. This will ensure that some other countries in the region will too, either on their own or through arrangements with powers like Pakistan to station nuclear weapons on their territory or otherwise extend nuclear deterrence against both Iran and Israel to them.

Israel and the United States, having done much to push Iran into this corner, have no common stand on how to help Iran out of it. What if Iran offers to accept truly credible verification measures to assure that it has forgone the development and fielding of weapons? There are hints that Iran may in fact be preparing such an offer for presentation after the November 6 U.S. elections. If Iran puts forward an offer that the United States considers acceptable, will Israel also accept it or try to move the goalposts? Given the Israeli hammerlock on U.S. Iran policy, could the United States actually take yes for an answer from Iran?

If the United States and Israel were to reject a forthcoming Iranian offer, should one be put forward, the entire region would have to live with the consequences. These include broader proliferation of nuclear weapons in the region. The hobbles such a bloom of nuclear deterrents in the region would impose on Israel's ability to attack its neighbors with impunity might lead Israel finally to try diplomacy with them. Other than that, it's hard to see what anyone would gain from the United States rejecting compromise with Tehran.

Meanwhile, U.S. diplomacy on the Israel-Palestine issue has become unsustainable. The half-truths with fantasy sauce that America's professional peace processors have cooked up for so long now have no takers. Neither the world nor a politically awakened Middle East will be fooled by happy talk about a nonexistent and unrevivable peace process. The day of reckoning is at hand. Israel must come to grips with the consequences of its successful territorial expansion. Palestinians must recognize the defeat of their aspirations for self-determination. America must acknowledge its political and diplomatic impotence. All sides must move on.

Israel has now effectively incorporated almost all the territory of Palestine, if not its inhabitants, under its sovereignty. There is no longer any prospect for a two-state solution in Palestine, unless one considers Indian reservations or Bantustans to be states. One state is a reality in Palestine. Within this state, Palestinians inhabit a jail administered by Palestinian trusties dependent on Jewish guards for their livelihood, personal safety, and authority. The Palestinians face an unpalatable but unavoidable choice between the security of prison life and a struggle for their rights in the only state they will ever live in, which is Israel. In short, the two-state *solution having been strangled by the success of scofflaw Israeli settlement* policies, the Palestinian question has ineluctably become one of human and civil rights within the state of Israel, not one of self-determination.

The consequences of the death of the two-state solution for Israeli Jews are already apparent. Ensuring that Israel is a democratic state that provides a national home for both Jews and Palestinians—rather than a country based on ethno-sectarian apartheid—is now the only way to realize Zionism on a basis acceptable to the world, including the vast majority of non-Israeli Jews. In default of this, Israel will suffer boycott, disinvestment, and sanctions in the West, escalating terrorism at home, rising tensions with ever more independent-minded and militarily competent neighbors, and widening international isolation. The immediate danger is that, before civil rights and democratic liberties can be extended to the Palestinian inhabitants of Eretz Yisrael, Israeli Jews will have sacrificed these values to aggressive medievalism and racism.

Americans cannot undo our past mistakes in the Middle East. We must learn from these even as we deal with their consequences. Among these consequences is a major reduction in U.S. prestige and influence in the region. Events there are now being driven as much or more by the policies of Iran, Saudi Arabia, Egypt, Turkey, Pakistan, India, Russia, and China or by forces on the Arab street as by American preferences. The situation is evolving amid intensifying animosity between Americans and the world's Muslims, not just those in the Middle East.

When President Obama entered office four years ago, he made a good-faith effort to deal with all of the issues I have discussed this morning. With more than a little help from our self-proclaimed friends in the region, he failed. The past four years have seen a great deal of change without much, if any, progress toward realization of any part of the U.S. agenda. They have also seen a shortage of American audacity and steadily diminishing hope for an effective U.S. role in resolving conflicts and reducing tensions in the Middle East.

Thirteen days from now, we Americans will elect a president. We will do so following a campaign in which the issues before this conference were dealt with, if at all, through exchanges of posturing, misleading sound bites, and invective. The next president, whoever he is, whether he wants to or not, will have to deal with these issues as they are, not as his campaign donors or our electorate would prefer them to be. He will do so with a weakened hand. He will not succeed by pursuing the course of least political resistance at home or by doing more of the same abroad. Our country's interests and those of our friends in the region will not prosper without painful adjustments in U.S. policy.

The United States, the Middle East, and China
June 5, 2013[4]

In foreign policy, national interest is the measure of all things. But interests, national or otherwise, are defined by the vectors of domestic politics. No region better illustrates this than the Middle East, the region that extends from the Eastern Mediterranean to Iran and Arabia. I want to speak to you today about the differing national interests of the states and peoples of this region, the United States, and China, which is emerging as a growing presence there as it is everywhere. One legacy of the Cold War is an American tendency to search for an arch-adversary and cast relationships with it in zero-sum terms. As I will explain, I don't think that is the correct prism through which to view China's engagement with the Middle East.

But before I get to China, let me begin with a few observations about where we Americans now stand in the Middle East with regard to Arab-Israeli peace, strategic transit, energy security, markets, and the effects of regional instability on our domestic tranquility.

For fifty years, we have treated the achievement of security for a Jewish homeland in Palestine as our top priority in the Middle East. We have sought to achieve this by military aid to foster and guarantee Israeli military hegemony in the region and by diplomacy aimed at brokering acceptance of it by its Arab and Muslim neighbors. The results are in. At no small cost to the United States in terms of the radicalization of Arab and Muslim opinion, oil embargoes, subsidies, gifts of war materiel, wars, and now anti-American terrorism with global reach, Israel has become a regional military Goliath, enjoying a nuclear monopoly and overwhelming superiority in the region's battle space. U.S. diplomacy has definitively failed.

In no small measure as a result of its own decisions, the Jewish state has no recognized or secure borders. Although acknowledged as an unwelcome fact, Israel remains a pariah in its region. In many ways, acceptance of Israel's legitimacy is receding, not advancing, under the impact of the racial and religious bigotry its policies are seen to exemplify. Israel appears to have decided to stake its existence on the dubious proposition that it can sustain military superiority over its neighbors in perpetuity. It

---

4. Remarks to the Far East Luncheon Group, Diplomatic and Consular Officers, Retired (DACOR), Washington, D.C.

has no diplomatic strategy for achieving their acceptance, nor does the United States.

The great American naval strategist Alfred Thayer Mahan was the first to call the region "the Middle East." The age of oil had not then quite arrived. Admiral Mahan wanted to highlight the area's strategic importance as the meeting place of Europe, Africa, and Asia and the focal point of the transportation corridors connecting Europe with the Indo-Pacific. The Middle East's geopolitical location remains a central but largely unremarked aspect of its importance. Logistics is everything in military strategy, but only logisticians seem to think about it. Without the ability to transit the Middle East at will, America would be much impaired as a global power. The maintenance of a permissive environment for such transit thus remains a vital U.S. interest. Our privileges in this regard rest on the value the region's rulers assign to our commitment to protect them. That, in turn, depends on whether they judge that they have an alternative to the United States as their protector. It's clear that, at present, no one else wants or can take on the role we have traditionally performed. So, though we are increasingly estranged from the region's peoples, our ability to travel through it to other parts of the globe is not in immediate jeopardy.

When someone mentions the Middle East, most people think first of oil. The United States ceased to be a net exporter of petroleum in 1970, when domestic oil production peaked. By 2005, we were importing 60 percent of the oil we consumed. Most of this came from outside the Middle East. Still, about 56 percent of the world's oil reserves are in that region, as is the only surge production capacity. What happens in the Middle East, more than anywhere else, determines both levels of global supply and prices. During the Cold War, the U.S.-led anti-Soviet coalition we called "the free world" was heavily dependent on imports from the region. Our economic and strategic interests combined to make secure access to its energy supplies a matter of vital concern. Our relationships with countries in the Middle East like Iran and Saudi Arabia reflected this. So did our emphasis on freedom of navigation in the Persian Gulf.

Our ability to extract oil and gas from shale and other previously unexploited sources at current price levels will alter these equations importantly. By the end of the decade, the United States may again be a net exporter of energy. Our reliance on imported oil could fall to as little as 10 percent before rebounding as shale reservoirs are depleted. Regardless of North American progress toward energy self-sufficiency, the world and most of its major energy consumers will remain dependent on oil from the

Middle East. What happens there will continue to have a decisive effect on energy prices. The availability of energy from shale means strategic immunity from supply disruptions outside North America. It does not mean independence from global markets.

What self-sufficiency does mean is that our interest in protecting access to the Persian Gulf's energy resources will soon derive entirely from our aspirations for leadership of a globally healthy economy rather than from our own import dependency. This will raise obvious questions about the benefits versus the costs to our country of our traditional "lone ranger" approach to preventing the disruption of supplies and shipping in the Persian Gulf. I wouldn't be surprised to find us looking for partners with whom to share the financial and military burdens of that mission in future.

The Middle East accounts for around 5 percent of global GDP. It is growing by about 5 percent annually and accounts for about 5 percent of U.S. exports. Arab cash purchases and generous U.S. taxpayer funding of arms transfers to Israel play a vital role in keeping production lines open and sustaining the U.S. defense-industrial base. Including military goods and services, the United States has a substantial but declining share of the region's imports—about one-fourth of them. By way of comparison, China's share is nearly two-fifths and India's one-fifth, almost all nonmilitary in nature. The Middle East is a significant market for American engineering, educational, and consulting services. Otherwise, as long as Arab oil producers' currencies remain linked to the dollar, the region's markets cannot be said to be of more than marginal importance to the U.S. export economy.

The Middle East has, however, become the principal focus of U.S. national-security policy. U.S. support for Israel and military interventions in the region have made it the epicenter of anti-American terrorism with global reach. Israel is threatening war on Iran to preclude it from developing nuclear weapons. Although other countries in the region dislike—even fear—Iran, none supports preemptive attack on the Islamic Republic. Meanwhile, our cooperation with the region's governments on counterterrorism is on the rise. So is the number of terrorists. There is a lot more hatred of America out there than there was before 9/11. We have added the resentment of most Sunnis to that of Iranian Shia, while igniting a civil war between these two sects of Islam and destabilizing the Fertile Crescent. No one can now say when or how any of this will end.

The peoples of the region share a desire for freedom from imperial or colonial dominance and for affirmation of their disparate religious, ethnic, or cultural identities. They are not much interested in our ideology or political practices but, by contrast with other regions, almost all seek foreign patrons to secure themselves against each other. Israeli Jews depend on us to support their ethno-religious uniqueness. Iranians believe that we menace their independence and cultural identity. Egyptians count on us because they do not know where else now to turn. Kurds hope we will back their self-determination. The Gulf Arabs seek our help and that of others to protect them against Israel and to balance Iranian power and preclude Persian hegemony.

Middle Eastern governments with oil or gas depend on energy exports to finance their defense and domestic welfare, development, and stability. Those without such resources seek subsidies for the same purposes. Despite varying degrees of foreign dependency, all jealously guard their independence and freedom of action. None is wedded to us or any other patron. All are looking around for alternative backers.

This is where many in the region believe China could come in. In China, the Arabs see a partner who will buy their oil without demanding that they accept a foreign ideology, abandon their way of life, or make other choices they'd rather avoid. They see a country that is far away and has no imperial agenda in their region but that is technologically competent and likely, in time, to be militarily powerful. They see a place to buy things they can use and enjoy. They see a country that unreservedly welcomes their investments and is grateful for the jobs these create. They see a major civilization that seems determined to build a partnership with them, does not insult their religion or their way of life, values its reputation as a reliable supplier too much to engage in the promiscuous application of sanctions or other coercive measures, and has no habit of bombing or invading other countries to whose policies it objects.

In short, the Arabs see the Chinese as pretty much like Americans— that is, Americans as we used to be before we decided to experiment with diplomacy-free foreign policy, hit-and-run democratization, regime change, drone wars, and other "neocon" conceits of the age. And they see a chance to rebalance their international relationships to offset their long-standing overdependence on the United States. But the political aloofness that makes China attractive as a partner also makes it unlikely that it would agree to compete with us for the privilege of acquiring and protecting foreign client states.

China has a long history of engagement with the Middle East. Islam entered China shortly after its seventh-century revelation, in 618, the year the Tang Dynasty began. The first official envoy of the Rashidun Caliphate arrived in Chang'an in 651. It's little known in the West that the great Ming admiral Zheng He, who commanded multiple voyages to South Asia, East Africa, and the Middle East from 1405 to 1433, was a Muslim whose grandfather and father had made the pilgrimage to Mecca and who had been tutored in Arabic. He was following long-established, well-mapped Arab and Chinese trade routes. Four of his seven voyages touched Arabia. He himself visited Mecca on the last of them. The connections between East and West Asia were severed and atrophied during the era of European imperialism and the Cold War. They are now being rebuilt with astonishing speed.

China's economy has grown more than sixfold over the past ten years. China became the world's largest energy consumer in 2010. It is the world's biggest investor in renewable energy, but last December it displaced the United States as its largest oil importer. China now consumes 21.3 percent of the world's oil. Not surprisingly, its main interest in the Middle East is uninterrupted access to the region's abundant energy supplies.

China imports over half its oil from the region, primarily from Saudi Arabia, though it also buys almost half the oil produced in post-Saddam Iraq, where Chinese oil companies now play a leading role, and more than two-fifths of the oil exported by Iran. To buy all that oil, China must sell goods and services to Middle Eastern oil producers. As has become so common in so many other places, China is now the top destination for the region's exports and the largest source of its imports. Chinese companies are the largest foreign investors in a growing number of Middle Eastern countries. For non-oil-producing countries that rely heavily on the tourist industry, Chinese visitors are now a significant source of hard currency. Chinese is taught in Confucius Institutes in Israel, most Arab countries, Iran, and Turkey.

American presidents up to Woodrow Wilson (and his immediate successors) would have understood today's China's reluctance to take sides in the quarrels of others. As a vulnerable new state, the People's Republic of China follows a policy analogous to that recommended by our founding fathers. As Thomas Jefferson put it, "Peace, commerce, and honest friendship with all nations—entangling alliances with none." China does not wish to be manipulated by Israel against the Arabs, by the Arabs against Israel or each other, or by either against Iran. It hopes for productive relations with all. Unique among great powers, China simultaneously maintains largely positive and substantive relations with all the region's peoples.

This is not an easy stand to take in an area prone to view events as a conflict between good and evil.

In dealing with the turmoil in Syria, China has clung to its vision of noninterference in the internal affairs of sovereign nations despite the damage this has done to its image in Saudi Arabia, its most important economic partner in the region and the principal sponsor of the Syrian rebels. Its unwillingness to support the Assad government against the insurgents has meanwhile earned it no points with Iran. China has excellent relations with Israel (including a lot of military-technology cooperation), but does not take the side of the Jewish state in its struggle to master and dispossess the Palestinians. Nor, as a country that seeks no enemies, is China prepared to play the role of mediator in the Middle East. It recognizes, as the Greek philosopher Bias did two and a half millennia ago, that "it is better to mediate between enemies than between friends, because one of the friends is sure to become an enemy and one of the enemies a friend."

China has sound domestic reasons to be cautious about involvement in the Middle East. There is not a single province in China without a native Muslim population. Increasing numbers of Chinese make the pilgrimage to Mecca. Although—for complex reasons—the official figures are much lower, well over 100 million Chinese are Muslim, and the number is growing. Some Uyghurs have raised the banner of Islam in a violent campaign for the secession of Xinjiang. Al-Qaeda has a Uyghur chapter. The contagious sectarian dogmas of the Middle East could adversely affect China's security and social tranquility.

In short, China shares neither the priorities nor the impulse to activism of the United States in the Middle East. It has no emotional commitment to the Jews of Israel or the Muslims of Arab countries, Iran, or Turkey. It did not have its diplomats taken hostage by raging students in Tehran. Its armed forces are configured to defend its national territory, not to project power on the global level or to the Middle East. China does not need security of transit through the region.

China is dependent on Middle East oil supplies but confident that the self-interest of vendors and diplomacy make the use of force largely irrelevant to the security of energy supplies. Where actual threats to this security have arisen, as from Somali piracy in the Gulf of Aden, China has independently deployed the People's Liberation Army Navy (PLA Navy) as part of an ad hoc, UN-authorized, multinational effort to restore freedom of navigation. Meanwhile, China has hedged against the possibility that the United States, India, or another great power might try to break its energy supply chains by diversifying its sources of oil and gas as much as it can. For sound strategic reasons, unlike us, China has kept its distance from the religious struggles of the Middle East. It has been content to buy what it needs and sell what it can to cover the cost, stay out of politics, and avoid taking stands on religious issues. If that sounds like the advice your grandmother gave you for dealing with other people, then that just confirms its essential wisdom.

Much as the countries of the Middle East would like to enlist China as a sponsor and protector, they are learning that China has neither the capability nor the inclination to take on these roles. Their disappointment with its distance from them has not impeded their development of a robust pattern of economic interdependence with China. The good news is that China does not seek to usurp our self-appointed role as the protector of the Middle East. That, I think, is also in some senses the bad news. We will not easily escape the burdens we have assumed in that region.

There is room for Sino-American cooperation in the Middle East. There is no inevitability about contention between us there. One must hope that we can, in fact, find ways to work together or in parallel. It would help to listen, not apply mirror-imaged stereotypes to each other. Perhaps we could both learn something from that. Neither coercion nor the use of force is the only way to advance the national interest. Diplomacy and other measures short of war are generally less costly and more effective. The politics of the homeland may define national interests but a clear-eyed view of the realities of the world beyond it is essential for their successful prosecution.

Despite the growing economic interdependence of the United States and China, the overall trajectory of our official relations is at present negative. We would do well to avoid adding needless elements of a zero-sum game in the Middle East to the mix. There, as elsewhere, we need to search for broader common interests within which narrow differences can be subsumed and on which policy coordination can take place. I hope the effort to do this will be a significant part of the summit meeting between Chinese Communist Party chairman Xi Jinping and President Obama that begins tomorrow.

Coping with Kaleidoscopic Change in the Middle East
October 22, 2013[5]

Much of the Middle East is now in turmoil. It has always been a mosaic of tribes, sects, and peoples, but its previously largely static tableau has become a kaleidoscope. The pieces are being moved by conflicts between states, religions, sects, ideologies, and ethnic groups. The situation reminds one of other circumstances in which chaotic change has overwhelmed existing order. I recall the Chinese classic, *Romance of the Three Kingdoms,* which describes such a time. Its first English translation was published about the time that Mr. Sykes and M. Picot gave the Levant its current borders. Its opening words are "Empires wax and wane; states cleave asunder and coalesce." The rest of the book vividly depicts the unpredictable course by which this can happen.

Our past actions in the Middle East account for more than a little of the current unpredictability of events there. Iraq continues the civil wars the U.S. occupation catalyzed. One thousand civilians are now dying there by political violence each month. The withdrawal of NATO and most, if not all U.S. forces from Afghanistan will leave behind a weak, incompetent, and corrupt regime, an unresolved insurgency, and a much bigger opium economy than before we decided to pacify the place. But why dwell on our strategic achievements when we have the future to talk about?

Too many forces are acting upon the Middle East kaleidoscope for anyone to know what pattern it will yield when it finally comes to rest, as—in time, perhaps after a considerable time—it will. The bitterly stalemated Israel-Palestine dispute was long the principal source of political radicalization and violence within the region. It has lost none of its power to inspire hatred but it has been joined in that role by other contests of equal or greater intensity. These include confrontations between Saudi Arabia, its allies, and Iran; between Iran and Israel; between Salafi Muslims, Copts, other Christians, Shia, Alawites, and Druze; between Sunni jihadis and Shiite apostles of both clerical rule and secularism; between traditions of *shura* led by an emir and winner-take-all electoral politics; between righteous secularism and Islamist populism; between generals and demagogues; between the street and security forces; between Arabs, Kurds, Persians, and Turks.

---

5. Remarks to the Twenty-Second Annual Arab-U.S. Policymakers Conference, Washington, D.C.

All of these contests find expression in multiple struggles. All have become tragic zero-sum games in which the interests of each side advance only at the expense of the well-being and domestic tranquility of another. The United States is implicated in many of them, but in none of them does or can it play a decisive role. How will these contests end? Will the geography of the region retain its Sykes-Picot contours? What new balances of power and relationships will emerge in the region? What the new mosaic will look like is, of course, of paramount importance to the shifting coalitions of states, sects, and tribes from which it is compounded, but it matters greatly to the United States and other great powers too.

That is because the Middle East occupies a pivotal geostrategic space. It lies athwart the routes between Asia, Africa, and Europe. It is where the world's energy resources are concentrated. It has become a hub for global finance and business. It is where three of the world's great religions originated and where they now collide. It is the epicenter of terrorism with global reach. What happens in the Middle East affects the world's economic, political, and strategic equilibrium. The Middle East is too important to be left solely to Middle Easterners.

Yet the Arab uprisings, revolutions, and coups of the past two and a half years have repeatedly demonstrated that, for all our unmatched military power, Americans no longer command the ability to shape trends in the Middle East. Almost no one now expects us to do so. Delusions of imperial omnipotence die hard, but the question of the day is no longer how we or other outside powers will act to affect the Arab future. Both colonialism and neocolonialism are no more. For better or ill, the states of the region have seized control of their own destiny. *Masha'Allah*—and good luck to them!

As the pieces shift in the Middle East, will the relationships between its states and outside powers shift as well? It is impossible to imagine that they will not. Recent events have marginalized Turkey. What role will it now play? We have already seen a measure of estrangement between the United States and our traditional Arab security partners. Saudi Arabia's refusal to take its seat in the UN Security Council reflects this. Riyadh has not just protested but opted to avoid daily interactions with the United States that would exacerbate bilateral tensions over regional issues. The course of events in Egypt, Bahrain, and Syria has exposed long-concealed differences in perspective between us and both Arabs and Israelis. Iran is now reaching out to us over the heads of both.

As America recedes in prestige in the region, Russia seems to be returning to a position of diplomatic influence. Will Europe, China, and others with a stake in restabilizing the Middle East also now assert themselves as independent actors there? Regional actors are redoubling their efforts to recruit outside powers to support them. This could produce some startling geopolitical realignments.

Before we get to some of these possibilities, let me briefly review current trends and events, beginning with the interactions between Israelis and Palestinians.

Attention is now focused elsewhere, but the Israel-Palestine issue remains at the core of Arab indignation and disbelief in America. Secretary of State Kerry's frenetic effort to drag Israel and the usual Palestinians into talks has not cured this. Very few, if any, in the region assign any potential value to this latest iteration of the now notoriously unproductive series of American-organized counterfeit "peace processes." The only effects to date of this latest round have been to delay Palestinian efforts to take Israel to the International Court of Justice and to accelerate the Jewish state's drive to Judaize the West Bank and set the stage for more ethnic cleansing when and if regional chaos produces the political cover to carry it out.

So far, the intermittent meetings between Tzipi Livni and Saeb Erakat look like yet another political distraction rather than a path to peace. It would be nice to be proved wrong, but it's hard to see anyone other than Israeli construction companies engaged in settlement-building gaining anything from what is mostly *not* going on.

The very structure of the talks emphasizes their futility. Most Palestinians are unrepresented in them. The Palestinian Authority is on the Israeli and American payrolls. It has been appointed to represent the Palestinians by Israel and the United States, but its authority to speak even for the inhabitants of the West Bank is in doubt. It certainly has no mandate to negotiate on behalf of those in Gaza, in the refugee camps, in diaspora, or living as second-class citizens in Israel. In the unlikely event that the PA were to come to some sort of agreement with its Israeli masters, few Palestinians anywhere would consider themselves bound by this. How Jerusalem is dealt with will decisively affect the stand of the world's 1.6 billion Muslims on any agreement. A peace viewed by most as contracted by an illegitimate party and by many as unjust would evoke violent backlash rather than acquiescence. By bringing the decades-long effort to produce a negotiated solution to a discreditable conclusion, it could ignite renewed terrorism against both Israelis and their American allies.

If, as most expect, the talks sputter to a fruitless end next July, the UN-recognized but largely fictive state of Palestine can be expected to take its case against Israel's violations of international and humanitarian law to the courts of international public opinion and the Hague. The movement to boycott, disinvest, and sanction Israel has already begun to take hold in Europe. It will gather global momentum. "Palestine" itself is nearly powerless, but neither Israel nor the United States have credible counters to Israel's progressive self-delegitimization through behavior that all but die-hard Zionist bigots find abhorrent.

The antipathies stoked by Israel's treatment of its captive Arab populations and its belligerence toward its neighbors are a longstanding factor in international resentment of the United States and in anti-American terrorism. Nothing is in train to change this. The Israel-Palestine issue is overshadowed at present by the dramatic events in Egypt, Syria, and elsewhere, but it remains a Pandora's box whose lid could blow off at any time.

The ongoing bloodbath in Syria is even more troubling and potentially at least as consequential. The use of nerve gas in a suburb of Damascus resurrected horrifying memories of mass death among both Israelis and Iranians, but sarin is irrelevant to the outcome in Syria—unless it falls into fanatic hands and is used to perpetrate the genocide that some justly fear. Apprehension about what Syria's rebels and their jihadi allies might do with chemical weapons is one reason—the ill-considered U.S. "red line" is another—that the Assad government agreed to turn them over to international control for destruction. The removal of chemical weapons from Syria will not prevent genocide. It will just keep massacres up close and personal.

Since March 2011, perhaps 130,000 Syrians have died at the hands of other Syrians and their foreign allies. The dead include about 17,000 rebels, 36,000 government troops, and 20,000 militia members, informers, and other regime supporters. Over 50,000 civilians have died—almost one-fourth of them children or women.

The carnage in Syria is beside the point for those determined to wrest it from Iranian influence, sever Hezbollah's supply lines, and flank the pro-Iranian regime in Iraq. Inconclusive conflict serves the interests of both jihadis and those who fear a victory by them in Syria. Fear of genocide or intolerable oppression by religious totalitarians guarantees that the religious minorities associated with the Assad regime will fight to the death. So the fighting goes on as outside suppliers ensure that Syrians are ever-better equipped and trained to kill each other.

One-third of Syrians have been displaced by the fighting. They are seeking safety in the company of their own kind. There are now at least three distinct zones in Syria, each ruled by a different mix of ethnic or religious communities, flying its own flag or flags and fielding its own armed forces. Could the ongoing fragmentation of Syria lead to partition along confessional and ethnic lines and the dismemberment of neighboring states like Lebanon? It is looking more and more as though it could.

If the Syrian slaughter does end in partition, what might that mean for the five countries that border Syria and for their allies in the region and beyond it? Partition would suit the interests of some inside and outside Syria, while others would oppose it. It's not too soon to think about its implications. When the blood dries and the dead are buried, will there still be a Syria, a Lebanon, an Iraq, or a Jordan as we have known them? Ninety-seven years after its birth, the Middle East Mr. Sykes and M. Picot conceived seems to be disintegrating. Outside powers created that Middle East. Indigenous forces are now tearing it apart.

Many aspects of the fighting in Syria remind us that the Middle East is where disregard of the United Nations Charter and Security Council resolutions and aggressive contempt by the strong for the sovereignty of weaker nations first became routine. It is where "might" again came to impersonate "right." It is the region in which the justifications for pernicious doctrines like preemptive attack and assaults on civilian populations in the name of counterterrorism were first elaborated. Intervening in a sovereign foreign state to overthrow its government is as much an act of war as attempting to conquer it. It used to be that, in deference to international law, those who engaged in such intervention did so on a basis that was plausibly deniable. In the Middle East no one now bothers to conceal attacks on states and societies through air and commando raids, official kidnappings and assassinations, arms deliveries, intelligence support, training, cyber-operations, or support for terrorist groups.

The Middle East has thus become a region where international law is routinely rebuffed, subverted, or ignored. Many norms of civilized behavior have been done to death there. So it is a particularly pleasant surprise that the most recent use of chemical weapons in the Middle East has finally led to their effective outlawing by the international community.

The Russian-brokered agreement to gather up and destroy Syria's chemical arsenal is a major step toward establishing an international norm banning the possession as well as the use of chemical weapons. Perhaps not incidentally, Russia has also given the world a stake in the integrity of the Assad regime's command and control of its forces. This is essential to prevent chemical weapons from being dispersed. But, beyond the danger of their use against Syria's beleaguered minorities, the disposition of chemical weapons has no bearing on the issues of concern to most Syrians or to others in the region. It does not shift the balance of power on the battlefield in Syria. It does not offer any hope of halting the continuing slaughter of civilians there.

If Russia has demonstrated the ability of sophisticated diplomats to seize opportunities to solve problems—even if they are peripheral problems about which few in the region care—it has also shown that resolving one problem almost always brings us to another. Syria built its chemical weapons to deter Israel's use of nuclear weapons. The orderly destruction of Syria's chemical stockpiles shifts the spotlight to Israel, which is now one of only two states in the world to threaten its neighbors with all three kinds of weapons of mass destruction (WMD): chemical, biological, and nuclear. (The other is the far less formidable but more vociferously aggressive Democratic People's Republic of Korea.) The issues presented by Israeli WMD can no longer be excluded from discussions of regional security.

This brings me to Iran. Iran is a resentful country that scares all but one of its Arab neighbors, as well as Israel. Ironically, however, despite the Israeli- and Gulf Arab–led campaign against Iran's effort to build the capacity to field a nuclear deterrent, Iran currently possesses no weapons of mass destruction: neither nuclear nor chemical nor biological. Iran's development of a deliverable nuclear weapon would cost Israel its nuclear monopoly in the region. It would very likely provoke other countries, like Saudi Arabia, to acquire their own deterrent capabilities through arrangements with one or more of the world's nine de facto nuclear-weapons states.

In practice, the choices for such extended deterrence arrangements come down to America, India, Israel, Pakistan, or Russia, with Pakistan the least problematic. Britain and France have neither the will nor the way to extend a nuclear umbrella. China is not interested in such foreign entanglements. Until it makes peace with the Palestinians, Israel will remain unacceptable as an overt partner and security guarantor for any Arab or Muslim country. Most Arabs see India as anti-Muslim but, in many ways, closer to Iran than to them. In Syria, Moscow has gone out of its way to show that its friends can depend on it, but it has yet to gain the trust of other Arabs. Recent events, including but not limited to the several changes of regime in Egypt, have convinced many that the United States is an unreliable protector. Pakistan has the weapons, the will, and the financial desperation to fill the need.

If it is not hard to see how Iranian nuclear weapons could be balanced and deterred by Israel and Pakistan, it is far more difficult to see how a stabilizing conventional balance of power in the Gulf region might be restored. Iraq is now aligned with Iran and no longer available to balance it. Arabs nervously recall that Iran, not Saudi Arabia and Egypt, was once the principal American security partner in the region. An end to hostile relations between Washington and Tehran remains unlikely but is no longer unthinkable. Suspicious minds in the Gulf imagine that a reduction in tensions between the United States and Iran might lead in time to renewed security cooperation between the two countries. This possibility, however remote, poses a major strategic dilemma for our Arab partners in the Gulf. As Egypt and the Gulf Arabs ratchet back their expectations and their reliance on America, to whom will they look for support?

The simple world of colonial and superpower rivalries is long vanished. The notion that one is either "with us or against us" has lost all resonance in the modern Middle East. No government in the region is prepared now to entrust its future to foreigners, still less to a single foreign power, so the role of great external powers is becoming variable, complex, dynamic, and asymmetric rather than comprehensive, exclusive, static, or uniform. There is room for new as well as old players, but all will dance to tunes composed in the region, not in their own capitals or those of other outside powers.

It is in this context that we must anticipate some expansion of Russian influence in the Middle East. Russia is on the other side of the Caspian Sea from Iran. If it can be persuaded to do so, Russia can balance and constrain Iran from the north without a footprint in the Gulf. It has a history of close relations with the armed forces in Egypt, Syria, and some other Arab countries. If the United States or other Western powers deny arms sales or suspend deliveries, Russia has the capacity to provide Arab armed forces with weapons and training. When the interests of the oil-rich GCC countries are at odds with those of Western powers, as they now appear to be in Egypt, Russia is a potential alternative partner. Gulf Arab credits or grants to Russian arms suppliers can offset Western weapons delivery or aid suspensions.

In this limited respect, China is also becoming a potential alternative to the West, as Turkey's recent purchase of a Chinese air defense system underscores. Old monopolies of influence and market dominance are giving way to a more competitive environment in the Middle East. In U.S.-Arab relations, much less can be taken for granted than before.

There is also a contest of ideas under way in the Middle East. Tolerance is almost everywhere in retreat. Passionate divisions favor extremism and the continuation of conflict. Drone warfare has helped anti-American terrorism to metastasize throughout the realm of Islam. Al-Qaeda and others of like mind are gaining ground. They spread by exploiting turmoil and popular resentment of worsening political, economic, and social problems. The use of force can't resolve these problems, but there are no obvious political solutions to them either, and expectations of progress are low. In the Middle East, diplomacy has come to serve mainly as camouflage for aggression, not as the antidote to it.

Given continuing regional and domestic disorder, could the totalitarian Islamist vision of al-Qaeda expand beyond the tiny minority of Muslims who now embrace it? Islamism and democracy have become increasingly identified. How can moderate forms of Islamist populism be prevented from degenerating into extremism and entrenching xenophobic dogmatism in places like Egypt and Palestine?

This is a problem for the West, which favors democracy but is disturbed by Islamism. Is the interest in stability of the United States and its allies consistent with the revolutionary idea of democracy? To put it that way is to shift the question from the realm of ideology to that of statecraft. So which is it? The domestic tranquility and regional stability imposed by autocracy, or the unrest and volatility that accompany democracy? These are issues that pose an even bigger challenge to countries in the region—and not just those with mass-based Islamist movements. Political Islam is a special threat to regimes that derive their legitimacy from piety but reject electoral politics in favor of *shura* and other traditional governmental practices.

The violent suppression of the Muslim Brotherhood and its radical offshoots risks creating conditions conducive to the long-term spread of instability, revolutionary Islamism, and terrorism. If Islamists who win elections cannot form governments or retain power till the next election, what is their alternative to violent politics? No one can hope to govern a country like Egypt for very long without a workable plan to reverse the deterioration of its economy and its investment climate. But neither those now in power nor their Islamist opponents have coherent economic philosophies or cures for the socioeconomic miseries of the Arab world beyond the oil-rich Gulf.

Economic desperation creates environments in which people can conclude that they have nothing to lose from self-destructive violence. Subventions from Gulf Arab countries are neither a short- nor a long-term solution to Arab poverty. Intelligent policies foster development; subsidies offset the absence of such policies. They underwrite underdevelopment, induce complacency, and facilitate dependency and sloth. The era when the countries of the Middle East could expect to depend on handouts from foreign aid agencies is coming to an end. The region has seized control of its own politics. It must now take responsibility for its economics.

What, then, is to be done by those of us outside the Middle East?

I think we must begin by acknowledging that we have lost intellectual command and practical control of the many situations unfolding there. The relationships we now have with regional actors are no longer the reliable ties of *wasta*, in which friendship and mutual regard compel mutual assistance. Our relationships, sadly in my view, are now mainly transactional, with each side weighing requests from the other in terms of what's in it for itself, not how it might best honor the norms of interdependence. If we are not responsive to the interests of our partners in the region, they will neither respect our interests nor avoid contradicting them. We need to listen more and prescribe less.

We must acknowledge the reality that we no longer have or can expect to have the clout we once did in the region. The practical implication of this is that we must cooperate with others—strategic competitors as well as countries with whom we are allied in other contexts—in order to serve our regional partners' interests as well as our own. The United States remains the most powerful external actor in the Middle East, but American primacy has been slain by the new assertiveness of the region's inhabitants. If we give others space to displace us, they will.

We need to rediscover diplomacy. By this I mean something radically contrary to our recent militarism and the related concept of "coercive diplomacy" through sanctions. Both assume that human beings are motivated only by threats and that their response to a credible threat will be a rational weighing of costs and benefits followed by capitulation. There is no evidence for either proposition—and a great deal of experience suggests that both are pernicious superstitions. Americans do not employ this approach to managing our own personal relationships; we should not assume it will work with foreign countries.

Diplomacy, like the successful management of interpersonal ties, lies in replacing our tendency to define problems as zero-sum with frameworks that promote the recognition of common interests. It presupposes empathetic, if reserved, understanding of adverse points of view. It incentivizes good behavior. It avoids vocal denial of the legitimacy of the other side's interests. It relies on convincing the other side that its objectives can best be achieved by doing things our way, and that it's in its own interest to change its policies and practices to do so. We seem have forgotten how to do diplomacy in this sense. At least, it's been a long time since we tried it in the Middle East.

We need to listen to our partners in the region and pay due regard to their interests. We cannot, for example, deal with Iran as though Israel is the only regional party at interest and the only one whose opinions we heed. What we do with Iran will have a profound effect on countries like Saudi Arabia, the UAE, Qatar, and Bahrain. It will affect our relations with Kuwait, Lebanon, Iraq, and Turkey as well as Syria. If we do not weigh the interests of our friends appropriately as we form our policies, they will respond with equal indifference to ours.

Most of all, we cannot afford to assume that the future will resemble the past in the Middle East. Whatever it looks like, it will certainly differ from what we have seen over the past century. We no longer have automatic partners in the region. Neither Israel nor our Arab friends trust us or are willing to defer to us. We will have to try harder to tend our relationships with them if we are to convince them to work with us toward common ends and not to suffer further estrangement from them. We owe it not just to our friends in the region but to ourselves to make the effort to acknowledge the multiple transitions now in progress and to work together to cope with them wisely.

The Middle East and China
February 17, 2015[6]

The Middle East is where Africa, Asia, and Europe come together and where the trade routes between China, India, and Europe converge. It has two-thirds of the world's energy reserves. It is also the epicenter of this planet's increasing religious strife. Relationships between this strategically crucial region and the rest of the world are now undergoing a sea change. I have been asked to speak to you about China's likely reactions and role in the region as this occurs.

By the Middle East, China means the mainly Arab- and Persian-inhabited areas of West Asia and North Africa. The collapse of the post-colonial order there has coincided with China's return to wealth and power. We in the West often include Central Asia in the Middle East. China does not. The Chinese see the post-Soviet state of affairs in Central Asia—in the mainly Turkic-speaking Muslim nations between China, Russia, and Europe—as developing satisfactorily within the framework of the Shanghai Cooperation Organisation (SCO). They are nowhere near as sanguine about their ability to manage trends and events in the Middle East.

Before I discuss the dilemmas Beijing confronts there, let me spend a few minutes talking about how the Middle East got to be the zone of intolerance and strife much of it is today. I'll then turn to China's current strategy—or rather the apparent lack of one. I'll wind up by briefly assessing the probability of more active Chinese engagement in the region, including the prospects for Sino-American cooperation or rivalry there.

Most historians date the modern Middle East to July 1, 1798. That was when Napoleon landed in Alexandria, proclaimed Egypt to have been liberated, and launched the first foreign effort to impose Western-style government on an Arab people. His well-intentioned but culturally insensitive actions—including repurposing some mosques as cafés—soon provoked a revolt by the devoutly Muslim citizens of Cairo. The French army put down that revolt and defeated the Ottoman forces arrayed against them. The ease with which French troops did this provided the world's Muslims with an impressive demonstration of the increasing superiority of Western military technology and organization.

---

6. Remarks to a Conference of the United States Institute of Peace and Georgetown University, Washington, D.C.

Napoleon's year in Egypt and Palestine set off a two-century Western rampage through the Middle East that subjugated its peoples and systematically subverted their traditional values, imposed unwanted states and borders on them, developed and extracted enormous profit from their energy resources, deposed and appointed their governments, sold avalanches of military hardware to their armed forces, and killed and displaced millions of them. The Middle East had produced a lot of human history. In the nineteenth and twentieth centuries, it was a passive and impotent object of contention between imperial powers and causes largely foreign to it.

The Islamic Revolution of 1979 in Iran and the Arab uprisings of 2011 mark the end of this epoch of passivity and victimization on the part of the core nations of the Muslim *umma*. *Dar al-Islam's* humiliated peoples *are now retaking control of their destiny. They are doing so amidst a wide*spread view that incumbent regimes are unjust, lack legitimacy, and remain in power only because they enjoy the protection of foreign, mainly Western—that is, American—patrons.

This simultaneously antiestablishment and barely concealed anti-Western sentiment could be heard on the streets of Cairo in 2011, when protesters chanted, "The people want the downfall of the regime." The same mentality is visible today in majorities in parts of the Arab region who condemn the meticulously provocative atrocities of the so-called "Islamic State" or Da'esh but take quiet pleasure in the Western outrage they evoke. Many in the region had earlier seen the assault on New York and Washington by a small gang of aggrieved fanatics on September 11, 2001, as not just blowback but payback—the beginning of iterative reprisal for past Western interventions and injuries. Subsequent events have reinforced rather than reduced the sympathy of many Muslims for what they view as justifiable counterattacks and counterhumiliations of the West that prove that Islam is no longer impotent.

The states established by European invaders were originally configured and their borders drawn to facilitate colonial policies of divide and rule. Colonial regimes were succeeded by autocracies that continued to govern on this basis. The recent overthrow of these autocracies has created a state of nature in which religious and ethnic communities, families, and individuals have been able to feel secure only when they are armed and have the drop on each other. Where foreign-supported regime change has occurred, violent politics, partition, and ethno-religious cleansing have almost everywhere succeeded unjust but tranquil order.

The anarchy brought to the Levant by the American removal of the Sunni-dominated secular regime in Baghdad in 2003 and the attempted removal of a similarly Shiite-managed secular government in Damascus since 2011 have kindled an ever-widening religious conflagration in the Islamic heartlands. Borders established in the colonial era no longer confine sectarian conflict. The region's rage has begun to spill far beyond it. Allegiances formed in the Cold War between states in the region and foreign patrons are meanwhile attenuating.

What happens in the Middle East is now decided in the Middle East. External forces can no longer intervene with impunity there. Developments in the Middle East no longer stay there. They affect nations and regions far beyond the region. China is no exception.

China's relations with the Middle East are ancient, but more distant and less obsessively linked to religion than those of the West. In 138 BCE, China's Han Dynasty dispatched emissaries to establish economic and political relations with it. This Chinese initiative inaugurated the so-called "Silk Road," which for more than a millennium linked China by land to Persia even as a parallel maritime route connected China to the Arabs.

Islam had already reached China by 651 CE, when the newly established Tang Dynasty received the ambassador of Caliph Uthman ibn Affan. Today there are at least 3,500 Qur'anic schools, nine Islamic universities, and about 45,000 mosques in China. Official statistics count about 25 million active Muslims in China, but much evidence suggests that the number of Chinese who consider themselves Muslim is much larger. Most are not members of ethnic minorities, though ten of China's fifty-five officially recognized ethnic groups are predominantly Muslim.

In the early fifteenth century, the Ming Dynasty admiral Zheng He reaffirmed China's ties to the Middle East as well as his own. Admiral Zheng was a nominal Muslim and the great-great-great-grandson of the Persian governor of Yunnan under the multinational Yuan Dynasty established by the Mongols. But China soon abandoned this outreach, and the arrival of seaborne European imperialists then severed communication between it and West Asia. This communication and links between Chinese and Arab Muslims are now being restored.

China's recent proposals for a new Silk Road, backed by a $40 billion infrastructure investment fund, evoke memories of its ancient trade and cultural connections to the Middle East and regions farther west. After the European Union (EU), China is the region's biggest trading partner. There is no question about the centrality of the Middle East to China's energy-related geopolitical calculations. The region already supplies half of China's oil imports, or about 30 percent of its domestic oil consumption. China is the largest foreign investor in Iraq's oil production. Qatar is China's biggest source of imported gas. (Turkmenistan is second.) Iran is a large potential source of gas as well as oil. China's energy imports from the region could well double over the coming decade and a half.

All three major Chinese oil companies gained significant access to oil in Iraq after the American WMD snipe hunt and failed hit-and-run democratization attempt there. Still, China remains cautious about the Middle East even as an energy source. West Asia and North Africa have received much less Chinese investment than their energy resources would justify. The relatively low level of Chinese commitment is, in part, a reflection of the fact that national oil companies like Saudi Aramco (from which China buys a fifth of all the oil it imports) have no need of foreign partners and offer them no significant openings to invest, except in refineries dedicated to importing their oil. Africa and South America have proven both more hospitable and easier for Chinese companies to understand. But China's attention deficit when it comes to the Middle East also reflects misgivings about the region.

Chinese society has traditionally inclined toward religious skepticism—that is, agnosticism tempered by cheerful tolerance of popular superstition. There is something inherently alarming to Chinese about a region where politics center on contests of religion and degrees of religiosity. Then, too, today's Middle East is not just politically volatile, it is a zone of frequent war. Israel periodically bombs and strafes its neighbors. The United States conducts vast, politically inconclusive interventions. Arabs and Persians engage in rivalry that mixes religious zealotry with geopolitics. Bearded men with guns kidnap and murder each other for perplexing reasons. Some people want the downfall of some regimes. Like the Balkans in the run-up to World War I, the states of the region manipulate and seek to enlist the support of outside powers against each other.

There is, of course, much more to the Middle East than this caricature, but what most Chinese know about it is more off-putting than enticing. They view the region with the same blurry myopia that Americans apply to Latin America—imagining it as an undifferentiated mass rather than the tapestry of distinctive societies it is. Unlike many Western expatriates there, Chinese are for the most part new and still personally uncommitted to careers in the Middle East. China seems for the most part to be following generic, rather than region-specific, policies there.

The Chinese cabinet—the State Council—has issued white papers on many foreign-policy issues and regions. It has offered no such guidance on relations with the Middle East. Beijing has belatedly begun a strategic dialogue and is discussing a free-trade agreement with the GCC, but it has not established a "strategic partnership" with any country or grouping of countries in the Middle East, as it has in every other region of the globe. Aside from access to energy and the sale of goods and engineering services, China has yet to define its strategic interests or intentions in the Middle East. There are, no doubt, many reasons for this.

Shortly after the establishment of the People's Republic, China proclaimed its adherence to "five principles of peaceful coexistence" that it crafted with India. The new doctrine stipulated that relations between states should be conducted on the basis of "mutual respect for each other's territorial integrity and sovereignty, mutual non-aggression, mutual non-interference in each other's internal affairs, equality and cooperation for mutual benefit, and peaceful coexistence." The five principles were an effective repudiation of the hegemonic tributary system by which China had traditionally conducted its foreign relations and a detailed affirmation and embrace of the Westphalian order that is the foundation of the United Nations Charter.

The People's Republic has since become one of the world's most committed advocates of the sovereign equality of states, their immunity from foreign dictation or intervention in their domestic affairs, and their right to their own ideology, regardless of what foreigners may think of it. China is now often criticized by Western bureaucrats and politicians for its insistence that business is business, politics is politics, and the two should not be mixed. By marked contrast, those doing business with China seem to find its apolitical approach to trade and investment both reassuring and refreshingly undomineering.

In the Middle East, it has suited both the Chinese temperament and China's national interests to stand on isolationist principles rather than develop a strategy. This has enabled China to avoid involvement in the region's uniquely turbulent and toxic politics. China has also avoided challenges to established powers—like the United States—that make periodic efforts to influence politico-military interactions there. For China, no rivalry means no spillover of differences about trends and events in the Middle East to relations with America or other great powers.

China's wary neutrality in the region's complex nationalist, religious, and geopolitical quarrels has frustrated the participants in these struggles. Beijing is happy to sell regional actors weapons or, in the case of Israel, buy military and internal security technology from them, but it has been completely unresponsive to efforts to enlist it as any party's patron. In recent years, the United States has developed an agenda in the Middle East independent of its traditional security partners there. Without exception, these partners now seek to dilute what they have come to regard as overdependence and overreliance on America. China, however, has not been willing to extend even implicit security guarantees to them, to offset their military dependence on the United States, Russia, or other great powers, or otherwise to compete for their allegiance.

Beijing has carefully dissociated itself from America's misadventures in Iraq, Libya, and Syria but has not exercised its veto to block Washington in the UN Security Council or otherwise tried to prevent what it has seen as U.S. miscalculations and misdeeds. China's aloof stance endears it to *no one in the Middle East*, still less Washington, but *its caution has so far* enabled it to avoid Islamist reprisal for offensive conduct abroad. It has yet to suffer externally directed terrorist acts of the sort that now ever more frequently disturb domestic tranquility in the West.

In both Africa and Central Asia, by contrast, China has policies of active engagement, clear strategies, and frameworks for implementing in them. In Africa, China is developing natural resources and markets for its goods and services. In doing so, it is acting much as the United States did in the post–World War II Middle East. In Central Asia, the SCO is not just a means of deconflicting China's and Russia's roles but also a guarantee and enforcement mechanism to counter Islamist politics and ethnic separatism in adjacent areas of China. The Uyghurs now fighting with Da'esh in Iraq and Syria—whatever their number—have leapfrogged the SCO's barriers to internationalize their anti-Chinese insurgency in Xinjiang and link it directly to the revolutionary theocracies of the Middle East. Religious affinities connect Chinese Muslims to the region. These bonds are becoming an avenue of religious and political contagion from the intensifying strife in the Arab world.

Da'esh's acquisition of a Uyghur component and constituency has led it to endorse armed jihad in China. For its part, China has pledged to aid the Iraqi government's fight against Da'esh "from the air." (Most likely this means arming Baghdad and Erbil with drones, a dual-use technology in which China is now a world leader.) This is a small but significant step toward military involvement in the politico-military affairs of a region far from the Chinese homeland.

Meanwhile, despite preemptive withdrawals, there are still many thousands of Chinese oil and construction company employees in Iraq to attract the malevolent interest of Da'esh. Chinese citizens working in current and potential conflict zones in the Middle East like Iraq, Egypt, Israel, Lebanon, Libya, Sudan, Syria, and Yemen, and their relatives back home, expect Beijing to look after them. Just so, a few years ago, Chinese shipping companies and their crewmen sought and eventually obtained action from the PLA Navy to protect them from piracy in the Gulf of Aden.

Clearly, there is mounting pressure from Chinese enterprises and individuals for China to take a more active role in the security of its companies' investments and the safety of their personnel in the Middle East. In the end, much as Beijing may wish to stick to economics, other elements of China's national power cannot remain totally unengaged. There are striking parallels with the way an infant United States was driven to develop power-projection capabilities in order to protect American citizens and shipping in the Barbary states of North Africa.

Still, there are clear limits to the potential for Chinese involvement in the Middle East outside the realm of commerce. China's interests in the region remain far narrower than our own. It has no allies anywhere whose economic or other interests it must defend on the battlefield or in international fora. It has no protectorates or client states in the region and pursues no ideological agenda there.

By contrast, the United States has unilaterally assumed responsibility for ensuring untrammeled access to Middle Eastern energy supplies to sustain the health of the global market economy. As a corollary, the U.S. Navy has undertaken to police the global commons to assure that merchant vessels of all nations can navigate to and from the region freely. This hegemonic role entails moral hazard. To the extent the United States is prepared to act to protect the interests of all the world's consumers of energy, other countries—like China—feel no need to develop the capability to do so or do anything at all to protect even their own interests.

Only when U.S. and other countries' efforts to protect Chinese interests prove inadequate—as happened with Somali piracy in the Gulf of Aden—does China move to project its own power to protect those interests. When it does this, the Somali precedent suggests, China will be prepared to recognize the parallel interests of others and coordinate its actions with them, but it will not put its forces under foreign command. Nor will it join a coalition outside the context of the United Nations (in whose peacekeeping operations the PLA has become a major participant).

As a country without entangling alliances, China has felt free to stand on principle in the UN Security Council. Beijing has cast a total of nine vetoes, all in support of noninterference in the internal affairs of member states. The four most recent such vetoes saw China join Russia in blocking calls to reorganize Syrian politics to facilitate the ouster of its government, to whose survival Russia, but not China, is bilaterally committed. By contrast, the United States has cast seventy-nine vetoes, forty-four of which were to prevent criticism of Israel or international interference in the Israel-Palestine problem.

So far China has managed to straddle the Israel-Palestine issue. It has supported both self-determination for the Palestinians and U.S.-led efforts to achieve acceptance for Israel as a legitimate part of the Middle East, but it has kept its own distance from these controversies. There is no reason to expect it will alter this stance anytime soon. As the international action on issues in the Holy Land migrates away from the United States to the international courts and Western consumer and investor boycotts, China will remain a bystander. It will try, as in the past, to maintain productive, if low-key, ties to Israel while remaining on untroubled terms with the Palestinians and their supporters. To the disappointment of both, it will not take sides.

How China will deal with the rising tide of Islamist terrorism is, however, an open question. Western counterterrorist operations have not just failed to contain Islamism and the extremist violence with which it is associated, they have helped it spread to many areas beyond the Middle East—in the Sahel, South Asia, Europe, Russia, and now China. A major unintended consequence of the "global war on terrorism" launched after 9/11 has been to institute or strengthen garrison states and to reverse earlier advances in both Muslim and Western societies toward expanded civil liberties and the rule of law. The spread of Islamist terrorism to China is now having the same illiberal consequences there.

Beijing has responded to terrorist attacks in Xinjiang by repressing Muslim religious practices. This Islamophobic overreaction increases the probability of escalating armed resistance by Uyghur and other Muslim minorities. It also risks a backlash against China from the fifty-seven member countries of the Organization of Islamic Cooperation and undercuts Beijing's efforts to cultivate good relations with them. The consequences of a bad image for China among Muslims extend well beyond the Middle East. Three-fifths of the world's Muslims live in China's own Indo-Pacific region. China's reputation among them has been much better than that of the United States. It is now worsening.

To sum up, China is not going to fix the mess in the Holy Land. Nor will it mediate between Saudi Arabia and Iran. It will not be a bridge between the Turks and Arabs. It will not conciliate Sunnis with Shia. It will neither help to impale America on its own mistakes in the Middle East nor take us off the hook there.

China is the champion and vindicator only of its own interests. It is determined to guard its independence while demonstrating respect for that of the states of the Middle East. It is neither a potential ally nor an enemy of any country there. It will not ally with one Middle Eastern country against another. In the Middle East, China's interests are limited to access to energy and markets, the safety of Chinese citizens who labor or do business there, and the avoidance of contagion from the region's religious wars. Barring direct challenges to these interests, Beijing is neither a potential rival nor a partner to Washington in the region. In the Middle East, China is a friend to all in a way that epitomizes the dispiriting insight of the late King Abdullah ibn Abdulaziz al-Saud, who said, "A friend who does not help you is no better than an enemy who does you no harm."

4

The Middle East and
U.S. Foreign Policy

Amerian foreign policy is everywhere adrift. Nowhere is this more evident than in the Middle East, where the military power of the United
States has never been greater. Yet American influence is foundering.
Almost every project Washington has undertaken—whether the achievement of peace in the Holy Land, regime change for the better in Iraq, Libya,
and Syria, the democratization of Arab societies, the elimination of Islamist
terrorism, or rapprochement with Iran—has faltered or failed or worse.

It would be easy to attribute America's loss of control over events in the
Middle East and elsewhere to the inability of the now notoriously dysfunctional U.S. government to marshal the will to apply more force in the region.
Many political activists in the United States make this charge. Some abroad
join them in it. But the lesson of U.S. military interventions in the Middle
East in the post–Cold War era is that there are a great many problems to
which the use of force is not an effective response. Diplomacy-free foreign policy does not work. The unique military prowess of the United States
does not make Americans omnipotent.

The inability of the United States to deal effectively with current events
abroad has a great deal to do with its failure to reconfigure its policies and
capabilities to deal with post–Cold War realities. Problems requiring political and economic solutions are proliferating. There are fewer predicaments
that can be solved by purely military means. Meanwhile, the globally coherent world order that American power organized itself to enforce after World
War II has disappeared. The world is in flux. America is not adapting to its
new circumstances.

In the Middle East, countries are no longer content to rely exclusively
on the United States for protection. Coalitions that would once have been

181

thought impossible are appearing. (As an example, consider the alliance of Russia with Hezbollah, Iran, the American-installed and supported pro-Iranian regime in Iraq, and the Syrian government against the so-called "Islamic State," which the United States is also seeking to crush.) Some argue that old enemies, like Iran, could become tomorrow's partners of the United States in the search for regional stability. Old friends, like Saudi Arabia and Israel, want to prevent this. Longstanding U.S. partnerships and patron-client relationships are wracked by mistrust and have lost their cordiality.

States formed within borders shaped by the Sykes-Picot Agreement of 1916 are disintegrating—to be replaced by what, nobody knows. International law is barely mentioned as multiple states openly fuel proxy wars in Syria directed at overthrowing its government and Israel conducts repeated massacres of Palestinian civilians with impunity. The region is convulsed by a broadening maelstrom of Islamist groups seeking revenge for Israeli and American interventions in Muslim societies. The most dangerous element of this phenomenon at present is a self-proclaimed "caliphate" of exceptional brutality. It now has more volunteers than it is able to induct and train for terrorist operations in Europe and America as well as the Middle East.

Finally, global energy security has been a major U.S. concern in the Middle East. But even this is changing. The United States has achieved strategic self-sufficiency of energy supply. American frackers and Saudi oilmen are currently engaged in a duel to determine which will be the swing producer in a future with more abundant oil and gas.

American policy has no answers to any of these trends and the perils they portend. They are challenges not just to American interests at home and abroad but to U.S. foreign-policy ingenuity, organization, and skill. The United States is not meeting these challenges. Geography, history, and geopolitics are coming together in new ways. In these globally amorphous and constantly shifting circumstances, it will not do to leave U.S. foreign policy on military-operated autopilot.

Paramountcy Lost:
Challenges for American Diplomacy in a Competitive World Order
August 29, 2012[1]

We've all heard that, according to the Mayan calendar, December this year will mark the end of a long historical cycle, bringing with it the end of the world as we have known it. Those of you in the audience who are worried about this know who you are. But, I wonder, how did the ancient Mayans so accurately forecast the budgetary apocalypse our Congresscritters have now crafted for us?

Let's be clear about the significance of the artificial "fiscal cliff" before us. It is a monument to a unique combination of political paralysis, fiscal dementia, and a compulsion to wage unaffordable and unwinnable wars. It symbolizes everything that the world now sees as wrong with our country. It also marks the addition of financial incapacity to the damage to American influence abroad that military blunders have already done.

The United States remains the world's only superpower, but the diffusion of wealth and power to regions beyond the North Atlantic has greatly reduced our military's ability to shape trends and events around the world. China, in particular, is emerging as an immovable military object, if not yet an irresistible military force. Our political influence, economic clout, and self-confidence are not what they used to be. The "sequester" and the political dysfunction that led us to it promise to weaken us still more. Major adjustments in U.S. policies and diplomacy are overdue.

Global governance was once mainly a vector of the struggle between the two superpowers and the blocs they led. After Moscow defaulted on the Cold War and dropped out of the contest for worldwide dominance, Americans briefly imagined that our matchless economic strength and unchallengeable military supremacy would enable us unilaterally to shape the world to our advantage. In the first decade of this century, however, the wizards of Wall Street brought down the global economy even as they discredited the so-called "Washington consensus" and emasculated the once-robust image of American capitalism.

Meanwhile, much of the world was disappointed by the lack of U.S. leadership on other issues, ranging from climate change to peace in the Middle East. People everywhere looked hopefully to worldwide institutions, like the United Nations, the G-20, the International Monetary Fund,

1. The American Foreign Service Association's Adair Memorial Lecture at the American University School of International Service, Washington, D.C.

and the World Trade Organization. None of them proved up to the job. Responsibility for the regulation of the planetary political economy began to devolve to its regions, if only by default.

The globally coherent worldwide order that American power configured itself to enforce after the Cold War is clearly morphing into something new. We can see the outlines of the new order, even if we cannot yet make out its details and don't know what to call it. The "post–Cold War era" is long past. The "American Century" ended eleven years ago, on 9/11. We are exiting the "age of antiterrorism." We are uncertain against whom we should deploy our incomparable military might or to what international purposes we should bend ourselves.

Call it what you will. This is an era of enemy-deprivation syndrome. There is no overarching contest to define our worldview. The international system is once again governed by multiple contentions and shifting strategic geometries. In such a world, diplomatic agility is as important as constancy of commitment—or more so.

Before the Cold War, the United States twice fought in coalition with Britain, France, Australia, Canada, and a few other countries, but we had no permanent alliances. The Soviet threat and the need to deal with the instabilities that attended the end of European empires in Asia and Africa led Americans to reverse our traditional aversion to foreign entanglements and to embrace them with a vengeance. The United States ultimately extended formal protection to about a fourth of the world's countries and informal protection to nearly another fourth. In our usage, the word "ally" lost its original sense of "accomplice" and came to mean "protectorate," not partner.

There have been huge changes in the global security environment since the collapse of our Soviet enemy, but there have been no adjustments at all in our alliance and defense commitments to foreign nations—other than their enlargement. The alliance structure we built in the Cold War has long outlived the foe it was created to counter. Remarkably, however, the preservation of our prestige at the head of that alliance structure seems to have become the principal objective of our foreign policy. Carrying on with approaches that address long-disappeared realities rather than adjusting to new circumstances is patently dysfunctional behavior. It represents the triumph of complacency and inertia over reason, statesmanship, and strategy.

With a few obvious exceptions like Israel, south Korea, and Saudi Arabia, the beneficiaries of our military protection do not agree that they face threats to their independence and prosperity that justify higher levels of defense spending. Our allies have been cutting, not increasing defense budgets. This has not, of course, stopped us from boosting our own military spending to the point that, depending on how you calculate it, it is somewhere between 87 percent and 120 percent as much as the rest of the world combined.

The power of the United States once spoke for itself. Americans expected automatic deference, but the new world order that is coming into being is multipolar, neither guided nor managed by the United States. Militarily powerful as we are and will remain, we cannot expect foreigners to follow our directives. We must instead help them see the need to do things in their own interest that happen also to be in ours. As Lester Pearson once put it, "Diplomacy is letting someone else have your own way."

Since they don't perceive much need for our protection, U.S. allies do not display much gratitude for it. They can't think why they should object to our spending money to relieve them of the burden of defending themselves against hypothetical or unknown threats. But—unlike the past—they also see no need to repay U.S. largesse by lining up behind us on issues in which their own interests are not directly engaged. Some might consider it astonishing that, for our part, we Americans haven't asked what specific interests of ours are still served by the alliance structure we built to deal with the late, unlamented USSR.

There are a lot of things wrong with a foreign policy that is mostly on mindless military autopilot. It deploys U.S. forces abroad to perpetuate our credibility as a superpower rather than to pursue well-defined politico-military or economic ends. It treats military spending as a perpetual industrial subsidy and ongoing fiscal stimulus rather than as a measured response to identifiable external threats. It drives diplomacy toward a futile effort to persuade allies to join us in disinvesting in the future by borrowing money to build military rather than civilian infrastructure and engaging in a constantly expanding list of wars of choice.

As we prepare to enter a still nameless new era, it's time for Americans to take a fresh look at the world. In this regard, the much-feared "sequester" could be a very good thing. It might compel us to rethink what is really necessary and to craft an affordable approach to national security as well as a foreign policy to implement it. Our present approach is neither affordable nor effective.

In a world where the United States no longer calls most of the shots and cannot hope to dominate every region of the globe, we must learn how to deal with other great powers on a basis of equality and mutual respect. China is the most obvious test of our ability to do so. In recent decades, it has been making a century of progress every fifteen years. It is now our economic competitor everywhere, if still a politico-military force only on its own East, Central, and South Asian peripheries.

Russia is again a regional, not a world, power. Its huge strategic arsenal simply demonstrates the irrelevance of nuclear weapons to anything but deterrence against the nuclear weapons of others. The European Union has made Europe a zone of peace, but it is an economic superpower that is too disorganized to act globally. Brazil may be *primus inter pares* in South America and India may reign supreme in South Asia, but both are in strategic regions disconnected from the global tensions that preoccupy Americans. By contrast, World War II showed us that the Indo-Pacific region was a coherent strategic zone from which hostile forces could marshal resources to project power globally, including to North America. (That same region was where the bloodiest proxy conflicts of the Cold War unfolded in Korea and Vietnam.) The strategic importance of the Indo-Pacific is hardwired into the American military consciousness.

China is now resuming its millennial place at the center of the Indo-Pacific region. Rather than exploring ways to peacefully accommodate this or bend it to our advantage, the United States seems determined to resist any diminution of our own role as the ultimate arbiter of regional security issues. As a result, we are being drawn into supporting claimants to islands, rocks, and reefs also claimed by China, but our capacity to dominate China's periphery has a limited half-life. Though China's defense burden remains low, its spending has been doubling every five years or so, apace with its civilian budget and economy. China is focused on defending itself in its own region, not on projecting power beyond it. Defense is cheaper than offense, which is what we specialize in.

It is not necessary to dominate a region to deter efforts by others to do so. We don't need to enjoy unchallengeable military superiority in Asia in order to enable our allies and friends there to learn to live with growing Chinese wealth and power, as we ourselves must do. Dominance of Asia is unaffordable. Even a less ambitious and more appropriate balancing role is going to be hugely expensive. We're talking about balancing the power of a country that is expected within forty years to have a GDP that's at least twice the size of ours. If we are determined for some reason to contest China's reassertion of influence in its own region, we had better have our economic act together.

Otto von Bismarck once commented that "God looks after fools, drunks, and the United States of America." I've always prayed that this was a valid religious revelation. But a belief in a special Providence for our country cannot excuse or offset the effects of self-destructive policies. We may not be in decline but we are clearly in denial. America is no longer setting the pace internationally.

It is pointless to blame others for this. Though our problems have sometimes been bound up in global supply chains, they have mostly been made in the U.S.A. by American politicians. The depression we're in was crafted by elected officials in Washington working with tax-pampered plutocrats on Wall Street. There's no denying that they did what they did with the mostly admiring endorsement of the American people.

America has shown uncommon resilience in the past. But there is no reason to believe that the structural predicaments now afflicting us will automatically correct themselves. We must change a wide range of policies and practices if we are to restore our traditional socioeconomic vigor and buoyancy. We need to do this for its own sake. But it's also the key to assuring ourselves the role in shaping the global future which our interests demand. Some aspects of our current condition are disheartening.

The United States was founded on a promise of equality of opportunity. Yet we now rank 100th out of the top 140 nations in income equality. Horatio Alger would be horrified to learn how much less social mobility there now is in America in comparison with much of Europe, not to mention China. Many here have come to doubt that hard work will pay off in financial and social success. But, then, it's now notoriously hard for Americans to find work at all.

John Maynard Keynes defined depression as "a chronic condition of subnormal activity for a considerable period without any marked tendency either towards recovery or towards collapse." We may not like the word "depression," but we're in one. The "unemployment rate" is going down largely because people are dropping out of the job market. Over the past five years, the labor participation rate—the percentage of our fellow citizens who are either employed or actively looking for work—has fallen to the point where there are now 100 million working-age Americans without jobs. There will be a lot more if our Congress does not rise to the challenges before it. Fiscal suicide will not cure the public policy problems Americans have made for ourselves.

The U.S. government is currently borrowing 25.9 percent of what it spends, an amount equivalent to 11 percent of GDP. Despite all this spending, our transportation and other infrastructure is decaying, the results of our educational system are ever more mediocre, our investment in science and engineering is going down, and our public health system, which costs more and delivers less for the money than any other in the world, is becoming an even costlier burden on our economy.

As other nations invest in competitiveness, we are disinvesting in it in favor of wasteful spending on hyperexpensive weaponry and insolvent welfare and pension programs. Our balance of trade and payments deficits are not being corrected. There is no prospect our budget will be balanced anytime soon. The only sector of our economy that is prospering is its bloated military-industrial complex. This cannot go on forever. So, sooner or later, it will end.

Technology has annihilated distance, linking people across the globe with unprecedented immediacy. As the Ghanaian diplomat Kojo Debrah put it, "Radio enables people to hear all evil, television enables them to see all evil, and the jet plane enables them to go out and do all evil." He might have added that the Internet enables them to tweet each other as they do it.

Businesses are no longer limited to national labor and capital markets. They locate their operations anywhere they want to maximize their profits. They hire where labor costs are lowest in relation to productivity and they borrow where rates are most favorable to their competitive participation in worldwide supply chains. Their executives may feel patriotism. Their business plans treat it as an advertising gimmick.

In this highly competitive environment, the advantage goes to those nations and regions that excel at the education of their workforces, the modernization of their infrastructure, and the crafting of intelligent industrial policies to empower entrepreneurial innovation and the exploitation of new technologies. The decisive factors in all these elements of competitiveness are the competence of a nation's politicians, the coherence of its policies, and the quality and timeliness of its decision-making. Now, more than ever, the domestic policies of societies determine the success or failure of their foreign interactions as well as their domestic conditions.

To restore American dynamism, we need a great deal more results-oriented reasoning on the part of our politicians than we've seen so far this century. Instead of railing at our foreign competitors, we should be learning from them. We have a tax code stitched together by a million special interests acting over the course of a century. This serves as our de facto industrial policy, directing investment and other business decisions in ways that subsidize vested interests and secure the status quo. Our tax system obstructs rather than facilitates economic restructuring to make our economy more productive, prosperous, and competitive. It's got to go.

It's been decades since the United States dominated global manufacturing or was the world's greatest creditor, not debtor, nation. And it's been a while since we drove the liberalization of trade and investment regimes at the global level. The Doha Round failed. There is no successor to it.

We can't afford to continue to base our trade and investment policies on assumptions drawn from circumstances that no longer exist. These policies badly need adjustment to promote innovation, ensure efficient infrastructure, improve the business climate, and raise the quality of the workforce. But many of the international trade agreements we're currently pursuing seem aimed less at leveraging foreign prosperity to our advantage, expanding our exports, attracting investment, repositioning our industry in regional markets, or increasing our competitiveness than at shoring up our ebbing standing abroad. We need to refocus our trade and investment policies on job creation.

For two centuries, North Atlantic societies set the pace of economic and technological advance and wrote the rules for the international system. Transatlantic solidarity enabled capitalism, liberal democratic values, the rule of law, and the idea of the nation-state to prevail over challenges from all the alternatives. The ideals of Atlantic civilization found expression in the universal acceptance of a rule-bound international system and institutions of global governance based on Western norms.

Sadly, this heritage is now slipping into the past or in danger of doing so. The North Atlantic is clearly being displaced by the Indo-Pacific as the global economic center of gravity. Most strikingly, Western societies no longer present compelling models that other nations and regions wish to emulate. Our democracy is increasingly equated with political venality, shortsightedness, indecision, and lack of strategic resolve, but the problem has been compounded by the foundering of the transatlantic consensus since 9/11. Our own divisions now cast doubt on the core values of Western civilization and their durability.

Europeans and Americans have come to disagree about an expanding array of issues bearing on the rights of the individual. These differences are passionate and fundamental. They include arguments about the propriety of "enhanced methods of interrogation" (otherwise known as torture), "extraordinary rendition" (meaning kidnapping and disappearance), the suspension of habeas corpus (in favor of indefinite detention without charge), the withholding of evidence from the accused, and the extrajudicial administration of capital punishment.

North Atlantic societies are still vastly more respectful of the dignity and rights of individuals than others, but the region as a whole no longer shares a coherent code of values with which to challenge the conscience of humanity. Lacking both consensus and conviction, its member states cannot effectively defend, let alone advance, the Western notion of the rule of law against competing ideologies derived from Islam or Confucianism. For the first time in centuries, non-Western values are coming to be seen as realistic alternatives to Western norms.

America's recent departures from the rule of law are in many ways the greatest menace our freedoms have ever faced. Our country faces no external existential threat comparable to that of the Cold War, yet we're building a garrison state that is eating away at our liberties in the name of saving them. Peace is the climate in which freedoms grow. We need an end to war in order to address the many threats to our ability to "secure the Blessings of Liberty to ourselves and our Posterity."

Americans believe that societies that respect the rule of law and rely upon democratic debate to make decisions are more prosperous, successful, and stable than those that do not. Recent efforts to impose our freedoms on others by force have reminded us that they can be spread only by our setting an example that others see as worthy of emulation. Freedom cannot be sustained if we ourselves violate its principles. This means that we must respect the right of others to make their own choices as long as these do not harm us. It also presupposes a contest of ideas. Our ideas will not prosper unless we maintain solidarity with others who value and also practice them.

That is why a first priority of American diplomacy must now be to re-forge the unity of the Atlantic community behind the concept of the rule of law. This cannot be done unless we confront and correct our own lapses from the great traditions of our republic. To re-empower our diplomacy by inspiring others to look to our leadership, we must restore our respect for our Bill of Rights as well as our deference to the dignity of the individual both at home and abroad. Let me be specific.

We must revive the Fourth Amendment's ban on searches and seizures of persons, houses, papers, and other personal effects without probable cause. No more "extraordinary rendition." No more universal electronic eavesdropping, warrantless seizure of paper and electronic records at the border, and intrusive inspection of anything and everything in the possession of passengers using public transportation.

We must reinstate the Fifth Amendment's protections against deprivation "of life, liberty, or property, without due process of law." No more suspension of habeas corpus or executive branch assertions of a right to detain or even kill people, including American citizens, without charge or trial.

We must return to respect for the Sixth Amendment's guarantee of the right of anyone accused of a crime to be informed of the charges and confronted with the witnesses against him and to be represented by a lawyer. No more "secret evidence."

We must reinstate the Eighth Amendment's prohibition of "cruel and unusual punishments," including torture, and we must reaffirm our adherence to the several Geneva Conventions. We Americans can have no credibility as advocates for human rights if we do not practice what we preach.

In short, the path to renewed effectiveness in American diplomacy lies not just in wise and dexterous statecraft and the professionalization of those who implement it abroad. It rests on the rebuilding of credibility through the rediscovery of the values that made our country great.

Nobody's Century:
The American Prospect in Post-Imperial Times
September 4, 2012[2]

In 1941, as the United States sat out the wars then raging in both the Atlantic and Pacific, Henry Luce argued that our destiny demanded that we, "the most powerful and vital nation in the world," step up to the international stage and assume the position of global leader. "The twentieth century must be to a significant degree an American century," he declared.

And so it proved to be, as America entered the war and led the world to victory over fascism, then created a new world order that promoted the rule of law and parliamentary institutions as the basis of global governance. Americans altered the human condition with a dazzling array of new technologies, fostered global opening and reform, contained and outlasted communism, and saw the apparent triumph of democratic ideals over their alternatives. But that era came to an end in 1989, with the fall of the Berlin Wall, the end of the Cold War, and the establishment of the United States as the only global power.

Americans then indulged in a dozen intercalary years of narcissistic confusion. We celebrated our unrivaled military power and proclaimed ourselves "the indispensable nation," but failed to define a coherent vision of a post–Cold War order or an inspiring role for our country within it. These essential tasks were deferred to the twenty-first century, which finally began eleven years ago, with the shock and awe of 9/11. In the panic and rage of that moment, we made the choices about our world role we had earlier declined to make.

Since 9/11, Americans have chosen to stake our domestic tranquility on our ability—under our commander-in-chief—to rule the world by *force of arms* rather than to lead, as we had in the past, by the force of our example or our arguments. We appear to have decided in the process that it is necessary to destroy our civil liberties in order to save them and that abandoning the checks and balances of our constitution will make us more secure. Meanwhile, our military-industrial complex and its flourishing antiterrorist sidekick have been working hard to invent a credible existential challenge to match that of the Cold War. This has produced constantly escalating spending on military and antiterrorist projects, but it has not overcome the reality that Americans now face no threat from

---

2. Remarks to the Twenty-Seventh Class of the Massachusetts Institute of Technology's Seminar XXI National Press Club, Washington, D.C.

abroad comparable to Nazi Germany, Imperial Japan, or the USSR. The only real menace to our freedoms is our own willingness to supplant the rule of law with ever more elements of a garrison state.

The so-called "global war on terror," or "militant Islam," as so many now openly describe it, has become an endless run in a military squirrel cage that is generating no light but a lot of future anti-American terrorism. It turns out that all that is required to be hated is to do hateful things. Ironically, as we "search abroad for monsters to destroy," we are creating them—transforming our foreign detractors into terrorists, multiplying their numbers, intensifying their militancy, and fortifying their hatred of us. The sons and brothers of those we have slain know where we are. They do not forget. No quarter is given in wars of religion. We are generating *the very menace that entered our imaginations on 9/11.*

On that day, the world felt our pain and stood with us. *Le Monde* famously proclaimed, "Nous sommes tous Américains!"[3] The world's solidarity with us reflected decades of goodwill for America, accumulated over the course of "the American century" that Henry Luce had foreseen. But does anyone here imagine that a second 9/11 would draw the same global reaction today? By surrendering the aspirations for a higher standard of behavior that once endeared us to the world, we have lost much of our international followership. We have thereby compromised our capacity to lead. To regain our influence, we must rediscover our values and return to the practice of them.

We remain the mightiest military power on the planet, but our multiple misadventures in West Asia have convincingly demonstrated the limitations of the use of force as a means to shape the world to our liking. We are engaged in proliferating wars of attrition with no war termination strategies in mind. Such wars kill and wound lots of people, do a lot of battle damage, and cost a lot. They produce no acceptable outcomes.

No one has been more outspoken about our national strategy deficit and the inadequacies of our diplomatic capabilities than our senior military leadership. This is to be expected. After all, as a nation, we look to our soldiers, sailors, airmen, and marines to repair the failures and deficiencies of our diplomacy. In recent times, we have asked them to double as diplomats where we've had none or too few to deploy.

By now it is widely accepted that our diplomatic establishment is understaffed, undertrained, overstretched, and generally inadequate for

3. Jean-Marie Colombani, "Nous sommes tous Américains," *Le Monde*, September 13, 2001, http://bit.ly/1mTkQjR.

twenty-first century missions. Twenty-eight percent of Foreign Service positions overseas are currently vacant or filled by officers serving above their grade. Former secretary of defense Bob Gates claimed that "the United States has more musicians in its military bands than it has diplomats." He was too tactful to point out that, if the State Department also had bands, they would in many cases be led by people without prior exposure to music. Alone among great powers, we retain the pre-modern habit of appointing many of our top diplomats through the spoils system rather than insisting upon rigorous training and proven experience in the field.

Auctioning off positions to the highest political bidder has never been a sound approach to staffing key national-security functions like diplomacy. As the *New York Herald-Tribune* put it in 1857, "Diplomacy is the sewer through which flows the scum and refuse of the political puddle. A man not fit to stay at home is just the man to send abroad." We didn't need much of a foreign policy back in 1857. We do now. No one would now allow campaign contributors to buy their way into military command. Diplomacy is skilled work that requires seasoned direction and execution. As our challenges mount, we will pay a rising price for a venal system that places affluent amateurs on point in one-third or more of our embassies abroad.

Lack of professionalism is, of course, far from the only shortcoming of our diplomacy. Underfunding is a big problem too. It will be an even bigger one if our national experiment with bungee jumping off a fiscal cliff doesn't work out, or if our politicians stick to the Evel Knievel school of budget planning they appear to have embraced. But the successful conduct of foreign affairs, like war, is less a matter of money and kit than of situational awareness, strategy, doctrine, professionally competent leadership, mentoring, training, and esprit. If we can no longer live entirely by our wallet or the brass knuckles on our fists, we must learn to live at least somewhat by our wits and charm.

It is said that when asked by allies for support, Athens would send an army, but Sparta would send a στραταγός, *strategos*—a strategist/general. We could learn from that. Intelligent judgment, experience, and shrewd calculation matter more than mass and enthusiasm. To move others, one must find their cognitive centers of gravity and push—or, better yet, pull. Coercion is never as reliable as persuasion. Nor is a forceful shove the only way to consign our enemies to perdition. As the witty American Caskie Stinnett once observed, "A diplomat is a person who can tell you to go to hell in such a way that you really look forward to the trip."[4] We need more people in government service who can do that.

It's even more important that we take a hard, new look at the emerging world order. This is not at all what we Americans expected as we waved the Soviet Union a joyous farewell. I am not speaking here of our recent antiterrorist obsessions or their origins. I am addressing something more fundamental and paradoxical—the deglobalization of politics and the emergence of self-regulating strategic zones, even as globalization continues. Globalization means that no country in a given zone is without the option of drawing on extraregional forces to buttress its freedom of maneuver. But regional powers increasingly treat such external forces— very often meaning the United States—as outsiders to be manipulated rather than as partners to be loyally served. Geography, history, and geopolitics are coming together in ways reminiscent of those before the age of Western dominance began five centuries ago. In these globally amorphous and constantly shifting circumstances, it will not do to leave our foreign policy on military-operated autopilot.

Organizations like NATO, various pan-European institutions, the Arab League, the Unión de Naciones Suramericanas, the African Union, and regional powers associated with them now lead efforts to address regional conflicts, like those in the former Yugoslavia, Libya, the Andean region and Central America, Sudan, and Syria. The UN and other global institutions have acted at the instance of such regional groupings, or not at all. Similarly, the global financial crisis brewed up by Wall Street's banksters did not stimulate effective reform proposals or coordinated responses from the G-20, the IMF, or anybody else at the global level. Rather, the affected parties and those seeking to escape being affected were left to cope more or less on their own or through regional initiatives. World Trade Organization–led negotiations to craft further liberalization of trade and investment have ended in gridlock. Responsibility for advancing economic prosperity has passed to a bewildering variety of bilateral and regional free-trade arrangements.

The United States is therefore finding ourselves compelled to replace global and functional approaches with regionally differentiated strategies focused on new and sometimes rapidly evolving subglobal realities. At their best, these are "grand strategies" that combine political, economic, cultural, informational, and military measures in a coherent effort to maximize our influence on outcomes. There is no longer an all-purpose

---

4. Freeman, *Diplomat's Dictionary*, 61.

enemy or any possibility of successfully imposing a "one-size-fits-all" policy on our relations with either our allies or competitors. Indeed, in the new world of the twenty-first century, our allies on some issues are our unscrupulous competitors on others. And vice versa.

Each region has inherited and is evolving its own power structure, which interacts with others even as it shapes decisions, events, and trends within its own sphere. In some regions, these power structures are dominated by a single subcontinent-sized country with comprehensive capabilities, like Russia in Eurasia or the United States in North America. Despite increasing challenges, giants like us face few constraints in our own regions.

In other cases, like those of India in South Asia or China in East Asia, regional preeminence is tempered by the existence of externally allied middle-ranking powers (like Pakistan or Japan). Such powers balance and constrain the regional giants' freedom of action in their immediate environs as well as globally. In still others, like Brazil in South America and, potentially, Indonesia in Southeast Asia, regional giants must enlist or neutralize other, smaller powers to able to realize their leadership potential both in their neighborhoods and in the world at large.

In Europe, Britain continues to leverage American power to its advantage, even if it is no longer prepared to play Tonto to our Lone Ranger. The confederal structure of the European Union allows former imperial powers like France and Germany—as well as rising nations like Poland—to aggregate the power of other Europeans to their own, enhancing their ability to play a leadership role at both the regional and global levels. For most purposes, they no longer need us.

It remains to be seen whether the Arab League will develop a similar pattern of global empowerment through the regional aggregation of power. Sub-Saharan Africa remains fractured into very many relatively small and weak countries that have so far proven incapable of effective collective action except on a very limited range of issues. Perhaps this will change as Africa's economies, which are now among the most dynamic in the world, build up its several potential middle-ranking powers.

The complexity and dynamism of the new order place a premium on diplomatic agility. Stolid constancy and loyalty to pre-existing alliance relationships are not the self-evident virtues they once were. We should not be surprised that erstwhile allies put their own interests ahead of ours and act accordingly. Where it is to our long-term advantage, we should do the same.

We need to rethink our commitments in light of our current interests as they are affected by a world order we no longer direct. We cannot afford to reject or defer adjusting these commitments out of fear that doing so might undermine our credibility. Over the course of the past decade and more, we have amply demonstrated our capacity for willful obstinacy. No one now doubts that we are prepared to persevere in failing policies for as long as it takes them to fail, but neither our allies nor our adversaries have been much impressed by our willingness to continue mindlessly to do things that neither serve our interests nor have any prospect of doing so. Reliable stupidity is still stupidity. Few admire it.

Judging by how things are going for us around the world, there is a lot for Americans to rethink. We have our work cut out for us!

In the new world order of regions, East Asia is once again the global center of economic gravity, as it was until the mid-nineteenth century. It is also increasingly Sinocentric. The factors driving this return to central-ity for China are mainly economic and political rather than military. We have nonetheless chosen to respond with a mainly *military* "pivot" that is transforming intrinsically trivial territorial disputes between China and its neighbors into broad U.S.-China strategic rivalry. The so-called pivot foretells a prolonged struggle by Americans to restrict China's influence in its own region.

To the delight of defense contractors, a major feature of our "pivot" is an arms race with China with a prefabricated procurement plan called "Air Sea Battle." To the distress of those in Asia who had hoped for American help in avoiding a fight with China while they made their peace with it, the "pivot" risks kindling a new Cold War. If so, this one will be a doozy.

American views of China often seem to have less to do with its re-alities than with the effects of enemy-deprivation syndrome on our na-tional strategic imagination. China is presented as a peer competitor compounded from past adversaries of the United States or as a sort of funhouse mirror-image of America as we rose to regional and then world power, combining putative aspirations for an Asian version of the Monroe Doctrine with an alleged lust for full-spectrum dominance of the global commons. This sort of misperception does wonders for defense budgets but provides a very poor basis for national strategy.

China presents many challenges to our interests but few of them are military. China is not the Soviet Union. It is not failing or isolated and cannot be "contained." Nor does it have an ideology aimed at global con-quest. Its military focus is self-defense in its own region. The defender has the advantage. So does the side with the short lines of communication. So does the contestant with the largest and most dynamic economy.

China's economy is projected to eclipse ours in a few years and to be more than twice as large by 2050. A Sino-American Cold War would thrust a fiscally fragile America already living beyond its military means into long-term contention with a country that has a relatively low defense burden, few budgetary constraints, and a graduation rate for scientists and engineers that is already ten times ours. No one in Asia wants to have to kowtow to China, but the United States would have few, if any, allies in any confrontation with it. No one wants to be caught in any kind of Sino-American crossfire. There has got to be a better way to secure our interests in the Indo-Pacific than by getting into yet another zero-sum competition with a great nuclear-armed power, this time one that will be able to out-spend us.

Our efforts to recruit India as an ally to counter China have come up against the reality that India, like the United States for most of our history, has a well-founded aversion to entangling alliances. It does not wish to subordinate itself to anyone else's strategic enthusiasms and is not prepared to be anyone's "protectorate." Our relationship with Pakistan has, meanwhile, resembled nothing so much as checking into the Hotel California with the Manson family.

In West Asia and North Africa, we have lost much of our political clout and most of our traction. Islamic populism is displacing the region's autocrats. Not surprisingly, leaders drawn from the Islamist tradition take a dim view of our so-called "war on militant Islam." The peace process we sponsored between Israel and the Palestinians is dead, leaving behind it a funeral pyre that is waiting to be lit by extremists. We should not be surprised if there is an IED or two hidden in that pile of broken promises, waiting to explode.

Our intervention in Iraq installed a pro-Iranian government and set off a war of religion. Our pacification effort in Afghanistan is going no-where. The good news, such as it is in our relations with the Muslim world, is that we are once again cooperating with Saudi Arabia in sponsoring Islamist *mujahidin* to effect regime change, this time not in Afghanistan but in Syria.

We remain fundamentally estranged from Iran. There's no diplomat-ic process in play to address this or to harmonize Iranian behavior with international law. Israel has spent a year and a half trying to blackmail us politically into committing ourselves to an assault on Iran's nuclear facil-ities. Israel admits that it cannot carry out a militarily effective attack on

Iran on its own but insists that, unless we agree to do for it what it cannot do for itself, it will go ahead and attack Iran anyway, expecting to drag us into the fight.

The latest twist is a campaign by prominent Israeli politicians and their American flacks to persuade us to give Israel still more weapons to improve its ability to attack Iran. This, they say, is the price we must pay to persuade Israel to agree to delay a unilateral assault on Iran till after our elections. As an astute observer of this interaction has pointed out, this is a bit like a pyromaniac demanding more matches to distract himself from setting fire to his neighborhood.

The person who comes up with the solution to these interlocked problems in what Alfred Thayer Mahan first called "the Middle East" will win a valuable prize. First prize is not to be sent there. Second prize is not to have to fight Middle Easterners here.

Turning to more congenial regions, the Atlantic community is our ideological and geopolitical homeland. But we are now joined to Europe as much by mutual annoyance as by common values. Even before our European allies got into financial trouble, they were cutting their military spending, reducing their commitment to the "Western defense effort." They don't see a convincing external military threat, and we can't identify one either. We have nonetheless taken on the burden of coping with the indefinable menaces we fear. So much for realism; so much for burden sharing, some might say.

In this respect, our relations with Europe now remind me of the poem: "As I was going up the stair, I saw a man who wasn't there. He wasn't there again today. Oh, how I wish he'd go away!" There is enough wrong with this picture to justify a serious American effort to work with Europeans to fix it. We should begin by admitting that our previous complaints about Europe may not have been entirely sound.

I don't need to tell you that, despite a "reset," our relations with Russia are still on the fritz. There's an economic boom on in Africa, where Chinese, Indian, and Brazilian companies have begun to make a lot of money. Americans are not making out so well, but the good news, I guess, is that AFRICOM finally has something to do. U.S. forces are now engaged in an expanding range of combat operations in sub-Saharan Africa. This is part of our growing alignment with the political status quo against "militant Islam" and against attempts at ethnic self-determination that would disturb the borders established by European colonial powers a century and more ago.

Meanwhile, South America has successfully decoupled itself strategically from the United States. After centuries of torpor, it is now among the most dynamic of the world's major regions, but we still have no strategy for drawing on its rising prosperity and power to buttress our own.

As I said, there's a lot in our foreign policy to rethink.

Beyond the policy review, we also need to conduct a fundamental re-examination of diplomatic doctrine. We've fallen into some pretty counterproductive foreign-policy practices. I'd like to cite one particularly pertinent example before closing.

In 1919, Woodrow Wilson proclaimed his faith in sanctions. Dean Acheson later called them a "persistent and mischievous superstition in the conduct of foreign affairs."[5] Wilson declared, "A nation that is boycotted is a nation that is in sight of surrender. Apply this economic, peaceful, silent, deadly remedy and there will be no need for force."[6] A century of experience shows that Wilson was spouting pernicious nonsense. Acheson was right.

Sanctions only work when they are tied to a negotiation. Negotiations only succeed when they are built around a proposition that can get to "yes." But sanctions have come routinely to be used as an alternative to negotiation. They allow politicians to buy time by pretending to be doing something bold, but they always become an end in themselves, evaluated in terms of the pain they inflict, not the behavior modifications they fail to induce. In a world in which the United States no longer enjoys undisputed economic primacy, sanctions that do not have the legitimacy and universality of the UN's endorsement are both ineffectual and an invitation to others to make inroads in the markets Americans forgo.

Simply put, sanctions are diplomatic ineptitude and military cowardice tarted up as moral outrage. They are a poor and mostly counterproductive response to international discord and dispute. In practice, they are not an alternative to war so much as a prelude to war or an empty threat of it. They are also integral to a strange and counterproductive mentality that asserts that one should only bargain with those who have previously agreed to one's bargaining position. But diplomatic dialogue is not a favor to those with whom one speaks. Rather, it is a way to present one's case directly to them, to understand the interests that underlie the positions they

---

5. Quoted in Freeman, *Diplomat's Dictionary*, 340.
6. Woodrow Wilson, speech delivered in Indianapolis, IN, September 4, 1919, in *Addresses of President Wilson* (Washington, D.C.: U.S. Government Printing Office, 1919).

take, and to gather intelligence about their intentions. In diplomacy as in war, one should never lose contact with one's adversary.

So I hope you're all in touch with your representatives in Congress.

The "American century" is now behind us. As a country, we have fallen pretty low. We are in an unacknowledged depression. Our politics are paralyzing and our fiscal situation is dire. Our longstanding grand strategy of containment succeeded—and thereby became irrelevant. We've failed to adjust to the new world this remarkable success created or to develop an effective strategy to deal with it. The lack of situational awareness can have serious consequences, as 9/11 should have shown us. Technology is now such that anyone we bomb anywhere in the world can find a way to bomb us back.

Yet I am optimistic about the United States of America. We have an overwhelming set of strengths going for us. We just need to get our policies right.

Our geostrategic location is unmatched. We are protected from most of the world by two great oceans to our east and west. Our neighbors to our north and south have no history of aggression against us. The only foreign threats to us are those that either envy or our own behavior provoke.

We have inherited a disproportionate endowment of the world's arable land, water, and mineral resources. We have a remarkably diverse population of 310 million, with a huge array of talent—anyone who watched the London Olympics will have seen that amply on display. As foreigners who have invested here can attest, amid all our diversity, we are united by being a diligent and productive people. Thanks to new technologies that exploit oil and gas in shale, we are once again about to become a major gas and petrochemical exporter.

We have a political system that, until we started cutting constitutional corners and allowing invective to rule our airways, gave us the freest and politically most appealing society on the planet. We may now be less free but, for now, we still have the world's most powerful economy. There is nothing—other than our own lack of resolve—to stop us from reviving the constitutional and cultural sources of our strength and prosperity.

Our once superior educational system and physical infrastructure were the products of sound fiscal practices and farsighted government policies. The steady deterioration in both as well as in our business climate reflects policies that are shortsighted, dogmatic, and disastrous. We used to learn from foreign best practices, not insist that we had all the answers. We have shown in the past that we can recognize our mistakes, correct them, and move on. There is no reason we cannot do these things once again. We can foster educational excellence, transportation efficiency, affordable public health, and cutting-edge business expansion, if we devote the resources and develop the policies to do so.

There are a lot of smart people in this country. We are blessed with a spirit of patriotism. Some Americans—though, frankly, too few—are also imbued with the ideology of public service. I think I see such people before me tonight. It is not unreasonable to believe that you can reimagine the United States of America and a foreign policy to serve our interests in our new circumstances.

May the Force be with you as you do this!

Obama's Foreign Policy and the Future of the Middle East
July 21, 2014[7]

A while back, the United States set out to reconfigure the Middle East. The result is that the region and our position in it are both in shambles. Much of what has happened seems irreversible. In the short time allotted to me, I want to talk about the region's dynamics. I will conclude with a few thoughts about what might be done but probably won't be.

To begin, if we are at all honest, we must admit that the deplorable state of affairs in the Middle East—in Egypt, Iraq, Israel, Jordan, Lebanon, Palestine, Syria, Iran, the Persian Gulf and Arabian Peninsula, and, peripherally, Afghanistan—is a product not only of the dynamics of the region but also of a lapse in our capacity to think and act strategically. We have answered the end of the bipolar order that characterized the Cold War with a mixture of denial, strategic incoherence, and inconstancy. False American assumptions and unrealistic U.S. objectives have helped create the current mess in the Middle East.

It is not news to anyone that American politics is uncivil and dysfunctional. We have a foreign-policy elite that has its head up its media bubble, prefers narratives to evidence-based analysis, confuses sanctions and military posturing with diplomacy, and imagines that the best way to deal with hateful foreigners is to use airborne robots to kill them, their friends, and their families. We have leaders who can't lead and a legislative branch that can't legislate. In short, we have a government that can't make relevant decisions, fund their implementation, enlist allies to support them, or see them through. Until we get our act together at home, those looking for American leadership abroad will be disappointed.

At West Point, President Obama accurately pointed out that "our military has no peer." He sensibly added that "U.S. military action cannot be the only—or even primary—component of our leadership in every instance. Just because we have the best hammer does not mean that every problem is a nail."[8]

True enough. Experience has amply justified hesitancy about the use of force. Our hammer blows in the Middle East were intended to showcase our power. Instead they convincingly demonstrated its limitations. These

---

7. Presentation to a Middle East Policy Council Capitol Hill Conference, Washington, D.C.
8. Barack Obama, speech delivered at the United States Military Academy Commencement Ceremony, West Point, NY, May 28, 2014, http://1.usa.gov/1Jk58G5.

interventions worsened—not improved—the region's stability, politics, and prospects. Our unmatched military prowess has not enabled us to impose our will in West Asia, in Eastern Europe, or elsewhere. The record of covert action for solving political problems in all of these regions has been no better.

The question, then, is, what alternatives to the military hammer and related kinetic instruments of statecraft does the U.S. presidency now have? Normally, the answer would be the political screwdriver of diplomacy or other nonpercussive means of influence, like subsidies and subventions. But there is a reason the Department of State is the smallest and weakest executive department of our government. The United States seldom resorts to diplomacy in resolving major differences with other states. Gladiators trump diplomats anytime in terms of the spectacle they provide. Even if they don't work, coercive measures like sanctions and bombing are much more immediately satisfying emotionally than the long slog of diplomacy.

Then, too, aside from our reflexive militarism, we are broke. Our military commanders have walking-around money. Our diplomats do not. And the amateurism inherent in the spoils system further reduces the effectiveness of our diplomacy.

Secretaries of state conducting jet-propelled seat-of-the-pants drop-by visits with foreign leaders have proven to be no substitute for either strategy or the patient cultivation of influence with those leaders or in their capitals. It's hard to think of any American project in the Middle East that is not now at or near a dead end. This includes our policies toward Israel and Palestine, democracy promotion, Egypt, Islamist terrorism, stability in the Fertile Crescent and the Levant, Iran, and the Gulf. Let me run very briefly through that list.

In April, our four-decade effort to broker a secure and accepted place for a Jewish state in the Middle East sputtered to a disgraceful end. In the tragicomic final phase of the so-called "peace process," instead of mediating, the United States negotiated with Israel about the terms of Palestinian capitulation, not with the Palestinians about self-determination. The U.S. effort to broker peace for Israel is now not just dead but so putrid it can't be shown at a wake. Israel didn't believe in it, so it killed it. May it rest in peace.

From the outset, Israel used the "peace process" as a distraction while it created facts on the ground in the form of illegal settlements. Israeli expansionism and related policies have now made Israel's peaceful coexistence with the Palestinians—and, thus, with Israel's Arab neighbors—impossible. The United States created the moral hazard that enabled Israel to put itself in this ultimately untenable position. Forty years of one-sided American diplomacy aimed at achieving regional and international acceptance for Israel have thus perversely produced the very opposite—increasing international isolation and opprobrium for the Jewish state.

We will now "cover Israel's back" at the United Nations as its ongoing maltreatment and intermittent muggings of its captive Arab population complete its international delegitimization and ostracism. We will pay a heavy political price for this stand globally, in the Middle East, and very likely in escalating terrorism against Americans abroad and at home. It may satisfy our sense of honor, but it more closely resembles assisted suicide than a strategy for the survival of Israel and our own position in the Middle East.

Americans like to have a moral foundation for policy. In the Middle East—and not just with respect to Israel—the geology has proven too complex to allow one. Take our professed desire to promote democracy. In practice, the United States has made a real effort at democratizing only countries it has invaded—like Iraq and Afghanistan—or those it despises—like Palestine, Iran, and Syria. The rest we carp at but leave to their hereditary rulers, dictators, generals, and thugs. When democratic elections yield governments to which we or our allies object—as in Algeria, Palestine, and Egypt—Washington contrives their overthrow and replacement by congenial despots. If democracy is the message, America is not now its prophet.

Our willingness to rid the region of troublesome democrats has appeased Israel and the Gulf Arab states, but it has greatly tarnished our claim to seriousness about our values. It has produced no democracies. It has pulled down several before they could institutionalize themselves.

Egypt is a case in point. After raising hopes of a democratic Arab awakening and electing an Islamist government that proved to be incompetent, Egypt is now an economically sinking military dictatorship, distinguished from other tyrannies only by the grotesque parodies of the rule of law it stages. There is not much we can do about this.

U.S. concerns about Israel's security dictate support for Egypt, regardless of the character of its government or how it put itself in power. America's Gulf Arab partners are committed to military dictatorship and suppression of Islamism in Egypt. It is hard to think of a place where there is a starker contradiction between American ideals, commitments to client states, and interests in precluding the spread of terrorism than in contemporary Egypt.

It's tempting to conclude that, if we're going to be hardheaded realists, we should just skip the off-putting hypocrisy about democracy and human rights and get on with it. That seems to be what we intend. How else is one to interpret the president's proposal for multiple partnerships with the region's security forces to repress Islamist terrorism? Today's Egypt is the outstanding example of regional cooperation in such repression. We have no other model to build on.

By leaving no outlet for peaceful dissent, Egypt is forcing at least part of its pious majority toward violent politics. This risks transforming the most populous of all Arab countries into the world's biggest and most deadly breeding ground for Islamist terrorists with global reach. It's true, of course, that Egypt is not the only incubator for such enemies of America.

Americans went abroad in search of monsters to destroy. We found them and bred more. Some have already followed us home. Others are no doubt on their way. That's why we have an expanding garrison state. Our counterterrorism programs are everywhere nurturing a passion for revenge against the United States.

We gave a big boost to the spread of Islamist terrorism when we invaded Iraq. Our stated purpose was to deny weapons of mass destruction that didn't exist to terrorists who weren't there. Having removed functioning government from Iraq, we thought we might as well engage in hit-and-run democratization of the place, so we replaced a secular dictatorship with a sectarian despotism. Not only did that not work, it set off a religious war that ultimately gave birth to the Jihadistan that now straddles the Syria-Iraq border.

What we did in Iraq has resulted in its breaking into three pieces. Now, in practice, we're working on dismembering the rest of the Levant. Israel is gnawing away at what remains of Palestine. A transnational coalition of jihadis is vivisecting Syria and Iraq. With our help, Syria is burning, charring Lebanon and scorching Jordan as it does. The Kurds are making their escape from the existing state structures.

The Syrian government is loathsome but we fear that, if—as we wish—it is defeated, it could be replaced by even more frightful people. Bombing can't prevent this, so in a triumph of magical militarism we propose instead to arm a force of mythical Syrian moderates. We expect this latest "coalition of the billing" to fight both the Syrian government and its most effective opponents, while nobly refraining from making common cause with the latter or transferring weapons to them. Sounds like a plan for pacifying Capitol Hill, if not Syria. If our objective is to keep Syria in flames, it's a plausible plan.

Perhaps that is what we really want. After all, the anarchy in Syria is a drain on Iran, which we have identified as our main enemy in the region. Destabilizing Syria arguably adds to the pressure on Iran to give up the nuclear weapons program that Israel's and our intelligence agencies keep telling us it doesn't have and that Iran's leaders have said they don't want because it would be sinful. Our frequent threats to bomb Iran seem to be a devilishly clever test of its leaders' moral integrity. If we give them every reason we can think of for them to build a nuclear deterrent, will they still not do it? Judging from our sudden decision to extend the deadline for a deal with Iran, this experiment will go on for at least four more months.

This brings me to a key point of policy difficulty. We've repeatedly told people in the Middle East that they must be either with us or against us, but they remain annoyingly unreliable about this.

Iran's ayatollahs are against us in Syria, Lebanon, and Bahrain but with us in Afghanistan and Iraq. The Assad regime and Hezbollah oppose us in Syria and Lebanon but are on our side in Iraq. The Salafi jihadis are with us in Syria but against us in Iraq and elsewhere. Israel's government is with us on Iran but against us in blocking self-determination for Palestinians while favoring it for Kurds. Saudi Arabia is with us on Iran and Syria but against us in Iraq. It was for us and then against us before it was for us in Egypt. It's against the Jihadistan in the Fertile Crescent, but nobody can figure out where it stands on Salafi jihadis in other places.

How can you have a coherent strategy to manage the Middle East when people there are so damnably inconsistent? The answer is that outsiders can't manage the Middle East and shouldn't try. It's time to let the countries in the region accept responsibility for what they do rather than freeing them to behave irresponsibly.

It's time to recognize that the United States can't solve the Israel-Palestine issue, can no longer protect Israel from the international legal and political consequences of its morally deviant behavior, and has nothing to gain and a great deal to lose by continuing to be identified with that behavior. Israel makes its own decisions without regard to American interests, values, or advice. It would make better decisions if it were not shielded from their consequences or had to pay for them itself. America should cut the umbilical cord and let Israel be Israel.

It's time to stop pretending the United States assigns any real importance to democracy, the rule of law, or human rights in the Middle East. We pay for gross violations of all three by Israel, support their negation in Egypt, and do not interfere in the politics of illiberal monarchies like Bahrain, Saudi Arabia, and the United Arab Emirates. Clearly, U.S. policy is almost entirely about interests, not values.

If that's the case, let's not violate our laws by dishonestly claiming that there have been no misuses of American weaponry by Israel and no coups, judicial horrors, or severe human rights violations in Egypt. We should not have laws that require us to be scofflaws. If the real interests of the United States in Syria relate to Iran and its contests with Israel and Saudi Arabia as well as to our new cold war with Russia, let's admit that and behave accordingly. This would mean axing the farcical format of the Geneva conference on Syria. That excluded key parties, making it a public relations stunt, not a serious effort to bring peace. Only if we include all the parties engaged in proxy wars in Syria, including Iran, can we hope to end the mass murder there.

It's time to do that for more than humanitarian reasons, compelling as those are. Ending the fighting in both Syria and Iraq is the key both to containing Jihadistan and to halting the further violent disintegration of the region. We should not be upping the ante in Syria by pumping in more weapons (many of which are likely to end up in jihadi hands). We should be trying to organize an end to external involvement in the fighting there and focusing on preventing the emergence of an expanding terrorist bastion in the Fertile Crescent and Levant that will serve as a homeland for the growing legions of enraged Muslims our drone warfare rallies to the black flag of Islamism.

The Jihadistan calling itself "the Islamic State" is a menace to both Iran and Saudi Arabia. Distasteful as they might find it to work with each other, they have a common interest to discover. The new "state" was born of geopolitical and religious rivalry between Riyadh and Tehran and can only be contained by their cooperation. Depending on how US-Iran relations develop, America might be able to help them do this. But, if the United States and Iran remain enemies, the obvious alternative for the United States would be to accept the inevitability of an expanded, Salafi-dominated state that will replace much of the political geography in the region, to work with Saudi Arabia to tame extremist tendencies within such a state, and to yoke it to a regional coalition to balance Iran, as the Iraq that U.S. intervention destroyed once did.

Any and all of these approaches would demand a level of diplomatic imagination and skill the United States has not shown in recent days. The more likely outcome of our current blend of baffled hesitancy, diplomatic ineptitude, and militarism is, therefore, that events will take their course. That means the growth of a credible existential threat to Israel, a prospective political explosion in Egypt, the disintegration of Iraq, Jordan, Lebanon, and Syria along with Palestine, and the diversion of a considerable part of the resources of these countries to terrorism in the region and against the American homeland. We can and should do better than this.

The Geopolitics of the Iran Nuclear Negotiations
September 29, 2014[9]

L ast July, negotiators from the Islamic Republic of Iran and the "P5+1" (China, France, Germany, Russia, the United Kingdom, and the United States) failed to reach a final agreement trading restrictions on Iran's development of its nuclear industry for sanctions relief. Having missed their deadline, they extended it, giving themselves until November 24 to agree. On September 19, they picked up the negotiations where they had left off, but made little progress.

The P5+1 and Iranian negotiators are meeting amid rapidly evolving international and regional circumstances. Whether they succeed or fail, their discussions will have an impact on much more than just nuclear proliferation in the Middle East. They will affect the geopolitics of that region, relations between the world's greatest powers, and the emerging multipolar world order.

Despite international anxieties about Iran's nuclear weapons program, the program itself remains a conjecture and allegation rather than an established fact. The world's most highly regarded intelligence agencies affirm only that *some Iranians* were doing *some work* on nuclear weapons until 2003, when the Islamic Republic ended this. The official worry is now that Iran's mastery of the full nuclear fuel cycle and its development of missiles will give it "nuclear latency"—the future capacity to weaponize nuclear materials on short notice. The intelligence agency consensus is that the Tehran has not made a decision to do this. Still, the seldom-rebutted popular narrative is that Iran is going all out to build a bomb. Even those who reject this narrative do not trust Iran *not* to make a decision to acquire nuclear weapons in future. This distrust is deep-rooted. It will not be easy to overcome. It is also not without its ironies.

Iran's supreme authorities have proclaimed that nuclear and other weapons of mass destruction are forbidden by Islam. They say that Iran is morally barred from building the bomb. Iran's history makes it hard to dismiss this declaration out of hand. After all, despite an estimated 100,000 deaths from Iraqi nerve-gas attacks, it was on this basis that Tehran declined to develop its own chemical-weapons capability during the Iran-Iraq war.

---

9. Washington, D.C.

The only threats to Iran from countries wielding weapons of mass destruction now come from those most agitated about Iran's possible acquisition of them—Israel, the United States, and (to a lesser extent) France and neighboring Russia—all of which have nuclear arsenals and a record of assaulting Muslim states. It is logical that Iran should want a nuclear deterrent to bar attack by such nuclear-armed enemies. Powerful interest groups and politicians in Israel, Saudi Arabia, France, and the United States assign more weight to this logic than to the findings of their own intelligence agencies. Israelis recall that they ran their own clandestine nuclear weapons program decades ago amid constant denials that they had such a program. Israel's government doubts that Iran is any more truthful about its nuclear programs and their objectives than Israel was.

Holocaust-inculcated paranoia disposes the Jewish state to treat the Iranian nuclear issue as a zero-sum game. The Netanyahu government opposes Iran's retention of any nuclear industry at all. It has repeatedly threatened to attack Iran to destroy its nuclear facilities.

Like its Gulf Arab neighbors, Iran plans increasingly to rely on nuclear energy for electric power, freeing fossil fuels for profitable export. Given past US-led efforts to shut off its access to nuclear fuel and materials, Iran insists on its own control of the nuclear fuel cycle. The P5+1 objective is to persuade Iran to cut its nuclear activities to the smallest possible scale and the lowest possible level of enrichment over the longest period of time to which Iran will agree.

Israel's views have decisive influence in Washington and substantial impact in Berlin, London, Paris, and Moscow. As a practical matter, if the talks produce agreement, it cannot be ratified by the United States or carried out by the U.S. and most other negotiating parties unless the Obama administration convincingly answers, obviates, rebuts, or rejects Israel's objections, which are sure to be forcefully advocated by its claque in the U.S. Congress. In the absence of a deal, Iran will continue to develop its nuclear sector without effective international constraint.

A breakdown in the negotiations or an agreement that falls apart due to opposition from Israel's American partisans would see Congress seek to ratchet up sanctions against Iran. Israel would be forced to decide whether to mount a unilateral attack on Iran or suffer a loss of credibility as its repeated threats to do so were revealed to be a bluff. Iran would have to choose between its professed aversion to weapons of mass destruction and its need to deter attack by Israel or the United States. Those Iranians, including President Rouhani and his government, who had gambled on doing a deal with the United States would be politically humiliated and discredited. Iran might follow north Korea in withdrawing from the Non-Proliferation Treaty. The role of international law in nonproliferation efforts would suffer a debilitating setback. The prospects for the proliferation of nuclear weapons in the Middle East would be greatly enhanced. The struggle to craft a strategy to deal with the spreading phenomenon of Islamist extremism, including the so-called "Islamic State" (IS) now straddling the Iraq-Syria border, would be further complicated.

Another extension of the negotiating deadline would lack credibility and—to one degree or another—entail some of the same negative consequences as a failure to close a deal or to implement one. There is a lot at stake in the current negotiations. Recent international trends and developments are both adding to their complexity and magnifying the consequences of their outcome.

Over the past year, relations among the P5+1 and the situation in the region have both changed substantially. Tensions between the EU, US, and Russia have become acute. Iran is less isolated internationally. Israel's influence in France, Germany, and the United Kingdom has weakened. The rise of IS and the drawdown of Western forces in Afghanistan have made cooperation with Iran on regional issues more attractive. Meanwhile, U.S. dollar hegemony has begun visibly to erode. The net effect of these changes has been to create new diplomatic options and opportunities for future sanctions avoidance by Iran.

As a result of the Ukraine crisis, Washington and Moscow are now barely on speaking terms. Berlin, London, and Paris have cut back engagement with the Putin government. Russia has moved to embrace China as an alternative to Europe. China, for its part, has been eager to secure its inner Asian rear. (A good relationship with Russia strengthens China's ability to fend off what it sees as a rising threat from the United States in the Western Pacific.) These developments have greatly lessened Western influence in Moscow and reduced Russian interest in deferring to Western policies when its own interests in the Middle East and elsewhere suggest a different course.

In August, Russia reportedly agreed to buy an initial 500,000 barrels of Iranian oil for resale on world markets, including China, with an option for twice as much. This directly undercut Western sanctions restricting Iran's oil trade. (Most sanctions on Iran have been imposed by the West without Security Council authorization, depriving them of binding force under international law. In the absence of UN legitimation of sanctions, China has been importing about 675,000 barrels of Iranian oil a day. India imports almost 300,000.) In the short term, the reported Russian deal reveals a damaging split in the political solidarity of the P5+1. It reduces financial pressure on Iran. In the longer term, it raises questions about the viability of current—let alone future—sanctions against Iran.

Most Europeans want a deal with Iran that reduces the prospects for Iranian development or deployment of nuclear weapons as well as follow-on proliferation in West Asia and North Africa. The EU has little appetite for more sanctions against Iran. Moreover, the limited sanctions relief of the interim agreement of November 24, 2013, predictably awakened interest in the Iranian market. European companies have been especially active in seeking sales and investment opportunities, stealing a march on their more cautious and presumably less favored American competitors. (Asian companies have all along been active in Iran.)

European interest in trade and investment in Iran is all the greater because the EU now seeks more than ever to reduce its energy dependence on Russia. European interest in achieving closure in the nuclear talks with Iran has risen. Meanwhile, distaste for Israel's domestic and regional policies has grown considerably in Europe but much less so in the United States. In this atmosphere, an Israeli effort to block or sabotage agreement with Iran would potentially split the P5+1 along yet another axis.

Recent gains by Sunni extremists in Iraq and Syria have served to underscore Iran's strategic influence in the Fertile Crescent, strengthening incentives for Western rapprochement with it. So far, deference to Gulf Arab animus toward both Iran and its Shiite clients in the region has prevented the United States and other leading (mostly Christian!) participants in the newly formed anti-IS coalition from active exploration of overt cooperation with Iran. Much has been made of the bravery of the Kurdish *peshmerga*, but the Shiite coalition of the Iranian, Iraqi, and Syrian governments and Hezbollah has been and remains the main force arrayed against IS on the ground.

In practice, Iran has the same enemies in the region as the West, if not the same friends. Unlike the Gulf Arabs, Iran has no ideological contradiction arising from a requirement to appease Sunni extremists at home or to oppose democracy in places like Egypt or Bahrain. Awkward as Western cooperation with Iran may be in terms of relations with the Arabs of the Gulf, the arguments for it are likely to seem increasingly compelling as the struggle against Sunni extremists in the region takes its predictably difficult course. Iran is about to be admitted to the Shanghai Cooperation Organisation. The need for Iranian and SCO actions to counter the Sunni extremist Taliban in post-NATO Afghanistan can only strengthen the case for cooperation with Iran. Such cooperation is incompatible with anything other than a relaxation of sanctions.

In the absence of consensus in the UN Security Council, most sanctions against Iran rely upon the fact that the dollar is not just the global medium of trade settlement and benchmark for currency exchange but also the U.S. national currency. Sovereignty over the dollar has allowed the United States to prohibit Iranian transactions in it and currencies linked to it, effectively excluding Iran from global trade and finance except as approved by Washington. But, as is always the case, the market distortions sanctions entail have created incentives to find ways to work around them. This means avoiding the use of the dollar in favor of gold, other currencies, or barter. The need to do this has been especially felt by countries like China, India, and Turkey, which need Iranian oil.

International transactions in the dollar and related currencies are facilitated by the Society for Worldwide Interbank Financial Telecommunication (SWIFT), from which the United States engineered the expulsion of Iranian banks in 2012. The U.S. resort to sanctions against Iran and other countries has inspired a variety of mechanisms designed to avoid not just the dollar but also SWIFT, whose databases enable the United States to monitor and punish transactions it has prohibited. Recent sanctions against Russia are spawning still greater creativity in this regard. This is reflected—*inter alia*—in recent initiatives by the BRICS group of countries to settle trade in their own currencies. The Chinese yuan, Hong Kong-Shanghai, and China's UnionPay seem now to be emerging as alternatives to the dollar, New York, and SWIFT in the conduct of interbank transactions supporting international trade.

The Indo-Pacific region's economies are already 1.5 times the size of either NAFTA or the EU and are growing more rapidly. The implications of this are clear. The era in which the United States and/or Europe can effectively sanction other countries without the support of the UN Security Council and the non-Western great powers excluded from it is drawing to a close. The opportunities for avoiding or undercutting sanctions available to countries like Iran are growing concomitantly with the redistribution of power in the global economy.

Iran has been seriously hurt by sanctions. But its pain—which, all too predictably, has not produced changes in its policy—is likely to diminish with time. Another round of Israeli-inspired, American-led tightening of sanctions will be difficult. Before long, it is likely to become impossible. If the current negotiations fail, there is every reason to believe both that Iran will be able to tough out the aftermath and that the straitjacket of sanctions that has constrained the Iranian economy will steadily loosen.

Iran's talks with the P5+1 have represented a gamble by Iranian moderates that improved relations with the West on terms respectful of Iranian sovereignty and national dignity are possible. A perceived Western rebuff of this thesis would severely undercut them. It would also sharpen the contradiction between Iran's professed moral principles and its military's perception that it needs a nuclear deterrent. Tehran might well respond by denouncing the NPT and ending international inspection of its nuclear facilities, as north Korea did. U.S.-Iranian reconciliation would likely be deferred for another generation or more.

Israel and the Gulf Arabs are disposed to welcome anything that delays or complicates Western rapprochement with Iran, which they judge is likely to come at their expense. Thus, they might initially welcome a failure by the P5+1 and Iran to reach agreement. But any such schadenfreude would be short-lived. The dashing of Iranian hopes for improved relations with the United States and European Union would seriously reduce prospects for the political compromises between Iran, its neighbors, and the West necessary to replace sectarian struggle and violent politics with stability in the Fertile Crescent. A definitive failure of Western efforts to broker less alarming nuclear policies in Iran would have the effect of exacerbating longstanding strategic antagonisms and increasing tensions in the Persian Gulf.

The lack of any internationally monitored cap on Iran's nuclear capabilities would be seen by its Arab neighbors as the removal of an essential external check on its imperial ambitions. In response, the several Gulf Arab states would likely carry out their oft-threatened preemptive acquisition of nuclear deterrents, whether imported or indigenous. (Once on the road to nuclear capability, they might also feel strong enough to pursue accommodation with Iran.) The Gulf Arab states would certainly insist on the right to their own nuclear enrichment, paralleling Iran's programs. Others beyond the Gulf, like Egypt and Turkey, might well feel compelled to follow suit with their own nuclear programs, leading to a spreading frenzy of nuclear proliferation. An unmanageably complex tangle of nuclear balances and doctrines would succeed Israel's current nuclear monopoly in a region notoriously prone to war.

By contrast, an agreement between Iran and the P5+1 that survived Israeli and Gulf Arab second-guessing could (and likely would) stall, if not preclude, further nuclear proliferation in the region. It could also catalyze progress toward Iranian rapprochement with the United States and other Western countries. Its regional impact would depend in part on whether it was judged as likely to prove effective in curbing Iran's presumed nuclear ambitions. If so, it could facilitate the regional accommodations necessary to restore stability in the Middle East and wider Muslim world. If not, it could trigger efforts by some Arab Gulf states to field their own nuclear deterrents before reconsidering how to coexist with the Islamic Republic.

One way or another, an agreement would produce a chance for all parties to discover common interests in combating and containing extremism, whether Sunni or Shiite in origin, and an opportunity for creative diplomacy to replace military contention with peaceful coexistence and competition. These opportunities might not be seized, of course, but they would not exist at all in the absence of a successful outcome to the current negotiations.

Saudi Arabia and the Oil Price Collapse
January 27, 2015[10]

Last June, oil sold at as much as $115 per barrel. Now it's between $45 and $50. That's a 60 percent collapse in price. There have been all sorts of speculation about why the Saudis let this happen and don't seem to want to do anything about it.

Elsewhere, I've expressed doubts about the wisdom of a number of Saudi Arabia's current foreign policies, but the Kingdom's approach to the oil market impresses me as intelligently calculated to serve its long-term economic interests, while yielding geopolitical benefits at no real political cost. Before I explain why I think this is so, bear with me as I briefly describe the market environment in which Saudi Arabia and other oil producers operate.

World demand for oil is now about 92 million barrels a day. Altogether, including Saudi Arabia, OPEC can supply about 40 percent of this demand. By itself, the Kingdom can meet about 13 to 14 percent of it. Saudi Arabia is the only oil producer that can ramp up output to fill an immediate supply shortfall. On pretty short notice, it can add a couple of million barrels a day—about 2 percent—to global oil supplies.

The Kingdom is also a very low-cost producer with reserves that will last for many decades. Many other OPEC members—like most non-OPEC countries—are high-cost producers whose costs per barrel are many times those in Saudi Arabia. Others are running out of oil.

Oil is a globally traded commodity. Its prices are determined partly by the current balance between supply and demand and partly by hopes and fears about future shifts in that balance. Estimates of trends in the balance between supply and demand by traders and guesses by speculators about future prices determine current prices of oil and other commodities. Speculators' expectations are often exaggerated and invite sharp corrections that create market volatility. In 2008 alone, oil prices were as high as $147 and as low as $47 per barrel.

In the relatively short term, *supply* can be affected by geopolitical events, like war and civil strife. Recent examples are what happened in Iraq and Libya as well as several times in Nigeria. Rough weather and labor unrest can prevent tankers from loading, leading to supply pinches, but the major factors determining whether supply can meet demand

10. Remarks to a Panel at the Center for the National Interest, Washington, D.C.

over the long term are investment in new exploration and production, new technologies for finding and extracting oil, and new ways of prolonging production in nearly depleted reservoirs.

Demand for energy is closely related to the rate of growth in the world economy and to seasonal factors. Natural disasters can have an impact on demand as well as supply. (For example, the Japanese tsunami forced a shut down in nuclear power in Japan and Germany and pushed both back into the fossil-fuels market.) In the long term, demand for oil is greatly affected by changes in technology that alter its costs of production, the efficiency with which it is used, and the availability of competitive alternatives to it.

If the companies that explore for oil and produce it think prices will stay high enough for them to make a significant profit, they will invest in finding and developing new oilfields or in prolonging output from existing fields. Efforts to find and produce oil from "conventional" sources may take nine years or more to begin to bring additional oil to market, if they succeed. After an initial, often massive amount of investment, investors then begin to get their money back. New infusions of capital are seldom necessary for many years. Once the original investment has been returned, it's all profit from then on in.

Fracking is different. The lag between discovery and production tends to be much shorter, but so is the time it takes to deplete fields—which must then be refracked to release new oil. The need to refrack on a regular basis means that, to keep production going, frackers, unlike conventional producers, must regularly inject large amounts of new capital into their companies. This makes them prisoners of their banks. They must not only repay current loans but constantly borrow new money.

For the past five years, prices and expectations about future prices have both been high. Interest rates, by contrast, have been very, very low. This situation encouraged a lot of investment projects, especially in unconventional sources of oil, like fracking and oil-sand development, some of which have been almost obscenely profitable at recent prices. In the United States, over the past four years, oil output rose by two-thirds, displacing imports and making an additional 5–6 million barrels per day available to markets abroad. Meanwhile, Iraq and Libya restored production to an aggregate total of about 4 million barrels a day.

Much of the world has been in recession since 2008. Demand for oil has continued to grow, but more slowly than supply and well below investor expectations. By late 2014, global oil supplies of about 93 million barrels a day exceeded demand by about 1 million barrels, or a bit more than 1 percent. Inventories of unsold oil were meanwhile growing rapidly.

To traders, the oversupply and growth in inventories signaled a clear trend toward lower future prices. Their apprehensions about an expanding oversupply of oil conspired to bring about a price collapse comparable to that in earlier speculative cycles.

Saudi Arabia is used to being blamed when prices seem too high. Now it's being blamed for prices being too low, but the Kingdom had nothing to do with either the increase in supply or the recession-induced decrease in demand for oil. Nor did it bring about the collapse in prices. Its position as the world's swing supplier gives it uncommon influence on expectations, but it cannot control prices. As Riyadh saw it, the rapidly falling prices for oil confronted it with some stark choices.

The Kingdom could lead OPEC in trying to reverse some or all of the drop in prices by curbing production to reduce supply, but shoring up prices would enable other producers to continue investing profitably in expanded production from shale and oil sands, as well as deep-sea drilling. It would therefore allow higher-cost producers to continue to gain long-term market share at Saudi and other OPEC members' expense. If OPEC members cut production, prices might rise somewhat but they would likely stabilize at levels that would still result in less revenue for the Kingdom and also slow, if not end, savings needed to fund the transition to an eventual post-petroleum Saudi economy. More damaging still, loss of future market share would cut the Kingdom's future revenue from oil as well as its global clout. Adding insult to injury, the main beneficiaries of an OPEC production cut and consequent stabilization of oil prices would be the Iranian and Russian governments and American and Chinese consumers, not Saudi Arabia or other Arab oil producers.

Alternatively, Saudi Arabia could do nothing, accepting the loss of significant current revenue but allowing prices to fall to levels at which its competitors could no longer produce profitably or invest with confidence in new capacity to meet future oil demand.

For Riyadh, this is a "no-brainer." It is clearly smarter to eliminate current and future competition and assure future market share than to help competitors remain profitable at the expense of Saudi and other Arab oil producers' patrimony and well-being in the decades to come. There are many reasons for this. I'll give you seven.

First, low prices don't hurt the Saudi national oil company, Saudi Aramco, much. The world's biggest oil company does not disclose its production costs, but estimates center around an average of $5 to $6 per barrel. In general, it appears to cost about $70 to produce a barrel of shale oil in the United States. (Some U.S. fracking is profitable at $40 per barrel, but some requires a price of $90 or more to break even.) Oil-sand-based production comes in at about $80 to $90 a barrel, plus transport, which can be expensive. Saudi Aramco and other Gulf Cooperation Council oil companies make a lot of money with oil at $50 a barrel. Many other producers can't turn a profit at that price.

Second, low oil prices halt investment by high-cost producers and inhibit any switch to energy sources other than oil. They affect not just fracking but deep-water drilling, Arctic exploration, expanded reliance on natural gas, and the development of alternatives to oil, including renewable energy sources (which have just become much less competitive than before). Lower oil prices also help force older, depleted fields out of production earlier, further reducing current and future supply. Major project investment will not go forward. Fracking and refracking will lose the access to bank loans they depend upon. All this sets the stage for a minor price rebound to $65 or so in a year or less—and a much bigger price rise a few years later. Better to maximize income over the long run than go for short-term revenue.

Third, the Kingdom's foreign-exchange reserves of about $900 billion are one-fifth larger than its GDP and almost four times its annual budget. Saudi Arabia can afford to take a revenue hit for a few years—long enough for others to be wrung out of the market.

Fourth, the countries most negatively affected by low prices are Saudi Arabia's enemies and competitors. The Kingdom cannot help but be pleased that low prices hurt the Assad regime's main backers, Russia and Iran, which depend heavily on revenue from oil exports. Saudi Arabia is not close to Venezuela. Nigeria has emerged as a competitor for the Chinese market. So what if these governments suffer? Meanwhile, low prices benefit American, Chinese, and Indian consumers and deepen their addiction to oil, ensuring a market for Saudi exports once prices return to high levels, as they will once demand again outstrips supply.

Fifth, cheap oil helps build markets in rising powers like China and India, where future energy demand is concentrated. (Asia already buys more than two-thirds of Saudi oil exports, while the Americas now take less than one-fifth.) The Kingdom is cultivating relations with Asian nations to dilute its dependence on the United States. Current prices help in this regard.

Sixth, both the prospect of several years of low prices and the timely reminder of market volatility that the price collapse has provided help discourage Chinese and Indian plans to develop domestic fracking and impede progress toward self-sufficiency of oil supply in the Kingdom's most promising markets.

Seventh, the effect of the price collapse has been to demonstrate that rumors of Saudi and OPEC irrelevance have been greatly exaggerated. The Kingdom's prestige has been enhanced.

In sum, the Kingdom's stance in OPEC and policies on oil pricing constrain future supply growth, inhibit the development of alternatives to oil, and preserve market share for it and other low-cost oil producers. Riyadh has reminded the world and the region of its power, demonstrated *its independence, and served its geopolitical interests. It can afford to stick* with its strategy and policies until investors in countries producing more expensive oil have been forced out of the market. In time, oil prices will rise, increasing the Kingdom's revenue stream. From the Saudi point of view, all this makes sense even without the geopolitical bonuses it brings. The new king, his crown prince, and the crown prince's heir apparent all participated in formulating the current policies. There is no reason to expect them to alter their calculus about what's in the Kingdom's interest anytime soon.

The U.S. and Saudi Arabia:
Marriage of Convenience on the Rocks?
March 11 and 12, 2015[11]

Saudi Arabia has done it again! On January 23, 2015, it dismayed foreign pundits by failing to sink into the anarchy they speculated might follow the death of its king, Abdullah. Instead, the Kingdom carried off yet another flawless passing of the leadership baton. What's more, the succession process indicated who the next two or three kings are likely to be, and the new king, Salman ibn Abdulaziz al-Saud, acted promptly and decisively to seize the reins of government and reorganize it.

This rightly attracted global attention. The world has a big stake in Saudi stability. Forget the cartoons about it! The Kingdom of Saudi Arabia is not a gas station full of oppressed, black-garbed women in the middle of a camel ranch. It is the heartland and focal point of Islam, the faith of at least one-in-four human beings alive today. It lies athwart transport routes between Asia, Europe, and Africa. The Kingdom is the custodian of a fourth or more of the world's oil reserves. Rumors that it is no longer relevant to oil markets have just been unambiguously refuted. (Ask any fracker in North Dakota about that!) Saudi Arabia is at the center of a growing concentration of global capital. Its puritanical religious doctrines inspire its—and our—most dangerous enemies.

In short, what happens in Saudi Arabia and between it and its neighbors matters greatly to Americans, American allies and friends, and American adversaries—but Saudi Arabia is little known, even less understood, and frequently caricatured. This is not surprising. The Kingdom is the only nation-state on the planet not to have been penetrated by Western colonialism. No European armies breached its borders, no missionaries, no merchants. Its capital, Riyadh, was long off limits to infidels; the holy cities of Mecca and Medina remain so today. It is said that hubris is the only reliably renewable resource of Western civilization, but when we Westerners finally came to Saudi Arabia, we came not as the vindicators of our presumed cultural superiority but as hired help.

As a result, some say that Saudis secretly see the world's peoples as divided into two basic categories: fellow Saudis and potential employees. Be that as it may, foreigners—Western, Asian, or Arab—who have lived in Saudi Arabia all see it as a very strange society—one that is not easy to

11. Remarks to the Sarasota Institute of Lifetime Learning and the Orlando Committee on Foreign Relations, Sarasota and Orlando, Florida

understand and that professes values at odds with those of non-Saudis. Some come to love it. Many don't.

The Kingdom has long stood apart from global norms. Its system of government draws on tribal and Islamic traditions rather than Western models. Its king *presides* rather than *rules* over the royal family and Saudi society. His responsibility is less to make decisions than to shape and proclaim consensus, while assuring a share of the national wealth to all, especially the least privileged.

Saudi Arabia levies no taxes on its citizens, other than the religious tithe on wealth known as *zakat*—a 2.5 percent annual donation of capital to charity and other public purposes. All Saudis enjoy free education and medical care from birth to death and can pursue these benefits at home or abroad, as they wish. The Kingdom has no elected parliament, though it does have elaborate informal mechanisms for consultation with its citizens on policy and personal matters. Saudi Arabia reverses and thereby affirms a basic principle of American political philosophy, "No representation without taxation." Most Saudis seem to like being on the payroll rather than the tax roll.

With rare exceptions, Saudis don't emigrate, though they go abroad in great numbers to study or vacation. The Saudi system may strike Americans as weird, but it clearly has the confidence of most Saudis. This is a reminder that legitimacy is derived from the consent of the governed, not from foreign opinion. Inveterate foreign muttering notwithstanding, the Kingdom is here to stay.

Saudi Arabia does not conform to European notions of monarchy, but it is not a democracy. The Saudi state is Islamist. Its constitution is the Holy Qur'an. Its basic legal framework is the Shariah—the Muslim code of religious law that parallels the Jewish Halakha. Saudis have never embraced the ideals of the eighteenth-century Atlantic Enlightenment and do not aspire to reorder their society along liberal lines. It would be difficult to imagine a society with values more different than those of the United States, yet U.S.-Saudi relations have been remarkably stable. The partnership between the two countries has been grounded in six areas of cooperation, reflecting vital interests that overlap. All of these, with the exception of the most recent—counterterrorism—have been seriously compromised by trends and events in this century.

King Salman has now inherited a very conservative country that his predecessor, King Abdullah, spent twenty years nudging toward greater religious tolerance, an expanded role for women in public life, increased integration with the global economy, and a more prominent role in both global and regional affairs. The Kingdom's tradition of successful top-down management of evolutionary change contrasts with the failure of revolutionary uprisings and coups d'état in its neighbors to engineer comparable progress. But Saudi Arabia's transformation remains both incomplete and animated by no clearly articulated vision. King Salman has promised continuity in policy. No one can yet say what that means, but Saudi Arabia now faces so many challenges abroad that it is likely to be extra cautious at home. The pace of reform may now slow. Saudi foreign policy may now be widening its focus.

The Kingdom has come to see itself as encircled by an ascendant Iran, the Gulf Arabs' traditional geopolitical rival which it is not powerful enough on its own to confront. An entirely counterproductive U.S. intervention in Iraq in 2003 ended Iraq's role in balancing Iran. By carelessly installing a pro-Iranian government in Baghdad, Washington greatly boosted Tehran's power at Riyadh's expense. Israel's 2006 maiming of Lebanon—which enjoyed enthusiastic U.S. support—then propelled Hezbollah, an Iranian ally and bitter enemy of Saudi Arabia, to the commanding heights of Lebanese politics.

The Arab uprisings of 2011 caused Saudi Arabia to doubt the value of relying on the United States. Saudi Arabia's most trusted regional partner, the Mubarak government in Egypt, was overthrown—to apparent American delight. Subsequent political instability and economic mismanagement then made Egypt a financial dependency of the Kingdom. The recent oil price collapse, while serving Riyadh's interests in other ways, has greatly reduced its revenue, raising serious questions about how long it can continue to subsidize Egypt.

Soon after the fall of Mubarak, mobs also toppled the government in neighboring Yemen and sought to oust the ruling family in Saudi Arabia's allied Kingdom of Bahrain. Yemen's capital has just been taken over by pro-Iranian Houthi tribal people. The country is sliding toward civil war. Iran continues to exploit the ongoing unrest by the Shiite majority in Bahrain, which threatens to spread to their kin in Saudi Arabia's oil-rich Eastern Province. Saudi and other Gulf Arab troops now garrison Bahrain, where no end to sectarian tensions is in sight.

When unrest came to Syria in the spring of 2011, King Abdullah's advisers thought that, with a little outside help, Syrians might be able to rid themselves of the Assad government and shift their country out of the Iranian orbit. Washington shared both Riyadh's loathing of Assad and this optimistic assessment, which turned out to be a tragic misreading of Syrian realities. With 225,000 dead and nine million Syrians displaced, Bashar al-Assad still rules in Damascus. Worse, Syria has become the incubator for a self-proclaimed "caliphate" ("Da'esh," to use the Arabic acronym for it), a renegade Muslim movement of truly satanic brutality that is at once an idea, a structure of governance, and an army.

Da'esh is the by-blow of the U.S. intervention in Iraq, raised to vicious maturity in Syria. It has already erased the Syrian-Iraqi border. It is determined to undo the legacy of colonialism in the Middle East, including the formation of the modern states of Iraq, Israel, Jordan, Lebanon, Palestine, and Syria, and to revenge past injuries to the world's Muslims at the hands of Western powers elsewhere. Da'esh wants to rule in Mecca and Medina. It now governs an area the size of Ireland with a population larger than Israel's or Jordan's. There may be more men in its armed forces than in Cuba's. It is attracting migrants, recruits, and statements of allegiance from all over the world.

At the outset, Riyadh saw Da'esh as a distastefully extremist but potentially useful instrument of armed opposition to Assad and Iran, but the Kingdom is now coming to view it as a rising threat to its interests, including its domestic tranquility. Under King Salman, Saudi policy seems to be evolving toward actively countering Da'esh as well as Iran. Part of this recalibration appears to involve a distancing of Saudi policy from Egypt's effort, under its latest military dictator, to crush the Muslim Brotherhood. Saudi Arabia may, like Qatar, now be coming to see the democratic Islamism of the Brotherhood as a potentially useful antidote to the violent Islamism of Da'esh.

It looks as though Riyadh may now be in the process of organizing a coalition with Ankara, Amman, Cairo, and Islamabad so as to be able to counter both Da'esh and Iran. This could change the regional balance and alter its political economy in important ways. With respect to Iran, Pakistan can provide a nuclear deterrent, Egypt can furnish military manpower, and Turkey has industrial strength. All three are producers of armaments as well as importers of them. Amman is on the frontline with Da'esh. Saudi money can help them cooperate or at least coordinate their policies to mutual advantage.

From an American perspective, such a coalition would be a mixed blessing. Certainly, Israel would not welcome it. But, if something like it came into being, there could at last be hope for an effective strategy that dealt with all three dimensions of the Da'esh phenomenon. Currently, there is a military campaign plan but no strategy. U.S. policy is especially unidimensional. We treat Da'esh as a bombing target, even though our military commanders all acknowledge that it is also an ideological and political problem that military means alone cannot address.

This is because we are no more credible or competent as commentators on Da'esh's connection to mainstream Islam than the Grand Mufti in Cairo would be to analyze the theological relationship between the Ku Klux Klan and Christianity. Only Muslims can deal authoritatively with theological issues and political strife within their religious community. There is no one more qualified to do this than Saudi Arabia.

The Saudis, like Da'esh, are Salafists—that is, adherents of the view that the revival or their faith requires reaffirmation of the way of the Salaf, the earliest Muslims, and the repudiation of subsequent innovations, superstitions, and corrupt practices. But the Saudis had their Salafi reformation in the eighteenth century. Salafism in the Kingdom is a conservative, stabilizing, if repressive, force. Beyond its borders, it is very often violent, reactionary, and disruptive in its effects.

Still, as the late King Abdullah showed, Saudi Arabia is uniquely positioned to counter negative aspects of Salafism and lead it in constructive directions. Salafi extremists argue that, to purify itself, Islam must return to its roots, an early Islam they portray as puritanical, xenophobic, intolerant, and oppressive of women. Under Abdullah, the Kingdom began to argue that this was incorrect. Early Islam was open-minded and receptive to Greek philosophy (which it preserved and later bequeathed to Europe, where it catalyzed the Renaissance). Its governments included Jews and Christian ministers. Its women were active in commerce and public life. It was a brilliant civilization at the center of scientific and technological advance.

This vision of the revival of Islam as a religion of peace, tolerance, and scientific innovation is one that only Muslims can put forward. It is needed to oppose the dark fantasies and constipated religiosity of Da'esh. Under Abdullah, Saudi Arabians had begun to make these arguments, if subtly. We must hope not only that they will continue this effort under King Salman but that we will have the wit to back them in this endeavor, in which we must lead from behind.

We also need Saudi help to deal with Da'esh as a political structure. It is as much a product as an enforcer of political exclusivity. Unless and until politics in Iraq and Syria can become inclusive, Da'esh will continue to be able to exploit sectarian divisions to its advantage. But these divisions and the extremist militias they generate are fed and inflamed by geopolitical rivalry between Saudi Arabia and Iran. Some sort of truce between Riyadh and Tehran will be necessary to tamp them down. Difficult as it is to imagine such a *modus vivendi*, I would not rule it out.

If handled skillfully, agreement in the international negotiations to cap and control Iranian nuclear programs could provide an opening for Saudi-Iranian rapprochement. Conversely, if there is no agreement or if an agreement is reached and then sabotaged, it is entirely possible that Saudi Arabia will seek its own nuclear deterrent to counter Iran. This might work for the Kingdom but it would make the region less stable, downgrade U.S. influence, and pose an additional nuclear threat to Israel.

Both the rise of Da'esh and the challenge of Iran's advance toward regional hegemony underscore the importance of Saudi-American strategic cooperation. Disquiet in Washington over the lack of a coherent strategy for dealing with either Da'esh or Iran is provoking a serious rethinking of policy. There is new leadership in Riyadh in a time of trial for the Kingdom. Saudi Arabia has emerged as a regional leader. This coincidence offers an opportunity for the reinvention and reaffirmation of the seven-decade partnership between the United States and the Kingdom. For the sake of both Americans and Saudis, we must seize this opportunity or suffer the consequences.

Too Quick on the Draw:
Militarism and the Malpractice of Diplomacy in America
June 13, 2015[12]

The late Arthur Goldberg, who served on our Supreme Court and as U.S. ambassador to the United Nations, once said that "diplomats approach every question with an open...mouth." No doubt that's often true at the United Nations, where parliamentary posturing and its evil twin, declaratory diplomacy, rule. The essence of diplomacy, however, is not talking but seeking common ground by listening carefully and with an open mind to what others don't say as well as what they do, then acting accordingly.

Diplomacy is how a nation advances its interests and resolves problems with foreigners with minimal violence. It is the nonbelligerent champion of domestic tranquility and prosperity. It promotes mutually acceptable varieties of *modus vivendi* between differing perspectives and cultures.

Diplomacy is the translation of national strategy into tactics to gain political, economic, and military advantages without the use of force. It is the outermost sentry and guardian of national defense. Its lapse or failure can bring war and all its pains to a nation.

But diplomacy is not just an alternative to war. It does not end when war begins. And when war proves necessary to adjust relations with other states or peoples, it is diplomacy that must translate the outcome of the fighting into agreed adjustments in relationships, crafting a better peace that reconciles the vanquished to their defeat and stabilizes a new status quo. By any measure, therefore, excellence in diplomacy is vitally important to the power, wealth, and well-being of the nation.

At its deepest level, diplomacy is a subtle strategic activity. It is about rearranging circumstances, perceptions, and the parameters of international problems so as to realign the self-interest of other nations with one's own in ways that cause them to see that it is in their interest to do what one wants them to do, and that it's possible for them to do it without appearing to capitulate to any foreign power or interest. Diplomacy is about getting others to play our game.

Judging by results in the complex post–Cold War environment, diplomacy is something the United States does not now understand or know how to do. I want to speak with you today about some of the beliefs and

---

12. Remarks to the Academy of Philosophy and Letters, Linthicum Heights, Maryland

practices that account for America's bungling of foreign policy in recent years. I will end by offering a few thoughts about how we might do better.

Since the fall of the Soviet Union liberated Americans from our fear of nuclear Armageddon, the foreign policy of the United States has come to rely almost exclusively on economic sanctions, military deterrence, and the use of force. Such measures are far from the only arrows in the traditional quiver of statecraft. Yet Americans no longer aim at leadership by example or polite persuasion backed by national prestige, patronage, institution building, or incentives for desirable behavior. In Washington, the threat to use force has become the first rather than the last resort in foreign policy. We Americans have embraced coercive measures as our default means of influencing other nations, whether they be allies, friends, adversaries, or enemies.

For most in our political elite, the overwhelming military and economic leverage of the United States justifies abandoning the effort to persuade rather than muscle recalcitrant foreigners into line. We habitually respond to challenges of every kind with military posturing rather than with diplomatic initiatives directed at solving the problems that generate these challenges. This approach has made us less—not more—secure, while burdening future generations of Americans with ruinous debt. It has unsettled our allies without deterring our adversaries. It has destabilized entire regions, multiplied our enemies, and estranged us from our friends.

South America no longer defers to us. Russia is again hostile. Europe questions our judgment, is audibly disturbed by our belligerence, and is distancing itself from our leadership. A disintegrating Middle East seethes with vengeful contempt for the United States. Africa ignores us. Our lust for India remains unrequited. China has come to see us as implacably hostile to its rise and is focused on countering our perceived efforts to hem it in. Japan is reviewing its inner samurai. Some say all these adversities are upon us because we are not sufficiently brutal in our approach to foreign affairs and that, to be taken seriously or to be effective, we must bomb, strafe, or use drones to assassinate those with whom we disagree and let the collateral damage fall where it may. What we have actually proved is that, if you are sufficiently indifferent to the interests of others and throw your weight around enough, you can turn off practically everybody.

Outside our own country, American military prowess and willingness to administer shock and awe to foreign societies are nowhere in doubt. In Vietnam, Kuwait, Afghanistan, Iraq, and many other places, Americans have provided ample evidence of our politico-military obduracy and willingness to inflict huge casualties on foreigners we judge to oppose us. As a nation, we nonetheless seem to doubt our own prowess and to be obsessed with proving it to ourselves and others. In truth, there is no credibility gap about American toughness to be remedied. That is not the issue. The issue is whether our policies are wise and whether military-campaign plans dressed up in domestically appealing rhetoric equate to strategies that can yield a world more congruent with our interests and values.

In recent years, the United States has killed untold multitudes in wars and counterterrorist drone warfare in West Asia and North Africa. Our campaigns have spilled the blood, broken the bodies, and taken or blighted the lives of many in our armed forces, while weakening our economy by diverting necessary investment from it. These demonstrations of American power and determination have inflicted vast amounts of pain and suffering on foreign peoples. They have not bent our opponents to our will. Far from yielding greater security for us or our allies, our interventions—whether on the ground or from the air—have multiplied our enemies, intensified their hatred for us, and escalated the threat to both our homeland and our citizens and friends abroad.

It is a measure of the extent to which we now see the world through military eyes that the response of much of America's political elite to the repeated failure of the use of force to yield desired results has been to assert that we would have succeeded if only we had been more gung ho and argued for the use of even greater force. What we have been doing with our armed forces has not halted dynamic change in the global and regional distribution of economic, military, and political power. There is no reason to believe that greater belligerence could yield a better result. Most Americans sense this and are skeptical both about the neoconservative agendas the military-industrial-congressional complex seeks to impose on our nation and the wisdom of staking our future on the preservation of a rapidly crumbling post–Cold War status quo.

Every nation's political culture is a product of its historical experience. The American way in national-security policy, like that of other countries, is steered by unexamined preconceptions drawn from the peculiarities of our history. In the aggregate, these convictions constitute a subliminal doctrine with the authority of dogma. Legions of academics now make a living by exploring applications of this dogma for the U.S. Department of Defense. They have produced an intellectual superstructure for the military-industrial complex in the form of an almost infinite variety of ruminations on coercion. (No one looks to the Department of State for support for research on less overbearing approaches to international relations. It has neither the money nor a desire to vindicate its core functions by sponsoring the development of diplomatic doctrine.)

Americans are right to consider our nation exceptional. Among other things, our experience with armed conflict and our appreciation of the relationship between the use of force and diplomacy are unique—some might say "anomalous." So, therefore, are our approaches to war, peace, and foreign relations.

War is the ultimate argument in relations between states and peoples. Its purpose is sometimes the conquest and subjugation of populations. More commonly, however, war is a means to remove perceived threats, repel aggression, restore a balance of power, compel acquiescence in a shift in borders, or alter the bad behavior of an adversary. Since war is not over until the defeated accept defeat and accommodate their new circumstances, other people's wars usually end in negotiations directed at translating military outcomes into mutually agreed political arrangements that will establish a stable new order of affairs. Not so the wars of the United States.

In our civil war, World War I, World War II, and the Cold War, the U.S. objective was not adjustments in relations with the enemy but "unconditional surrender," that is, a peace imposed on the defeated nation without its assent and entailing its subsequent moral, political, and economic reconstruction. The smaller wars of the twentieth century did not replace this idiosyncratic American rejection of models of warfare linked to limited objectives. We fought to a draw in Korea, where to this day we have not translated the 1953 armistice into peace. We were bested in Vietnam. In Grenada in 1983, Panama in 1989, and Iraq in 2003, we imposed regime change on the defeated, not terms for war termination and peace.

Americans have no recent experience of ending wars through negotiation with those we have vanquished, as has been the norm throughout human history. Our national narrative inclines us to equate success in war with smashing up enemies enough to ensure that we can safely deny them the dignity of taking them seriously or enlisting them in building a peace. Our wars are typically planned as military campaigns with purely military objectives, with little, if any, thought to what adjustments in foreign relations the end of the fighting might facilitate or how to exploit the political opportunities our use of force can provide. As a rule, we do not specify war aims or plan for negotiations to obtain a defeated enemy's acceptance of our terms for ending the fighting.

The absence of clearly stated war aims for U.S. combat operations makes it easy for our politicians to move the goal posts. Our wars therefore almost invariably entail mission creep. Our armed forces find themselves in pursuit of a fluid set of objectives that never solidifies. With victory undefined, our soldiers, sailors, airmen, and marines cannot say when they have accomplished their missions enough to stand down.

Our habit of failing to define specific political objectives for our military also means that, in our case, war is less "an extension of politics by other means" (as Clausewitz prescribed) than a brutally direct way of punishing our foes linked to no clear conception of how they might take aboard the lessons we imagine they should draw from the drubbing we give them. Our chronic inattention to the terms of war termination means that U.S. triumphs on the battlefield are seldom, if ever, translated into terms that reward military victory with a stable peace.

The U.S. armed forces are highly professional and admirably effective at demolishing our enemies' power, but their expectation that civilian policymakers will then make something of the political vulnerabilities they create is almost always disappointed. The relevant civilian policymakers are almost all inexperienced amateurs placed in office by the spoils system. Their inexperience, the theories of coercive diplomacy they studied at university, the traditional disengagement of American diplomats from military operations, and our now heavily militarized political culture converge to assure that American diplomacy is missing in action when it is most needed—as the fighting ends.

Thus, our military triumph in the 1991 war to liberate Kuwait was never translated into terms to which Saddam Hussein or his regime were asked to pledge their honor. Instead, we looked to the United Nations to pass a one-sided omnibus resolution imposing onerous restrictions on Iraqi sovereignty, including inspections, reparations, and the demilitarization of portions of Iraq's territory. Saddam assumed no explicit obligation to comply with these dictates. To the extent he could get away with ignoring them, he did. The war never really ended. In our 2003 reinvasion of Iraq, U.S. planners assumed apolitically that military victory would automatically bring peace. No competent Iraqi authority was left in place to accept terms and maintain stability. Subliminal doctrine instead prevailed. The U.S. government devised no mechanism to translate its success on the battlefield into a legitimate new order and peace in Iraq.

In Iraq, we were guided by the historically induced, peculiarly American presumption that war naturally culminates in the unconditional surrender and moral reconstruction of the enemy. The Department of State was excluded from all planning. The notion that a political process might be required for war termination on terms that could reconcile the enemy to its defeat never occurred to the White House or Department of Defense. Afghanistan, Bosnia, Kosovo, and Libya offer different but analogous examples of Washington's blindness or indifference to the utility of diplomacy in translating battlefield results into political results. As a result, our military interventions have nowhere produced a better peace. We Americans do not know how to conclude our wars.

American confusion about the relationship between the use of force and political order-setting extends to our approach to situations that have the potential to explode in war but have not yet done so. Our country learned how to behave as a world power during the four-decade-long bipolar stalemate of the Cold War. The Cold War's strategy of containment made holding the line against our Soviet rivals the central task of U.S. diplomacy. Americans came to view negotiated adjustments in relations as part of a great zero-sum game and as therefore, for the most part, infeasible or undesirable or both. After all, a misstep could trigger a nuclear war fatal to both sides.

The Cold War reduced diplomacy to the political equivalent of trench warfare, in which the absence of adjustments in position rather than advantageous maneuvering constituted success. It taught Americans to deter conflict by threatening escalation that might lead to a mutually fatal nuclear exchange. It conditioned us to believe that it is often wiser to stonewall—to freeze a situation so as to contain potential conflict—than to waste time and effort exploring ways of mitigating or eliminating it.

We Americans have yet to unlearn the now largely irrelevant lessons of the Cold War. We still respond to adverse developments with threats of escalating pressure calculated to immobilize the other side rather than with diplomatic efforts to resolve the issues that motivate it. We impose sanctions to symbolize our displeasure and to enable our politicians to appear to be doing something tough, even if it is inherently feckless. Sometimes we decline to speak with our adversary on the issue in question until it has agreed to end the behavior to which we object. Almost invariably, the core of our response is issuing deterrent military threats.

The ostensible purpose of sanctions is to coerce the targeted country into submission. Once imposed, though, sanctions invariably become ends in themselves. Their success is then measured not by how they modify or fail to modify the behavior of their targets but by the degree of pain and deprivation they are seen to inflict. There is no recorded instance in which the threat or actual imposition of sanctions not linked to negotiations about a "yes-able" proposition has induced cooperation. Sanctions do not build bridges or foster attitudes that facilitate concessions. They harden and entrench differences.

In many ways, sanctions backfire. They impose the equivalent of a protectionist wall against imports on the target nation. This often stimulates a drive for self-sufficiency and induces artificial prosperity in some sectors of its economy. Sanctions hurt some U.S. domestic interest groups and benefit others. Those who benefit develop a vested interest in perpetuating sanctions, making them hard to use as a bargaining chip.

Perversely, sanctions also tend to boost the political authority of the leaders of the countries they target. They place decisions about the distribution of rationed goods and services in these leaders' hands. To the extent that sanctions immiserate populations, they unite nationalist opposition to the foreigners imposing them. As the examples of north Korea, Mao's China, and Cuba attest, sanctions prolong the half-life of regimes that might otherwise fall from power as a result of patriotic resistance to their misrule. Eventually, as we now see with Cuba (and China before it), sanctions have the ironic effect of transforming the places we have walled off into exotic tourist destinations for Americans.

The pernicious effects of sanctions are magnified by the American habit of combining them with diplomatic ostracism. Refusal to talk is a tactic that can gain time for active improvement of one's bargaining position, but meeting with another party is not a favor to it. Insisting on substantive concessions as the price for a meeting is self-defeating. Diplomatic contact is not a concession to an adversary but a means of gaining intelligence about its thinking and intentions, understanding and seeking to reshape how it sees its interests, looking for openings in its policy positions that can be exploited, conveying accurate messages and explanations of one's own reasoning, manipulating its appreciation of its circumstances, and facilitating concessions by it.

Efforts at deterrence invite counterescalation by their target. Controlling this risk necessitates reassuring one's adversary about the limits of one's objectives. Reassurance requires accurate messaging. That cannot be assured without direct communication with the other side. This underscores the importance of the diplomatic relations and contacts we sometimes unwisely suspend. It is a sound rule that one should never lose contact with an enemy, on the battlefield or in the diplomatic arena.

Our frequent violation of this rule is a special problem for our practice of deterrence, now virtually the only technique of statecraft in our kit other than sanctions and military assault. To avert perceived challenges to our interests or those of the nations we have undertaken to protect, we declare that attempts by another country to seek unilateral advantage will invoke retaliation to impose unacceptable levels of loss. The penalties we promise can be political and economic, but in the case of the contemporary United States they are almost invariably military.

Deterrence substitutes military confrontation designed to freeze risk for diplomacy directed at eliminating its underlying causes. It sets off a test of will between the two sides' armed forces as each considers how best to demonstrate its resolve while causing the other to back down. Deterrence can, of course, be the starting point for a diplomatic effort to resolve conflicts of interest, but if it is not paired with diplomacy, such conflicts are likely to fester or intensify. Then, too, with the end of the Cold War, the danger of escalation to the nuclear level has lessened. The threats of escalation inherent in deterrence are now less intimidating and more likely to face challenge.

In our attempts to limit uncertainty through deterrence alone, without diplomatic efforts to resolve the underlying crises that generate the uncertainty, Americans preserve the status quo even when it is disadvantageous. By assuming that the immensity of our power makes deterrence in itself an adequate response to threats to our interests as we see them, we inadvertently perpetuate the danger of armed conflict, store up trouble for the future, and give potential adversaries time to increase their power relative to ours. This is the approach we are currently applying to China in the East and South China Seas and to Russia on its western borders. It is no more likely to succeed now than on the multiple occasions in the past in which it failed. The same is true of our latest attempt to apply military technical solutions to the political problems of a disintegrated Iraq.

This brings me to the question of whether and how we can learn from our mistakes. George Santayana famously warned that "those who do not remember the past are condemned to repeat it." He was right.

But what if every four or so years, you administered a frontal lobotomy to yourself, excising your memories and making it impossible to learn from experience? What if most aspects of your job were always new to you? What if you didn't know whether something you propose to do had been tried before and, if so, whether it succeeded or failed? To one degree or another, this is what is entailed in staffing the national security functions of our government (other than those assigned to our military) with short-term political appointees selected to reward not their knowledge, experience, or skill, but campaign contributions, political sycophancy, affiliation with domestic interest groups, academic achievements, success in fields unrelated to diplomacy, or social prominence.

Alone among major powers, the United States has not professionalized its diplomacy. Professions are composed of individuals who profess a unique combination of specialized knowledge, experience, and technique. Their expertise reflects the distillation into doctrine—constantly refreshed—of what can be learned from experience. Their skills are inculcated through case studies, periodic training, and on-the-job mentoring. They are constantly improved by the critical introspection inherent in after-action reviews.

By contrast, Americans appear to believe that the formulation and conduct of foreign relations are best entrusted to self-promoting amateurs, ideologues, and dilettantes unburdened by apprenticeship, training, or prior experience. The lower ranks of our diplomatic service are highly regarded abroad for their intellectual competence and cross-cultural communication skills. With some notable exceptions, our ambassadors and the senior officials atop the Washington foreign affairs bureaucracies are not similarly admired. The contrast with the superbly professional leadership of the U.S. armed forces could not be greater. It should surprise no one that our soldiers, sailors, airmen, and marines often wait in vain for guidance and support from the civilian side of the U.S. government's national security establishment. Current trends suggest they may have to wait a long time for their civilian counterparts to shape up.

The post–Cold War period has seen major expansion in the numbers of political appointees and their placement in ever lower foreign-policy positions, along with huge bloat in the National Security Council staff. This has progressively deprofessionalized U.S. diplomacy from the top down in both Washington and the field, while thinning out the American diplomatic bench. Increasingly, the U.S. military is being thrust into diplomatic roles it is not trained or equipped to handle, further militarizing U.S. foreign relations.

In the absence of major curtailment of the spoils system, the prospects for improved U.S. diplomatic performance are poor. Amateur ambassadors and senior officials cannot provide professional mentoring, yet the United States invests little in training its career personnel in either the lore or core skills of diplomacy. No case studies of diplomatic advocacy, negotiation, reporting and analysis, or protection of overseas Americans have been compiled. There is no professional framework for after-action reviews in American diplomacy, and they seldom occur. (To the extent that examining what went right or wrong and why that might reflect adversely on ambitious political appointees or the administration itself, it is actually discouraged.) This ensures that nothing would be learned from experience even if there were career diplomats in senior positions to learn it.

Diplomacy, as such, is not part of civic education in the United States. A large percentage of our political elite has no idea what diplomats do, can do, or ought to do. Not for nothing is it said that if you speak three or more languages, you are multilingual. If you speak two languages, you are bilingual. If you speak only one language, you are American. And if you *speak only one language*, have never studied geography, and do not have a passport, you are probably a member of Congress.

It is also said that if we can't get our act together at home, there is little reason to hope that we will get it together abroad. But we cannot afford not to. We are entering an era of strategic fluidity in which there are no fixed lines for Cold War–style diplomacy to defend, there is declining deference to our leadership, and there are ever more challenges that cannot be solved by military means. We need to raise the level of our international game.

It is time to rediscover the deep diplomacy that creates circumstances in which others become inclined, out of self-interest, to make choices and do things that serve our interests and that advance those interests without war. It is time to rediscover noncoercive instruments of statecraft that can persuade others that they can benefit by working with us rather than against us. It is time to exempt the foreign-affairs elements of our national security policy apparatus from the venality and incompetence that the spoils system has come to exemplify. It is time to staff our diplomacy as we have staffed our military, with well-trained professionals, and to demand from them the best they can give to their country—our country.

Conclusion

Fixing the Mess
in the Middle East

The Middle East is the region where Africa, Asia, and Europe come together. It is also the part of the world where we have been most compellingly reminded that some struggles cannot be won, but there are no struggles that cannot be lost.

It is often said that human beings learn little useful from success but can learn a great deal from defeat. If so, the Middle East now offers a remarkably rich menu of foreign-policy failures for Americans to study:

- Our four-decade diplomatic effort to bring peace to the Holy Land has sputtered to an ignominious conclusion.
- Our unconditional political, economic, and military backing of Israel has earned us the enmity of Israel's enemies even as it has enabled egregiously contemptuous expressions of ingratitude and disrespect for us from Israel itself.
- Our attempts to contain the Iranian revolution have instead empowered it.
- Our military campaigns to pacify the region have destabilized it, dismantled its states, ignited ferocious wars of religion among its peoples, and generated new terrorist threats to us.
- Our efforts to democratize Arab societies have helped to produce anarchy, terrorism, dictatorship, or an indecisive juxtaposition of all three.
- In Iraq, Libya, and Syria we have shown that war does not decide who's right so much as determine who's left.

- Our campaign against terrorism with global reach has multiplied our enemies and continuously expanded their areas of operation.
- Our opposition to nuclear proliferation has not prevented Israel from clandestinely developing nuclear weapons and related delivery systems and may not preclude Iran and others from following suit.
- Deference from regional security partners like Saudi Arabia has become a thing of the past.
- At the global level, our policies in the Middle East have damaged our prestige, weakened our alliances, and gained us a reputation for militaristic fecklessness in the conduct of our foreign affairs. They have also distracted us from challenges elsewhere of equal or greater importance to our national interests.

That's quite a record.

One can only measure success or failure by reference to what one is trying achieve. So, in practice, what have U.S. objectives been? Are these objectives still valid? If we've failed to advance them, what went wrong? What must we do now to have a better chance of success?

Our objectives in the Middle East have not changed much over the course of the past half century or more. We have sought to:

- Gain acceptance and security for a Jewish homeland from the other states and peoples of the region.
- Ensure the uninterrupted availability of the region's energy supplies to sustain global and U.S. security and prosperity.
- Preserve our ability to transit the region so as to be able to project power around the world.
- Prevent the rise of a regional hegemon or the deployment of weapons of mass destruction that might threaten any or all of these first three objectives.
- Maximize profitable commerce.
- Promote stability while enhancing respect for human rights and progress toward constitutional democracy.

Let's briefly review our progress with respect to each of these objectives. I will not mince words.

Israel has come to enjoy military supremacy but it remains excluded from most participation in its region's political, economic, and cultural life. In the sixty-seven years since the Jewish state was proclaimed, Israel has not made a single friend in the Middle East, where it continues to be regarded as an illegitimate legacy of Western imperialism engaged in racist removal of the indigenous population. International support for Israel is down to the United States and a few of the former colonial powers that originally imposed the Zionist project on the Arabs under Sykes-Picot and the related Balfour Declaration. The two-state solution has expired as a physical and political possibility. There is no longer any peace process to distract global attention from Israel's maltreatment of its captive Arab populations.

After years of deference to American diplomacy, the Palestinians are beginning to challenge the legality of Israel's cruelties to them in the *International Criminal Court* and other venues in which Americans have no veto, are not present, or cannot protect the Jewish state from the consequences of its own behavior as we have always been able to do in the past. Israel's ongoing occupation of the West Bank and siege of Gaza are fueling a drive to boycott its products, disinvest in its companies, and sanction its political and cultural elite. These trends are the very opposite of what the United States has attempted to achieve for Israel.

In a stunning demonstration of his country's most famous renewable resource—chutzpah—Israel's prime minister made contempt for America a mainstay of his reelection campaign while simultaneously transforming Israel into a partisan issue in the United States. His use of the U.S. Congress as a campaign prop failed. He has been forced to form a governing coalition that defers to the most defiantly racist elements in Israel.

This is the very opposite of a sound survival strategy for Israel. Uncertainties about their country's future are leading many Israelis to emigrate, not just to America but to Europe. This should disturb Americans, if only because of the enormous investment we have made in attempts to gain a secure place for Israel in its region and the world. The Palestinians have been silent about Mr. Netanyahu's recent political maneuvers. Evidently, they recall Napoleon's adage that one should never interrupt an enemy when he is making a mistake.

This brings me to an awkward but transcendently important issue. Israel was established as a haven from anti-Semitism—hatred of Jews—in Europe, a disease of nationalism and Christian culture that culminated in the Holocaust. Israel's creation was a relief for European Jews but a disaster for the Arabs of Palestine, who were either ethnically cleansed by

European Jewish settlers or subjugated, or both. But the birth of Israel also proved tragic for Jews throughout the Middle East—the Mizrahim.

In a nasty irony, the implementation of Zionism in the Holy Land led to the introduction of European-style anti-Semitism—including its classic Christian libels on Jews—to the region, dividing Arab Jews from their Muslim neighbors as never before and compelling them to join European Jews in taking refuge in Israel amidst outrage over the dispossession of Palestinians from their homeland. Now, in a further irony, Israel's pogroms and other injustices to the Muslim and Christian Arabs over whom it rules are leading not just to a rebirth of anti-Semitism in Europe but to its globalization.

The late King Abdullah of Saudi Arabia engineered a reversal of decades of Arab rejectionism at Beirut in 2002. He brought all Arab countries and later all fifty-seven Muslim countries to agree to normalize relations with Israel if it did a deal—any deal—with the Palestinians that the latter could accept. Israel spurned the offer. Its working assumption seems to be that it does not need peace with its neighbors as long as it can bomb and strafe them. Proceeding on this basis is not just a bad bet, it is one that is dividing Israel from the world, including Jews outside Israel. This does not look like a story with a happy ending.

It's hard to avoid the thought that Zionism is turning out to be bad for the Jews. If so, given the American investment in it, it will also have turned out to be bad for America. The political costs to America of support for Israel are steadily rising. We must find a way to divert Israel from the largely self-engineered isolation into which it is driving itself, while repairing our own increasing international ostracism on issues related to Israel.

Let me turn, very briefly, to the second U.S. objective in the region, security of access to energy supplies. Triumphalist nonsense about North American energy independence has just suffered a major comeuppance, as Saudi Arabia has shown its capacity to let oversupply rip, bankrupting or sidelining frackers and forcing mass layoffs in our previously booming oil and gas industry. The Middle East, where two-thirds of global fossil fuel reserves are located, still matters.

The question, therefore, is not whether untrammeled access to the energy resources of the Persian Gulf is essential to global prosperity. It is. Rather, it is whether the United States should or even could indefinitely bear the sole burden of ensuring access to Gulf energy resources on our own. Should we seek to share responsibility for assuring energy security with Europe and countries like China, India, Japan, and Korea that are far more dependent on Middle East oil than we are? Current U.S. policy assumes that "no" is the answer. Watch that space!

The third U.S. objective, sustaining freedom of transit through the region, is more subtle still. Tens of thousands of U.S. military flights transit Saudi and Egyptian airspace annually en route between Europe and Asia. Flight clearance is a fundamental privilege of sovereignty. It is done in the region on an incredibly labor-intensive ad hoc basis. There are no agreements obligating countries there to grant it. The prevailing overflight regime reflects relationships with the countries of the region that are now fraying. Transit is not currently in jeopardy, but it cannot be counted upon. Every once in a while, to remind us of this reality, the Saudis refuse permission for overflight. These refusals remind us of the importance to our position as a world power of cordial relations with Saudi Arabia, Egypt, and the other countries of the Red Sea–Persian Gulf area.

Our fourth objective has been preventing the rise of a serious threat to Israel, energy flows, or freedom of navigation through the region's air and sea space.

First, a little history.

During the Cold War, the Soviet Union and regional allies like Egypt and Syria seemed to pose such a threat. The United States balanced it with our own security partnerships. In 1964, we dropped our arms embargo on Israel. Nine years later, in 1973, we delivered massive military assistance to Israel to enable it to avoid defeat in war with Egypt and Syria. We have since become committed to sustaining Israel's military supremacy in the region. To keep Egypt at peace with Israel, since 1979 we have provided it with generous subsidies. In 1994, we added Jordan to this equation.

After the fall of the Shah of Iran in 1979, we bolstered Saudi Arabia as a counter to the Islamic Republic of Iran, then helped Iraq avoid defeat in its eight-year war with Iran. In 1990, when Saddam Hussein's Iraq annexed Kuwait and threatened to dominate the region and hence global oil prices, we and the Saudis organized coalitions including Egypt, Pakistan, and Syria to dislodge Iraq from Kuwait, reduce its power to levels that Iran could balance, and thus end the threat it posed to the Gulf Arab states. So far, so good.

In 1993, the Clinton administration abruptly abandoned the effort to use Iraq to balance Iran. Instead, it proclaimed a policy of "dual containment," under which Washington undertook unilaterally to balance both Baghdad and Tehran simultaneously. This made sense in terms of our interest in protecting Israel from either Iraq or Iran, but it placed the primary burden of defending Persian Gulf energy resources on the United States rather than on the Gulf Arabs or the international community. It secured a place for U.S. forces astride the routes between Asia and Europe. But it also required the creation of a long-term U.S. military presence in the Gulf Arab countries, especially Saudi Arabia. The Kingdom was strapped for cash, but we wanted it to pay for our presence and, amid popular resentment, it did. The stationing of U.S. troops on soil considered by many Muslims to be sacred and off-limits to unbelievers was a political irritant that helped stimulate the September 11, 2001, terrorist attacks on New York and Washington.

A fully justified and brilliantly executed U.S. punitive raid on al-Qaeda and its Taliban hosts in Afghanistan somehow morphed into a military campaign to pacify Afghanistan and save it from militant Islam. Most Muslims, like the rest of the world, stood with Americans on 9/11. We have long since squandered that support. Over time, we began to kill Muslims we suspected of opposing us with drones—remote-controlled robots that rain death from the sky, killing militants along with their families, friends, and coreligionists as well as innocent bystanders. The practical effect of this is that we kill one (possible) terrorist and get ten free.

Meanwhile, our invasion of Iraq in 2003 accomplished none of its declared objectives but ended domestic tranquility in that country and resulted in a huge number of Arab deaths. No country, other than Israel, had urged us to attack Iraq. No weapons of mass destruction were found there. We were not welcomed as liberators. We staged elections but did not transform the country into a democracy. Iraq neither embraced Israel nor became our ally. In 2011, at Iraqi insistence, we withdrew, leaving behind a divided, shattered, and embittered country. We not only failed to impress the world with our power, as the proponents of the war hoped we would, we demonstrated our limitations. We showed that our military can defeat armies and militias but that it cannot bend foreign societies to our will, pacify their populations, or refute their ideas.

The net effect of our invasion and occupation of Iraq was to install a pro-Iranian, Shiite-majority government in Baghdad. That government then tyrannized Iraq's Sunni minority. Thus, we at once added Iraq to the list of Iran's client states and incubated a new crop of anti-American terrorists.

Earlier, we had driven Iran's enemies from power in Afghanistan. In 2006, Israel's aerial maiming of Lebanon elevated the Iranian-supported

Shiite Hezbollah to the commanding heights of Lebanese politics. We did not respond to Damascus's efforts to dilute its dependence on Iran by establishing a more cooperative relationship with us.

In sum, we carelessly sponsored the rise of the very sort of anti-Israel and anti–Gulf Arab alliance our policies were aimed at precluding. We handed Iran dominant influence in Iraq, Lebanon, and Syria. The Arab uprisings of 2011 added Bahrain to the list of places where Iran can exploit Shiite grievances. Now pro-Iranian Houthi tribesmen have seized control of much of Yemen. The Gulf Arabs see Iran encircling them and are attempting to rectify this without regard to the interests and advice of the United States.

The Saudis and others in the Gulf remember the days when the United States saw the Shah's Iran as the regional gendarme. Their fears that those days might come again are far-fetched but understandable, given all that has happened. As a result of U.S. bungling in Iraq and elsewhere, Iran has, after all, greatly expanded its reach in the region. Gulf Arab apprehension about the proposed agreement to cap and constrain Iran's nuclear programs is less about a military threat from Iranian nuclear weapons than about the possibility that we and other members of the UN Security Council will effectively acknowledge, if not endorse, Iran's new proto-hegemony in the region.

America is at war with the renegade Islamist insurgency that calls itself "the Islamic State." (I see no reason to dignify it with that title and, like most people in the region, prefer to call it by its less pretentious Arabic acronym, "Da'esh.") For many reasons, the Gulf Arabs doubt our reliability. Iraq has emerged as the most effective regional opponent of Da'esh. The Gulf Arabs fear that we Americans may be driven to make common cause with Iran to combat Da'esh.

Despite Mr. Netanyahu's public hysteria about Iran and his efforts to demonize it, Israel has traditionally seen Iran's rivalry with the Arabs as a strategic asset. It had a very cooperative relationship with the Shah. Neither Israelis nor Arabs have forgotten the strategic logic that produced Israel's entente with Iran. Israel is very much on Da'esh's list of targets, as is Iran.

For now, however, Israel's main concern is the possible loss of its nuclear monopoly in the Middle East. Many years ago, Israel actually did what it now accuses Iran of planning to do. It clandestinely developed nuclear weapons while denying to us and others that it was doing so. Unlike Iran, Israel has not adhered to the Nuclear Non-Proliferation Treaty or subjected its nuclear facilities to international inspection. It has expressed no interest in proposals for a nuclear-free zone in the Middle East. It sees its ability to bring on nuclear Armageddon as the ultimate guarantee of its existence.

Unlike Israel, Iran does not have nuclear weapons and seems prepared to settle for more conventional means of ensuring its security. Despite all the pain our sanctions have inflicted and whether the current nuclear negotiations with it succeed or fail, Iran seems destined to exercise strategic suzerainty in a major part of the Middle East.

Like the Israelis, the Saudis do not trust Iran to halt at nuclear latency if there is a deal with it by the United States and its Security Council partners. Unlike the Israeli prime minister, Riyadh judges that, if the negotiations with Iran fail to produce an agreement, this will precipitate an Iranian decision actually to build a nuclear deterrent. An agreement would confer added prestige on Iran. That's bad. A nuclear deterrent would give Iran added freedom from U.S. or other coercion. That's worse.

The Saudis have little confidence in U.S. protection, given America's inadvertent empowerment of Iran and incubation of Da'esh, as well as its erratic behavior during the Arab uprisings that toppled Egyptian president Hosni Mubarak. They are building their own coalitions to counter Iran and contain Da'esh, with or without the United States.

After taking the throne, King Salman quickly found sought common ground with Qatar and Turkey on the issue of the Muslim Brotherhood. The result has been the emergence of an Islamist front in Syria that has put the Assad regime on the defensive, while curtailing inroads by Da'esh. King Salman also formed a coalition with other Gulf Arab countries and Egypt to counter the pro-Iranian Houthi movement in Yemen. For the first time since World War II, the Saudi armed forces have taken the offensive in the region.

King Salman's main concern has been how to balance and contain Iran. He appears to have concluded that he cannot rely upon the United States to do this and must take action himself. The diplomatic and military actions he has launched, including the war in Yemen, are enormously popular in his kingdom. They have helped him to achieve a concentration of power in Riyadh that is the greatest since the death of his father, the Kingdom's founder, Abdulaziz al-Saud. They have also made it clear that Saudi Arabia will no longer automatically follow the United States' lead.

In 2006, Secretary of State Condoleeza Rice infamously proclaimed the birth of a "new Middle East." A new order in the Middle East is now belatedly coming into being. But it is not the one Secretary Rice envisaged. The influence of the United States and the prospects for the peaceful integration of Israel into the region have both been adversely affected by the events of the past fifteen years.

To many, Israel now seems to have acquired the obnoxious habit of biting the American hand that has fed it for so long. The Palestinians have despaired of American support for their self-determination. They are reaching out to the international community in ways that deliberately bypass the United States. Random acts of violence herald mayhem in the Holy Land.

Da'esh has proclaimed the objective of erasing the Sykes-Picot borders and the states within them. It has already expunged the border between Iraq and Syria. It is at work in Lebanon and has set its sights on Jordan, Palestine, and Israel.

Lebanon, under Saudi influence, has turned to France rather than America for support. Hezbollah has intervened militarily in Iraq and Syria, both of whose governments are close to Iran. Egypt and Turkey have distanced themselves from the United States as well as from each other. Russia is back as a regional actor and arms supplier.

The Gulf Arabs, Egypt, and Turkey now separately intervene in Bahrain, Libya, Syria, Iraq, and Yemen without reference to American policy or views. Iran is the dominant influence in Iraq, Syria, parts of Lebanon, and now Yemen. It has boots on the ground in Iraq. Saudi Arabia seems to be organizing a coalition that will manage its own nuclear deterrence and military balancing of Iran.

To describe this as out of control is hardly adequate. What are we to do about it?

Perhaps we should start by recalling the first law of holes—when stuck in one, stop digging. It appears that "don't just sit there, bomb something" isn't much of a strategy. When he was asked last summer what our strategy for dealing with Da'esh was, President Obama replied, "We don't yet have one." He was widely derided for that. He should have been praised for making the novel suggestion that before Washington acts, it should first think through what it hopes to accomplish and how best to do it. Sun Zi once observed that "tactics without strategy is the noise before defeat." America's noisy but strategy-free approach to the Middle East has proven him right.

Again the starting point must be what we are trying to accomplish. Strategy is, in the words of John Lewis Gaddis, "the discipline of achieving desired ends through the most efficient use of available means." Our desired ends with respect to the Middle East are not in doubt. They have been and remain to gain an accepted and therefore secure place for Israel there, to keep the region's oil and gas coming at reasonable prices, to be able to pass through the area at will, to head off challenges to these interests, to do profitable business in the markets of the Middle East, and to promote stability amid the expansion of liberty in its countries. Judging by results, we have been doing a lot wrong.

Two related problems in our overall approach need correction. They are "enablement" and the creation of "moral hazard." Both are fall-out from relationships of codependency.

Enablement occurs when one party to a relationship indulges or supports and thereby enables another party's dysfunctional behavior. A familiar example from ordinary life is giving money to a drunk or a drug addict or ignoring, explaining away, or defending their self-destructive behavior. Moral hazard is the condition that obtains when one party is emboldened to take risks it would not otherwise take because it knows another party will shoulder the consequences and bear the costs of failure.

The U.S.-Israel relationship has evolved to exemplify codependency. It now embodies both enablement and moral hazard. U.S. support for Israel is unconditional. Israel has therefore had no need to cultivate relations with others in the Middle East, to declare its borders, or to choose peace over continued expansion into formerly Arab lands. Confidence in U.S. backing enables Israel to do whatever it likes to the Palestinians and its neighbors without having to worry about the consequences.

Israel is now a rich country, but the United States continues to subsidize it with cash transfers and other fiscal privileges. The Jewish state is the most powerful country in the Middle East. It can launch attacks on its neighbors, confident that it will be resupplied by the United States. Its use of U.S. weapons in ways that violate both U.S. and international law goes unrebuked. Forty-one American vetoes in the UN Security Council have exempted Israel from censure and the application of international law. We enable it to defy the expressed will of the international community—including, ironically, our own.

We Americans are facilitating Israel's indulgence in denial and avoidance of the choices it must make if it is not to jeopardize its long-term existence as a state in the Middle East. The biggest contribution we could now make to Israel's longevity would be to ration our support for it, so as to cause it to rethink and reform its often self-destructive behavior. Such peace as Israel now enjoys with Egypt, Jordan, and the Palestinians is the direct result of tough love of this kind by earlier American administrations. We Americans cannot save Israel from itself, but we can avoid killing it with uncritical kindness. We should support Israel when it makes sense to do so and it needs our support on specific issues, but not otherwise. Israel is placing itself and American interests in jeopardy. We need to discuss how to reverse this dynamic.

Moral hazard has also been a major problem in our relationship with our Arab partners. Why should they play an active role in countering the threat to them they perceive from Iran, if they can get America to do this for them? Similarly, why should any Muslim country rearrange its priorities to deal with Muslim renegades like Da'esh when it can count on *America to act for it? If America thinks it must lead, why not let it do so?* But, as our Arab friends now seem to realize, responsible foreign and defense policies begin with self-help, not outsourcing of military risks.

The United States has the power-projection and war-fighting capabilities to back a Saudi-led coalition effort against Da'esh. The Saudis have the religious and political credibility, leadership credentials, and diplomatic connections to organize such an effort. We do not.

Since this century began, America has administered multiple disappointments to its allies and friends in the Middle East, while empowering their and our adversaries. Unlike the Gulf Arabs, Egypt, and Turkey, Washington does not have diplomatic relations with Tehran. Given our non-Muslim identity, solidarity with Israel, and recent history in the Fertile Crescent, the United States cannot hope to unite the region's Muslims against Da'esh. Da'esh is an insurgency that claims to exemplify Islam as well as a governing structure and an armed force. A coalition led by inhibited foreign forces, built on papered-over differences, and embodying hedged commitments will not defeat such an insurgency with or without boots on the ground.

There is an ineluctable requirement for Muslim leadership and strategic vision from within the region. Without it, the existing political geography of the Arab world—not just the map drawn by Sykes-Picot—faces progressive erosion and ultimate collapse. States will be pulled down, to be succeeded by warlords, as is already happening in Iraq and Syria. Degenerate and perverted forms of Islam will threaten prevailing Sunni and Shiite religious dispensations, as Da'esh now does. If indeed Saudi Arabia is finally prepared to organize a regional coalition to enable it to deal directly with these issues, we should welcome this and give it our backing, while seeking to assure that it does not damage Israel's security, impede our transit through the region, or otherwise harm our interests.

I come at last to our objectives of promoting trade and liberal values.

The need for considered judgment and restraint extends to refraining from expansive rhetoric about our values or attempting to compel others to conform to them. In practice, we have insisted on democratization only in countries we have invaded or that were otherwise falling apart, as Egypt was during the first of the two "non-coups" it suffered. When elections have yielded governments whose policies we oppose, we have not hesitated to conspire with their opponents to overthrow them. The results of our efforts to coerce political change in the Middle East are not just failures but catastrophic failures. Our policies have nowhere produced democracy. They have instead contrived the destabilization of societies, the kindling of religious warfare, and the installation of dictatorships contemptuous of the rights of religious and ethnic minorities.

Frankly, we have done a lot better at selling things, including armaments, to the region than we have at transplanting the ideals of the Atlantic Enlightenment there. The region's autocrats cooperate with us to secure our protection, and they get it. When they are nonetheless overthrown, the result is not democracy or the rule of law but sociopolitical collapse and the emergence of a Hobbesian state of nature in which religious and ethnic communities, families, and individuals are able to feel safe only when they are armed and have the drop on each other. Where we have engineered or attempted to engineer regime change, violent politics, partition, and ethno-religious cleansing have everywhere succeeded unjust but tranquil order. One result of our bungled interventions in Iraq and Syria is the rise of Da'esh. This is yet another illustration that, in our efforts to do good in the Middle East, we have violated the principle that one should first do no harm.

Americans used to believe that we could best lead by example. We and those in the Middle East seeking nonviolent change would all be better off if America returned to that tradition and forswore ideologically motivated hectoring and intervention. No one willingly follows a wagging finger. Despite our unparalleled ability to use force against foreigners, the best way to inspire them to emulate us remains showing them that we have our act together. At the moment, we do not.

In the end, to cure the dysfunction in our policies toward the Middle East, it comes down to this: We must cure the dysfunction and venality of our politics. If we cannot, we have no business trying to use an

8,000-mile-long screwdriver to fix things one-third of the way around the world. That doesn't work well under the best of circumstances—but when the country wielding the screwdriver has very little idea what it's doing, it really screws things up.

About the Author

Ambassador Chas W. Freeman, Jr. spent three decades as a U.S. diplomat, winding up his government service as Assistant Secretary of Defense for International Security Affairs. In the course of his unusually varied and distinguished career, he was the principal American interpreter during President Nixon's breakthrough visit to Beijing; played a key role in shaping relations with China as it reformed and opened up; helped negotiate the deal with the leaders of Cuba, South Africa, Angola, and the Soviet Union that ended the colonial era in Africa by terminating South African rule in Namibia and removing Cuban troops from Angola; served as U.S. Ambassador to Saudi Arabia during Operations Desert Shield and Desert Storm; designed NATO's transformation into a Europe-wide security system; and set up military-to-military relations with China. Since his retirement from government, Freeman has remained actively engaged on five continents and has continued to speak and write widely on issues of international relations and U.S. foreign policy.